Surrogacy in Russia

Emerald Studies in Reproduction, Culture and Society

Series Editors: Petra Nordqvist, Manchester University, UK and Nicky Hudson, De Montfort University, UK

This book series brings together scholars from across the social sciences and humanities who are working in the broad field of human reproduction. Reproduction is a growing field of interest in the UK and internationally, and this series publishes work from across the lifecycle of reproduction addressing issues such as conception, contraception, abortion, pregnancy, birth, infertility, pre and postnatal care, pre-natal screen and testing, IVF, prenatal genetic diagnosis, mitochondrial donation, surrogacy, adoption, reproductive donation, family-making and more. Books in this series will focus on the social, cultural, material, legal, historical and political aspects of human reproduction, encouraging work from early career researchers as well as established scholars. The series includes monographs, edited collections and shortform books (between 20 and 50,000 words). Contributors use the latest conceptual, methodological and theoretical developments to enhance and develop current thinking about human reproduction and its significance for understanding wider social practices and processes.

Published Titles in This Series

Lived Realities of Solo Motherhood, Donor Conception and Medically Assisted Reproduction
By Tine Ravn

When Reproduction meets Ageing: The Science and Medicine of the Fertility Decline
By Nolwenn Bühler

Egg Freezing, Fertility and Reproductive Choice
By Kylie Baldwin

The Cryopolitics of Reproduction on Ice: A New Scandinavian Ice Age
By Charlotte Kroløkke, Thomas Søbirk Petersen, Janne Rothmar Herrmann, Anna Sofie Bach, Stine Willum Adrian, Rune Klingenberg and Michael Nebeling Petersen

Voluntary and Involuntary Childlessness
Edited by Natalie Sappleton

Surrogacy in Russia: An Ethnography of Reproductive Labour, Stratification and Migration

By

CHRISTINA WEIS

De Montfort University, UK

United Kingdom – North America – Japan – India – Malaysia – China

Emerald Publishing Limited
Howard House, Wagon Lane, Bingley BD16 1WA, UK

First edition 2021

British Library Cataloguing in Publication Data
A catalogue record for this book is available from the British Library

ISBN: 978-1-83982-897-3 (Print)
ISBN: 978-1-83982-896-6 (Online)
ISBN: 978-1-83982-898-0 (Epub)

Printed and bound by CPI Group (UK) Ltd, Croydon, CR0 4YY

ISOQAR certified
Management System,
awarded to Emerald
for adherence to
Environmental
standard
ISO 14001:2004.

Certificate Number 1985
ISO 14001

INVESTOR IN PEOPLE

To my parents, Hildegard and Karl Weis

Table of Contents

List of Figures

Note on Conversion

In this book, I provide an average conversion rate from the Russian Rouble to British Pound Sterling calculated for the time of my second data collection in 2014/2015.

In the winter of 2014, the Russian currency experienced a strong inflation. To illustrate, a common final compensation of 800,000 ₽ for a surrogacy arrangement in St. Petersburg fluctuated between approximately £13,300 in August 2014, £9,950 in December 2014 and £10,200 in May 2015.

Payments for surrogacy pregnancies in Russia commonly entail the details as listed in the table below. Because of the fluctuation of the Russian Rouble over the course of my research, I am rendering a conversion to British Pound Sterling based on an average for 2014/2015.

Costs	Russian Rouble	British Pound Sterling
Final compensation (full term, healthy delivery)	800,000–950,000	13,280–15,770
Addition for twin pregnancy	150,000–200,000	2,490–3,320
Addition for caesarean section	150,000–200,000	2,490–3,320
Monthly allowance	20,000–25,000	332–415
Monthly allowance (twins)	25,000–35,000	415–581

Acknowledgements

There are so many people who supported me, inspired me and contributed to this book.

I want to start with those who allowed me to study their work and lives, the surrogacy workers and client parents in Russia. Thank you for trusting me and sharing openly with me your experiences, feelings, worries and hopes – that you so often concealed so carefully from your own families and friends. For sake of confidentiality I cannot name you, and the same applies to all the medical professionals who acted as gatekeepers and consultants. Thank you for giving me your time, for helping me get insights and access and slowly building a network.

Thank you to everyone who listened to my stories of fieldwork, the happy and ecstatic ones, the ones that brought tears of sadness or rage to my eyes, the too descriptive or too bloody ones, and the ones I struggled to put into words. Thank you for letting me rant and vent, for giving me space to reflect and a safe space of comfort, and for asking me the right questions at the right time, prompting me to put my emotions and knowledge into words. Thank you for nurturing my resilience.

Heaps of this book are based on my MSc and doctoral research. I therefore want to thank Prof Ton Robben and Dr Hans de Kruijf, who were my supervisors during my first fieldwork period in 2011/2012 during my MSc studies in Cultural Anthropology at Utrecht University. A massive thank you to Prof Nicky Hudson and Dr Sally Ruane (De Montfort University), who supervised me during my doctoral research from 2013 to 2017, and provided me with expert guidance and advice, inspiration and encouragement, tireless patience and kindness, and throughout my doctoral studies gave me the feeling that I will succeed. I could not have imagined better supervisors!

In addition, I would like to thank Dr Robbie Davis-Floyd, with whom I interned in 2016 and 2017, while writing up my PhD thesis, and Prof Sharmila Rudrappa, who I met during these stays in Austin, TX, and whose insights and advice continue to guide me in my work. I also want to thank and acknowledge Dr Aurelia Weikert, who taught me in the 'Anthropology of Assisted Reproduction' during my undergraduate studies in Social and Cultural Anthropology at the University of Vienna. You were the first to draw my attention to assisted reproduction and sparked what was to come. Thank you Dr Michal Nahman for your ongoing support, friendship and academic mentorship, and staying faithful to coffee with olives (only in Barcelona!) despite your (else) culinary excellence.

Thank you to all members of the Centre for Reproduction Research (CRR) at De Montfort University for being the most wonderful and supportive colleagues and friends from the moment I joined the CRR. Thank you for supporting my growth from a doctoral student to an early career researcher. Thank you, in particular, Dr Wendy Norton, my companion in surrogacy research, Sasha Loyal, Jess Turner, Dr Kriss Fearon, Caroline Law, Dr Cathy Herbrand, Dr Kylie Baldwin, Dr Esmeé Hanna, Dr Raksha Pandya-Wood and Prof Lorraine Culley. Thank you, in particular, Esmeé for the encouraging mentoring, Kriss for the countless hours of dedicated proofreading, and Zaheera Essat and Wendy for answering my countless medical questions on IVF and pregnancy.

Огромное спасибо to my friends and colleagues in Russia: Zhanna Yureva, captain of the White Nights Furies, the St. Petersburg roller derby team. From the first moment I set foot into St. Petersburg for my MSc research in 2012 and met you at the Netherlands Institute ('Can I ask you a straight-forward question? Where do the not straight people meet?') to hugging me goodbye on my last day of my doctoral research, you were there, unconditionally, whenever and wherever I needed you. I will never forget that you bought and set up a Christmas tree for me at your home and invited me on Christmas Eve to make sure I am not alone for 'my' Christmas. Alena Lysenkina, my housemate and soulmate during my second research visit in 2014/2015. Rarely one meets a person as kind and loving to all creatures, green-leaved, two-legged, four-legged or one-eyed, as you are. Thank you for your friendship and sharing a home full of rescue animals, plants, home-baked bread, pancakes and art. Serghey Poliyanski, without batting an eye, you stayed back evening after evening at the end of our weekly Dutch lessons at the Netherlands Institute to help me in translating the tricky bits of my Russian interviews. Thank you for the Saturdays at yours, filled with coffee and laughter. And thank you for insisting on my hot water footbath after returning from the New Year's party, while watching and waiting with sleepy eyes. Thank you to the three of you, for your tireless transcription and translation help, and for continuing to support my research by sending me news and updates from Russia, and answering my questions long after I had left. And Kirsi Kalliomäki! Thank you for sharing the assortment of biscuits that accompanied your most expensive coffee of your life (to be had in the St. Petersburg Kempinski Hotel on the opening of the 2014 LGBT film festival). You truly were a ray of sunshine during the dark winter days, and the many coffees that accompanied our friendship well needed.

Thank you to the Netherlands Institute in St. Petersburg (NISPb) for the research grant that supported my MSc research visit, and especially Mila Chevalier for so generously extending your welcome for me to continue using your facilities throughout my field research (including the access to the coffee machine). Thank you Mila, as well as Luuc Kooijmans and Petra Couvée, for making sure I learned Dutch while living in Russia and helping me out so many times when I got myself stuck, including getting me out of a tricky housing situation. By making me part of the NISPb community, you did not just gave me a place to work and fuel on coffee but also a place to recharge and a kitchen to go to for a chat, kindness and comfort.

Thank you to the Centre for Independent Social Research (CISR) in St. Petersburg for hosting my seminar in 2014, and in particular Dr Olga Tkach for your continuous support and feedback on my work! Thank you to the University of St. Petersburg and State University of Technology and Design for inviting me and organising my stay in Russia as a visiting research student and visiting researcher, respectively.

More words of thanks go to Dr Aghogho Ekpruke – my good friend and confidant since I came to the United Kingdom for my doctoral studies. We both know how sometimes you believed more in me than I did myself, and how so often you just check in at the right time and find the right words to lift me up. I celebrate our friendship.

Thank you to Dr Sayani Mitra, my other companion in surrogacy research and an inspiration throughout our doctoral journeys and beyond. Thank you, Dr Marcin Smietana, who never fails to be kind and encouraging. Thank you for the valuable discussions and feedback on drafts and the cheerleading. Likewise, thank you, Dr Anindita Majumdar, for the neverending encouragement. Thank you also Maria Kirpichenko for all the chats on surrogacy and reproductive politics in Russia and the insights you gave me.

Thank you to my friends Eva, Sabrina and Vroni, who have been sharing and encouraging my excitement in studying (medical) anthropology from the very beginning, and thank you for all your love.

Sabrina, thank you also for reading first drafts and providing detailed feedback. Likewise thank you, Cameron, for appearing as a proofreader out of nowhere just weeks before submission after coming to my yoga classes! That was so unexpected and so helpful!

Thank you, Olga Yegorova, for helping me to assemble the desk from which I wrote this book!

Thank you, Emerald Publishing Team! It was lovely and so easy to work with you. I can only recommend you!

Thank you to a long list of friends (and colleagues) who were just there while I was doing this research and as this book took shape, and who listened and were kind and wonderful: Ryan James Ludlam, Dr Bruna Alvarez, Dr Yuliya Hilevych, Dr Aamir Hussein, Rita, Rob, Phil, Jason Finn, Filipe Machado Ferreira, Eric and Marcia and Emma and the Mount of Oaks Community, Joseph Akande, Dr Goffredo Polizzi, Suz Coughtrie, Dr Sara Thornton, Dr Anika König, Paschal Gumadwong Bagonza, Prof Christa Craven, Dr Linda Toledo, Dr Periklis Papaloukas, Dr Sebastian Cordoba, Lindsay and Rose, and James Kerr, who is especially dear to me.

And finally, coming last, but not least, because they held me and all of this together: thank you mum and dad, Hildegard and Karl Weis, and my brothers Felix and Philipp (who designed the cover image)! Thank you for your love and support – your daughter and sister, always travelling, always 'somewhere', yet always close.

Prologue: From Moldova to Russia for Surrogacy. Gabriela's Story

I met Gabriela for the first time in person on an evening in early February 2015.[1] The streets of St. Petersburg were laden in frozen sludge, the wind cold. A short period of warmer days had turned the snow-covered city into a landscape of ice puddles and crusty, brown snow piles before the temperature dropped again below freezing.

Gabriela is from the Republic of Moldova, the 'fruit basket and vineyard' of the Soviet Union, a small landlocked country south of Russia with long, warm summers and mild winters. Like many women I met in St. Petersburg, Gabriela had come to Russia to be a surrogacy worker. We had arranged this first personal encounter after being in touch via phone and email for nearly four months, after I responded to her online advertisement offering her services as a surrogacy worker, asking her to participate in my research. In this first online post, she included the following information:

> My name is Gabriela, I am 32. I have two children (11 and 4 years).
> I live in Pieter [St Petersburg], but have Moldovan citizenship.
> Slavic appearance, 160 cm, 55kg, all [medical] analysis present.

She further detailed her financial expectations of 800,000 Roubles [£13,280] for a successful surrogacy pregnancy (to be paid after the delivery of a healthy child), an additional 150,000 Roubles [£2,490] in the case of a twin pregnancy, an additional 100,000 Roubles [£1,660] in case of a caesarean section and 20,000–25,000 Roubles [£332–£415] as a monthly living allowance. She closed the ad with her contact details and the note that she was 'expecting a serious attitude' from interested client parents.

For the first few months, as we were exchanging emails and phone calls, and communicating in a blend of Romanian, her native language, and Russian, for surrogacy specificities, I learned that she had come to St. Petersburg specifically for surrogacy. Out of necessity and so as not be entirely dependent on agencies or client parents, she had also taken up employment in a factory, rented her own accommodation and taken care of her Russian work permit.

---

[1]All names in this book are pseudonyms.

Surrogacy in Russia, 1–3
Copyright © 2021 Christina Weis
Published under exclusive licence by Emerald Publishing Limited
doi:10.1108/978-1-83982-896-620211002

At first, she was lucky. She had found her first client parents, a couple from Russia's Arctic seaport Murmansk, within weeks of beginning her search. Soon they reached an agreement, signed contracts and the first embryo transfer was scheduled within a few months. However, the embryo transfer failed due to a medical error. Even though Gabriela liked the client parents and likewise they wanted to continue working with her, with a heavy heart, she decided against a second attempt with them: the client mother struggled to produce oocytes, and the doctors could not guarantee whether and when she would be able to undertake a next attempt. Gabriela couldn't afford the wait and the uncertainty. She had left her two young children in her mother's care in Moldova and wanted to return as soon as she could, with the money from the surrogacy arrangement in her pocket, to sort out her dire housing situation. Furthermore, her mother was unaware of the surrogacy work – to her community she had simply left for Russia for work, like so many people of her generation from Moldova.

In the beginning of February 2015, four months later, she found a new arrangement. That was when she offered me to meet for the first time to share her experience in detail.

We agreed to meet at the entrance of a metro station in a working-class district of St. Petersburg. I had told her how to recognise me, and, punctual to the agreed time, a young woman in a dark blue winter coat stepped over towards me. 'Christina?' I nodded. 'I am Gabriela'. After a quick exchange of 'how are you', and before I could thank her for agreeing to meet me, she took charge of the situation and started walking. She immediately came to the point, 'You wanted to ask me things'. 'Yes, about your surrogacy experiences and your attempts', I replied and asked whether I could invite her for a tea as the wind was icy and we both were pulling our shoulders up to our ears. She declined, apologising that she wouldn't have time for that and so we continued to walk. She sighed. Moving to St. Petersburg was hard, she started her story. When she moved here the previous year, in the beginning of winter, she struggled with the cold climate and the darkness of St. Petersburg's winter months. The winter was 'horrible', she had felt despondent in the unfamiliar surroundings, the harsh weather and the solitary and difficult search for the right surrogacy arrangement without a person to turn to for advice or support.

As we arrived back at the metro station, Gabriela tells me she was left with no choice but to come to Russia to search for client parents. Finding and securing an arrangement from Moldova was not an option.

> Because people [client parents or commercial surrogacy agencies] want to see you. So I came here. But the conditions are harsh. My current contract with the agency says that I may not tell anybody about it and that I am not allowed to show the contract to anybody. Literally, I am not even allowed to talk to you right now.

As we embarked on walking the same route a second time, I understood why conditions had set us to walk in the darkness of the night, far from the city centre, rather than sitting in a café.

'The contract is horrible', Gabriela continued, and provided some details upon careful request. 'I don't have any rights. The parent have all the advantages and I have none. All I have are enormous risks. And if nothing works out, I get nothing'. I asked her on what grounds she had chosen the agency. 'Because I am tired of waiting! I have been away from home for a year and I want to get it done now. No sex: that is not difficult, but being forbidden to leave the city once pregnant and not travel home to see family is hard!'. She paused and added, in a downcast voice, that because of the current economic situation and the unexpected devaluation of the Russian rouble, the value of her surrogacy earnings has dropped tremendously and living expenses in St. Petersburg have gone up.

The last thing she told me before we reached the metro station for the third time was that she had already had an embryo transfer with the new client parents and was scheduled for a pregnancy test in a few days from today. Before she left, she assured me that she would consider giving me a recorded interview and possibly let me see the contract, and if so, she would get in touch.

My field notes of that day ended with a monologue with myself: *I really would like to get this interview before she knows the result, because if it's negative, she might not want to meet again.... I am aware how selfish that thought is. But as there is no certainty in working as a surrogate, there is no certainty when researching on surrogacy.*

In this book about the social organisation and cultural framing of commercial gestational surrogacy in Russia, I am bringing together the experiences of women who acted as surrogates, the people who bought their services, and the medical professionals and agency staff involved in implementing and monitoring surrogacy pregnancies and births. As an ethnographer who spent 15 months interacting and conversing with these actors, visiting clinics, agencies and homes, and observing interactions, I am also sharing my personal and methodological considerations, decisions, emotions and struggles to give a transparent account of how I produced this knowledge and to offer in writing what ethnographers often only share in private.

Chapter 1

Introduction: Surrogacy in Russia

I absolutely understood, from the beginning, that those are *their*
children. That there is nothing of me. I was like a nanny. A good
nanny during the time of the pregnancy. And so, these are completely
their children. [Emphasis hers.]
(Daria, surrogacy worker (two pregnancies including one
twin pregnancy), November 2014)

Surrogacy is commonly defined as an arrangement whereby a woman conceives
in order to give birth to a child or children for another individual or couple to raise.
However, we cannot talk about 'surrogacy' as a single category. In other words,
'surrogacy' does not exist, but surrogacies.[1] A first distinction needs to be made
between genetic and gestational surrogacy arrangements, and commercial and
'altruistic' forms of surrogacy. In a genetic surrogacy arrangement, also referred to
as 'traditional' or 'host' surrogacy, the 'surrogate mother' provides her own eggs
and is inseminated to conceive. It is impossible to trace the beginnings of genetic
surrogacy. It has been practiced in various cultural contexts, with some 'surrogate
mothers' voluntarily engaging in genetic surrogacy arrangements for altruistic
or commercial reasons, while others were and continue to be forced to do so. In
gestational surrogacy arrangements, the 'surrogate mother' does not provide her
own egg(s) and is, therefore, not genetically related to the child. Gestational surrogacy has become possible with the invention of in vitro fertilisation (IVF) (Spar,
2006). It emerges from a plethora of arrangements, in which intended parents'
sperm or ova are used, or gametes are provided by or purchased from third-party
donors. In commercial surrogacy, as the name implies, the gestating woman is
financially compensated for her reproductive labour, whereas in altruistic
arrangements, she is expected to receive compensation only for immediately related
expenses, such as medication, travel or childcare provision, but no additional
financial reward is to be paid. Further to these four distinctions, surrogacy
arrangements are shaped within their varying legal, social, cultural and religious

---

[1]See also König (2018, pp. 282–283) for her elaboration on how 'one cannot even speak of
surrogacy as one specific practice, as in fact surrogacy means many different things, is done
under very diverse conditions, and the actors involved participate in it for a variety of
reasons'.

Surrogacy in Russia, 5–22
Copyright © 2021 Christina Weis
Published under exclusive licence by Emerald Publishing Limited
doi:10.1108/978-1-83982-896-620211004

settings (Berend, 2016b; Gerrits, 2016; Jacobson, 2016; König, 2018; Majumdar, 2017; Rudrappa, 2015; Twine, 2015; Whittaker, 2018). Surrogacy arrangements continue to be controversial. They are a topic of ongoing debates, such as whether they constitute women's exploitation, a commodification of women and children, whether they should be prohibited or not and who should have access and who should not (Anderson, 2000; Dworkin, 1983; Ekman, 2013; Lewis, 2019; Majumdar, 2014; Mamo & Alston-Stepnitz, 2015; Rothman, 1988; Svitnev, 2012b).

In this book, I address commercial, gestational surrogacy, as it is practiced in Russia.

Surrogacy in Russia

In Russia, the first gestational surrogacy pregnancy was conceived in St. Petersburg in 1995 and resulted in the birth of twins (Isakova, Korsak, & Gromyko, 2001). In the years that followed, surrogacy arrangements were barely regulated and sparsely practised due to the high cost and the novelty of the procedure. Yet about two decades later, the practises of assisted reproduction have been normalised (Burfoot, 1990), and St. Petersburg and Moscow have developed into reproductive hubs with the numbers of surrogacy arrangements increasing, especially since 2010. In comparison to the United States, surrogacy costs in Russia are low. Recent clampdowns on surrogacy arrangements in countries popular for transnational surrogacy arrangements, such as India, Nepal and Thailand (Rathi, 2020; Zimmerman, 2016), have contributed to a steady increase of international client parents accessing the Russian market. Russia's most recent increase in demand has come from client parents from China (Weis, 2021).

In 2013, the Russian Public Opinion Research Center survey (WCIOM, 2013) found that 51% of respondents considered surrogate mothers to be 'doing something necessary and useful'. Likewise, 16% of respondents regarded the act 'completely acceptable', whereas 26% rated surrogacy to be 'morally intolerable'. Analysing Russian print media, Nartova (2009, p. 79) found the widespread message that 'the only legitimate, normal and morally approved uses of surrogate motherhood (...) are those related to overcoming infertility' in heterosexual, ideally married, couples. Many conservative and influential religious voices publicly oppose surrogacy and repeatedly demand its prohibition (Agadjanian, 2017; Kirpichenko, 2017; ROC, n.d.); in 2013, for instance, Yelena Mizulina, then chairperson of the Duma Committee on Family, Women and Children, likened surrogacy to nuclear weapons in its threat to humanity, by '[destroying] natural ways of giving birth to children and natural ways of human reproduction' (SVPRESSA, 2013) (see Chapter 5 for a detailed discussion). Supporters of surrogacy, especially fertility doctors, in turn consider it to be a timely method of infertility management and a way of taking action against national fertility decline (see for instance Konstantin Svitnev in an interview with Rossiyskaya Gazeta, Novoselova, 2006). Discussing the societal and political attitudes towards surrogacy with the endocrinologist Dr Alexey, he summarised his and his colleagues' approach boldly: 'If a woman does not have a uterus, let another woman *with* a uterus carry the pregnancy for her'. In his opinion, opting for surrogacy to resolve infertility is the only 'sane attitude' a woman with fertility impairments can display. Whereas women who decide against surrogacy, despite the possibilities it offers and despite their financial capacity to do so, not only showed backward attitudes incompatible with a modern society but also failed in fulfilling their societal roles as mothers, according to Dr Alexey. Motherhood continues to be considered 'the highest embodiment of the feminine' in Russia (Vasyagina & Kalimullin, 2015, p. 61; see also; Rusanova, 2013). Highlighting the country's fertility decline, the proponents of surrogacy press for wider access and even state-subsidised IVF cycles to boost Russia's population growth (Svitnev, 2007). As Sarah Franklin (2013) remarks, trying to have children – by any means that are accessible – has become a new norm, and Russia is no exception.

Even though surrogacy is legal (for more details, see below) and increasingly well established as an infertility treatment, many surrogacy workers and client parents prefer to not disclose their identities (see also Khvorostyanov & Yeshua-Katz, 2020). For surrogacy workers, non-disclosure often is a strategic choice to avoid censure, belittling as 'breeders', or discrimination against their own children. Surrogacy workers themselves do not regard their occupation as morally reprehensible (see Chapter 2); on the contrary, many perceive surrogacy to be a sincere and even commendable way to support themselves and their families, taking the stance *men'she znaesh', kreptche spish'* ('the less you know, the better you sleep') to spare their families from public scrutiny and their parents from unnecessary worry. To achieve this, some surrogacy workers ceased visiting family and friends, or even relocated from their social surroundings to another part of the city or to another city altogether once their belly started showing. Others continued their everyday lives and jobs while covering up the absence of a child after birth with the 'white lie' of stillbirth. Ilya, for instance, who worked as a surrogacy worker three times, jokingly narrated how she bought her teenage son's compliance of silence with computer games and twice cunningly faked grief over alleged miscarriages at work. Karina, who carried three surrogacy pregnancies, always took paid maternity leave, then gave notice after the delivery and cut all ties with her former colleagues. In a less drastic manner, Olesya arranged herself in family pictures so that she hid her protruding belly. By posting the photos below (Fig. 1.1, reproduced as sketches) on her public social media account during her pregnancy while she was concealing the pregnancy, Olesya was actively writing her own (social media) history as 'not pregnant'.

Client parents' reasons for non-disclosure included shame over their impaired fertility, fear of discrimination, and paramount, the fear that their children would suffer discrimination. To maintain their secret, client mothers strapped on artificial bellies to suggest a pregnancy and had their husband stroke these bellies for others to see. However, many client mothers reported their fear of being found out as well as the effort and discomfort of strapping on a silicon 'pregnant belly' that weighed several kilos. Client mother Katarina described that she felt like 'I was carrying my own personal sauna on my belly. It was like a real sauna. I was constantly dripping sweat', and Anastasia recalled how she feared surprise visits from relatives, or simply going out on the street and possibly getting involved in an accident and having paramedics notice the fraud. Prior to the birth, many client mothers even

Fig. 1.1.   Sketches of Olesya Concealing Her Surrogacy Pregnancy.
Fieldnotes.
Left: Olesya is lifting her jacket off her protruding belly and pulling it forward as she is holding her son's shoulder to conceal the shape of her pregnancy. Right: Olesya, in swim wear, is posing hugging her husband, hiding the pregnancy.

rented a hospital room and took advantage of their maternity hospitals' offer to photo-document 'their birth'. After the birth, many cut all ties with the surrogacy worker to avoid information about the surrogacy being leaked or the need to live with the fear that the woman might one day contact them again.

Setting the Scene: The Legal Settings and Social Organisation of Surrogacy in Russia

The legal regulations and medical guidelines for surrogacy in Russia are minimal. In fact, regulations are so limited that lawyer, legal expert and member of the Russian Association of Human Reproduction (RAHR), Konstantin Svitnev,

> …[considers Russia] as a sort of reproductive paradise, being the country with the most favorable legislation for intended parents, where no specific federal law regulates any aspect of assisted reproduction.
>
> (Svitnev, 2011, p. 155)

The Federal Law on Citizens' Health No. 323 permits altruistic and commercial surrogacy and defines surrogate motherhood and the requirements for a woman wanting to be a surrogate as follows:

Surrogate motherhood is the gestation and birth of a child (including premature birth) under a contract concluded between a surrogate mother (a woman who gestates the foetus after receiving an embryo transfer of a donated embryo) and potential parents whose gametes were used for fertilization, or a single woman, for whom the gestation and birth of a child is impossible for medical reasons.

A surrogate mother may be a woman between the age of twenty and thirty-five, who has at least one healthy child of her own, who has received a medical certificate attesting satisfactory health status, and has given written, informed and voluntary consent for this medical intervention. A woman who is married, registered in accordance with the procedure established by the legislation of the Russian Federation, may be a surrogate mother only with the written consent of her spouse. A surrogate mother cannot simultaneously be an egg donor.

Further, the Medical Order 107 lists the medical testing required to determine whether a woman is suitable to be a 'surrogate mother'. In addition, although it is not listed in the requirements, agencies and most doctors require surrogacy workers to have delivered vaginally to qualify. According to Russian law, the 'surrogate mother' is the legal mother and guardian of the child she births. In order to obtain legal parenthood status, client parents need to register as the child's parents at the civil registry after the child's birth and provide documentation from the fertility clinic, the maternity ward and show evidence of the 'surrogate mother's' written consent. Only then does a child's birth certificate list the client parents as the parents.[2]

According to the current Russian law (as constituted in 2011), seeking a surrogate in Russia is permitted for married and unmarried heterosexual couples and single women (Russian citizens, residents and foreigners alike). Single men are not mentioned in the law, but over the past decade, surrogacy agencies and specialised lawyers have developed different strategies to enable single men to become fathers through surrogacy. Two strategies that I have witnessed during my fieldwork in St. Petersburg included involving a specialist lawyer to fight for the single father's paternity in court, or taking an informal route whereby the surrogacy worker does not relinquish the child, but registers as the mother and arranges with the client father for him to have parental rights and duties. One of my participants, Matvey, a single man in his early 60s, opted for this route. He also entrusted me with the information that he is gay and that neither his surrogacy worker nor his agency were aware of this. Instead:

---

[2]If a person born through surrogacy wants to learn about their surrogate (against their parents' wishes or when parents have not kept contact details), the only place that stores the evidence would be the civil registry that provided the birth certificate.

> I believe Olya [the surrogacy worker] thinks that I am a lost cause and so on... and here my age [63] obviously helps me to maintain that impression. She might think 'ah well, maybe he has had broken marriages'. She never asked. I believe, the older the man, the less likely one is to have to answer questions about one's sexual life.
>
> (Matvey, client father, February 2015)

According to Matvey, as long as he lives in Russia, nothing further would be needed from Olya. However, if he wanted to move or travel abroad, he would need her permission, certified by a notary.

As same-sex marriage is not permitted and the Russian state doesn't acknowledge two fathers as a child's legal parents, only one man in a same-sex relationship can act as a father. Nevertheless, some agencies offered gay couples the opportunity to each provide a sperm sample to create two batches of embryos, each fertilised with one man's semen, to subsequently transfer one embryo from each and 'with a bit of luck', have a twin pregnancy to ensure each man's genetic connection. The resulting children would then be genetic half-siblings, sharing origin from the same egg provider. But, as of 01 January 2021, this very arrangement is no longer possible, as the newest amendment to the family law prohibits assisted reproduction without using at least one intending parent's gamete (Loktionova, 2020). That means, in a married couple, either the client father or the client mother have to provide either egg or sperm, and in case of a gay couple, only the provider of the sperm can be recognized as the father. Two fathers, even if genetically related to two children carried by their surrogacy worker in a twin pregnancy, are not legally recognized by the law on Citizens' Health, and recognizing a father who has no genetic link is prohibited by the recent amendment to the family law. Furthermore, surrogacy for single and gay men in Russia could be prohibited in 2021 if the Russian State Duma accepts the draft bill proposed in January 2021 (for details, see Chapter 5).

Thus, the current Russian legal framework defines the contract partners, regulates the initiation of a surrogacy programme and, to some extent, its ending. However, as has already been raised by feminist and legal scholars (Khazova, 2013; Kirillova & Bogdan, 2013; Kirpichenko, 2017; Sokolova & Mulenko, 2013), the legal framework around surrogacy in Russia is riddled with shortcomings that may expose surrogacy workers to risks; it is not clear whether a surrogacy contract is legally binding (Khazova, 2013, p. 317). This means that if the client parents abandon the child during the commissioned pregnancy or after delivery, the surrogacy worker remains the legal guardian and is confronted with the option of keeping and raising the child, or giving the child up for adoption. The client parents are not obliged to pay the surrogacy worker for her labour. There is no upper limit of how many embryos can be transferred at once, or guidance for spacing between embryo transfers. According to the Federal Law No. 323, the surrogacy worker has the right to terminate the pregnancy like any pregnant woman up to the 12th week, or for medical reasons, at any point during the pregnancy. However, having entered a surrogacy contract, the contract commonly stipulates that the rights to make these decisions lie with the client parents, pitching state law against contract law. Hence, if a surrogacy worker aborts without the client parents' consent, the client parents can sue her and demand that she reimburses all the expenses they have incurred (medical expenses, travel expenses, etc.). There is no guidance on what measures should be undertaken if a child is born disabled. Further, there is no legal age limit for the client parents (Rusanova, 2013), and various agencies in my sample obliged their surrogacy workers to undergo amniocentesis if their client mothers provided their own eggs and were older than 40. Moreover, surrogacy workers in agency arrangements don't have the right to know prior to the transfer whether their client mother is the egg provider and her age, so that she can decline the arrangement, as eggs of women with advanced age have a lower chance of resulting in pregnancy.

There are two main ways to arrange surrogacy pregnancies in Russia: either through commercial surrogacy agencies or through direct arrangements. Surrogacy agencies are private commercial enterprises. They select suitable surrogacy workers among interested women, match them with client parents, provide client parents with legal guidance, supervise the pregnancies, provide a notary to take surrogacy workers' consent to hand the baby over after childbirth, administer the payment of the surrogacy workers and, finally, guide the client parents through establishing legal parenthood.[3] In Russia, no consideration of statutory conditions or licencing is required to open a surrogacy agency, or in the words of agency owner Alexander, '[opening a surrogacy agency] is as simple as opening an ice cream parlour'. When agencies match surrogacy workers and client parents, they commonly advise their clients to not seek personal contact with their surrogacy worker and prefer to match according to availability by menstrual cycle and blood type rather than clients' preferences. For a surcharge, client parents can choose from the agency's catalogue, decline a match or request a personal 'viewing'. However, agencies advise against personal contact during the arrangement. One agency employee, for instance, remarked that if client parents insisted, they advised them to at least wait until the pregnancy had survived the 'critical first trimester', so they did not get emotionally invested in the foetus or the surrogacy worker, in case the pregnancy failed. Not only would that spare them avoidable emotional turmoil, but it would also speed up the process of starting the next attempt with the next available and suitable surrogacy worker, rather than insisting on waiting for the doctor's approval to repeat an attempt with their first match because of their emotional investment. Unlike the client parents, the surrogacy workers receive no information about their client parents and may never meet them during the entire arrangement.

In direct arrangements, surrogacy workers and client parents conclude a contract directly between one another. They commonly find each other on relevant online sites, such as on infertility forums or under the surrogacy section of the medical service website 'Meddesk.ru'. Once contact is established, surrogacy workers and client parents exchange questions of interest, including details of the arrangements and financial aspects before they meet in person to gauge whether or not the other

---

[3]For an excellent analysis of commercial surrogacy agency websites and their use of imagery and text to promote surrogacy and surrogacy workers, see Kirpichenko (2020).

party seems a suitable and appropriate person with whom to enter into a contract. (See Chapter 2 for more detail on relationships between surrogacy workers and client parents.)

Surrogacy arrangements in Russia happen exclusively in the private sphere; that means they take place in private fertility clinics, and if the client parents choose, with the guidance and support of private commercial agencies. However, the birth and medical supervision of the pregnancy may happen in a state institution if the client parents choose to do so, as it saves money. In Russia, every citizen and legalised resident is guaranteed universal access to health-care service by mandatory health insurance (signed into law in 1993); maternity care is included in the free of charge provisions.[4] Prenatal appointments are taken at the *zhenskaya consultatsiya* (maternity centre), and births take place at the *roddom* (short for *rodilniy dom*; the maternity hospital). In both places, women can make appointments without a referral. In direct arrangements, regardless of whether the client parents choose a private or state *zhenskaya consultatsiya,* and regardless of whether the client parents attend or are absent from the appointment, I observed the tendency among surrogacy workers and client parents to conceal that it was a surrogacy pregnancy. For instance, Nastya, who carried twins, only informed her gynaecologist that the twins were conceived via IVF to make sure no medical nuances would be missed. In another case, client mother Nadezhda and surrogacy worker Ilya, even when inviting me to the five-month scan, did not inform their doctor about the surrogacy arrangement; instead, Ilya presented both of us as close friends who she desired as her supporters (see p. 151 in Appendix 2 for a description of the situation).

Finally, I want to give some insights into how surrogacy contracts are made and payments are calculated. In direct arrangements, client parents and surrogacy workers agree over the conditions and payment in one direct contract. Generally, the contract stipulates the number of embryo transfers, the financial aspects, each party's rights and responsibilities, and provisions for worst-case scenarios (such as miscarriage, stillbirth, death of the surrogacy worker or medical emergencies). Depending on the client parents, the surrogacy workers may have a say in the contract's content. In agency arrangements, two or three sets of contracts are concluded: between the agency and the client parents, the agency and the surrogacy worker and, depending on the agency, between the client parents and the surrogacy worker.[5] Here, surrogacy workers have no say in the contract

---

[4]While mandatory services are free of charge, the rapid commercialisation of what was previous the Soviet health-care system has led to pronounced inequalities across income groups and geographical regions, as well as to under-the-counter payments for benefits and an influx of private services, especially in the fields of dentistry, ophthalmology and infertility, for those able to afford them (Blam & Kovalev, 2006; Larivaara, Dubikaytis, Kuznetsova, & Hemminki, 2008).

[5]The contract between the client parents and the agency includes selecting and supervising the surrogacy worker, arranging the delivery and the bureaucratic aftermath of arranging for the client parents to be recognising as the legal parents. Depending on the agency, client parents are offered a range of pre-tailored programmes and contracts, or the more expensive option of individualised programmes and contracts.

contents and cannot refuse terms or make amendments. Unlike in direct arrangements, where client parents tend to include up to three embryo transfers with their surrogacy workers, agencies prefer moving the client parents on to the next available surrogacy worker if an attempt fails (for more details on matching, see Chapter 2). No governmental guidance exists regarding the contents of a surrogacy contract. This, and novice surrogacy workers' lack of familiarity with specific legal and medical vocabulary, puts surrogacy workers at risk of exploitation. The following statement by Daria, whose vocational training as a medical technician and previous experience as a surrogacy worker gave her unique expertise, illustrates the point:

> When I saw the [agency] contract with all the demands, I told them that I don't want that. (…) I didn't like that it included all those different penal sanctions. Some of them were crazy (…) after [reading] two pages I asked them to give me the contract to have a thorough read at home and they told me that I could read it only here, on electronic view. 'We will not provide you with a printed version to take with you', they said. I didn't like that. I was alert! I told them 'Why on earth do you think that's acceptable? That I sign it like a cat in a bag, not knowing what I am getting myself into?!' [The contract included] such phrases as 'if the child is not born healthy, then the clinic might suspend the final compensation'. But the concept of health is relative. (…) and they neither defined what a full term and a pre-term baby is (…). When you give birth to twins, they are usually born a bit earlier. (…) and in such cases [pre-term delivery], the contract stipulated there would be a significant reduction in the final compensation.
> (Daria, surrogacy worker, November 2014)

Daria decided against this offer, not least because she felt in no hurry to enter a second arrangement. Surrogacy worker Gabriela, whose story opens this book, by contrast, felt under immense pressure to find an arrangement, and she, therefore, signed a 60-page long contract which she likewise was not allowed to take home to study and ask questions for clarification, but given an hour to sign or leave. In one of our meetings, she brought the signed contract – in confidence, as it included penalties for sharing its contents – to show me the paragraphs she had pencil-marked as those that she didn't understand. Carefully turning the pages, I thought at a moment that one of my dark long hair had fallen onto the page, but when I tried to brush it off, I realised appalled that Gabriela had marked an entire page as incomprehensible to her.

As surrogacy is a private business, there are no regulations regarding the prices. Instead, users, providers and mediators of surrogacy services closely monitor their competitors, online discussions and advertisements in order to set their prices. Though the costs and compensations for surrogacy services are steadily rising, the compensation surrogacy workers receive is not keeping up with the increasing living costs and, especially, not with the real estate market. Doctors and nurses confirmed that while, in 2000, the money earned through surrogacy gestation bought women a one- to two-room apartment, in 2015 surrogacy workers already calculated for themselves the need to carry at least two pregnancies to afford a similar apartment.

Surrogacy workers are paid in the local currency, Russian Roubles (₽).[6] Their compensation is commonly broken to a monthly instalment during the pregnancy for food and transport (20,000–25,000₽/£332–415, and in case of twins: 25,000–35,000₽/£415–581), and the final compensation of 800,000–950,000₽ (£13,280–15,770) (in St. Petersburg). In case of a multiple pregnancy or a caesarean section, 150,000–200,000₽ (£2,490–3,320) are added.[7]

Pre-term births are compensated at a much lower level, such as for a birth in the 32nd–34th week, the surrogacy worker is entitled to 60% of the stipulated payment.[8] In general, the money surrogacy worker in Russia earn far exceeds her annual income; in 2015, the average monthly salary in the Siberian Federal District was 15,000₽ (£249) and the national average 18,500₽ (£307).

Surrogacy workers are required to abstain from any harmful substances and activities, at a minimum alcohol, nicotine, narcotics and any medicine unless prescribed by their doctor. In stricter cases, surrogacy workers are also prohibited from driving or using certain public transport, playing certain sports and engaging in sexual intercourse. Non-compliance is punished via financial penalties, which are subtracted from the final remuneration. Penalties are also given for non-compliance with dietary requirements or a prescribed exercise regime, or not answering phone calls. The severity of these penalties depends on the contract. Discussing the practice of penalties with an agency owner and his colleague, the owner explained that he fines surrogacy workers upon their first violation – without

---

[6]These are the prices for 2014–2015, when I conducted the longest period of fieldwork in St. Petersburg.

[7]The compensation for a caesarean section is intended to compensate the surrogacy worker for the trauma and loss of opportunity to become a surrogacy worker again. If complications demand a hysterectomy, additional compensation is paid on a discretionary basis. In case of failed embryo transfers, first trimester pregnancy loss, spontaneous abortion or abortion on request of the client parents, the surrogacy worker is entitled to a compensation, calculated according to the gestational week and the respective rates of agencies/client parents. Compensation in case of pregnancy loss is not calculated in a direct proportion to the stage at which the pregnancy was lost, but it is at the discretion of the agency whether to compensate the first three months at all. From the fourth months on, every week of pregnancy is compensated at a certain rate, whereby the rate for the second trimester is lower than the third trimester.

[8]Several doctors and agency workers related their suspicion that some surrogacy workers would try to induce labour, accepting the risk of potentially damaging to the child in order to reduce the duration of the pregnancy. In order to prevent this, agencies introduced salary reduction for pre-term birth to incentivise full term gestation.

One contract (of a direct arrangement that I was given for insight, but not allowed to keep or photo-document) stipulated that there would be no compensation for the surrogacy worker should the child be born dead, or die shortly after birth and before parental rights were assigned to the client parents (for more information see further below), or be born with severe disability caused by the birth.

prior warning – a minimum 10% of her prospective earnings. Responding to the astonishment written in my face, his colleague added 'Our Russian girls only speak "Rouble"'.

Why Yet Another Piece of Surrogacy Research Matters – Or Locating Research on Surrogacy in Russia within Existing Work

In 2011/2012, when I began preparing for my research on surrogacy in Russia, to my knowledge, no empirical research on surrogacy in any country of the former Soviet Union had been undertaken. Early empirical surrogacy research concentrated on arrangements in the United States, from where commercial surrogacy originated (Spar, 2006), and the United Kingdom, which banned commercial forms of surrogacy right at the outset and has since been implementing both genetic and gestational arrangements on altruistic bases. In the early 2000s, empirical surrogacy research began shifting to newly emerging transnational hubs in South Asia, such as India (Pande, 2014b).

The empirical research on surrogacy in the United States and United Kingdom started in the early 1980s and mainly focused on the surrogate mothers' motivation, their personality traits and character, including testing for psychopathologies, and the attitude of the general public (Aigen, 1996; Einwohner, 1989; Franks, 1981; Kanefield, 1999; Kleinpeter & Hohman, 2000; Parker, 1983, 1984; Pizitz, Joseph, & Rabin, 2012). It is important to note that with IVF only recently being invented, the majority of arrangements were genetic surrogacy arrangements, and therefore, without explicitly mentioning it, early empirical research was based predominantly on genetic surrogacy arrangements. This includes Helena Ragonés (1994) US-based ethnography *Surrogate Motherhood: Conception in the Heart*, which is the first extensive qualitative surrogacy study, examining surrogacy in light of American kinship ideology. At about the same time, political scientists, philosophers and feminist scholars debated whether surrogacy should be understood as the commodification of women or children (Anderson, 1990; van Niekerk & van Zyl, 1995), the disenfranchisement of surrogate mothers (Oliver, 1989), women's liberation to use their bodies and reproductive capacities as they pleased (Andrews, 1988; Berkhout, 2008; McLachlan & Swales, 2000) or a reduction of women's capacity to be reproductive vessels (Weiss, 1992).

A decade later, India emerged as the most popular destination for transnational fertility travel mostly for North Americans and Western Europeans who were promised surrogacy arrangements giving 'First World skill for Third World prices'. At this point, the topic came back into the focus of empirical research. Amrita Pande (2009, 2010), who began her fieldwork in 2006 in Anand, India, pioneered the 'second wave' of qualitative surrogacy research. Her book *Wombs in Labor. Transnational Commercial Surrogacy in India* (2014) is the first to centre the analysis of surrogacy practices around the concept of labour and its new forms that arise from (reproductive) globalisation. More ethnographies on surrogacy in India soon followed, such as Sharmila Rudrappa's (2015) *Discounted Life*, Daisy Deomampo's

(2016) *Transnational Reproduction*, Anindita Majumdar's (2017) *Transnational Commercial Surrogacy and the (Un)Making of Kin in India* and Sayani Mitra's (2017) *Disruptive Embodiments*. These monographs address the experience of intending parents and surrogacy workers in transnational surrogacy, the risks of exploiting surrogate mothers in developing countries, the making, unmaking and meaning of kinship in different cultural contexts and imaginaries of race and ethnicity. At the same time, Elly Teman's (2010) ethnography *'Birthing a mother'* was published. It describes the Jewish–Israeli context, where surrogacy is endorsed by the state, yet restricted to heterosexual, married citizens, and it pays particular attention to the relationships between surrogate and intended mothers, and Israel's pro-natalist quest of reproducing the nation. In 2018, Andrea Whittaker published *International Surrogacy as Disruptive Industry in Southeast Asia*, addressing how surrogacy spread from India to countries in South Asia, taking on new patterns characterised by new flexible hybrid forms. Yet alongside the growing body of empirical research on surrogacy developments in the United States, Israel and South-East Asia, commercial surrogacy arrangements were also being practised in the countries of the former Soviet Union, yet remained at the margins of scholarly attention. Accounts of the practice of surrogacy in Russia were limited to the print media discourse analysis of the Russian sociologists Olga Tkach, Olga Brednikova and Nadya Nartova (Brednikova, Nartova, & Tkach, 2009; Nartova, 2009; Tkach, 2009). In 2013, first empirical contributions on surrogacy in former Soviet Union countries have been made by myself in form of my Msc thesis (Weis, 2013) and Michelle Rivkin-Fish (2013), who analysed online forum posts by surrogate and intending mothers; in the following years, Anastasia Dushina, Kersha, Larkina, and Provorova (2016) interviewed surrogacy agency staff in Russia, Veronika Siegl (2018a, 2018b) conducted ethnographic research on surrogacy in Russia and the Ukraine, Natalia Khvorostyanov and Daphne Yeshua-Katz (2020) analysed Russian surrogates online forum conversations, and Sigrid Vertommen and Camille Barbagallo (2021) conducted empirical research on surrogacy in Georgia.

Expanding surrogacy research and theoretical conceptualisations of women's reproductive labour from Europe and Northern America to South Asia, Pande (2010) argues that the Western controversy over the morality of surrogacy is ill-suited as a way to understand the lived experience of surrogate mothers in India. In India, surrogacy had become a survival strategy, and cultural understandings of surrogacy differ. In a similar vein, I demonstrate in this book that the common tropes of (transnational) surrogacy, such as the North–South exploitation and brown bodies carrying white babies (Harrison, 2016; Hochschild, 2011; Pande, 2014a, 2014b; Twine, 2017) and the framing of surrogacy as a labour of love (Jacobson, 2016) or an altruistic or heroic act (Berend, 2012, 2016b; Teman, 2010), fail to address the practice of surrogacy in Russia and other countries of the former Soviet Union.

In his book, I contribute to our understanding of surrogacy practises around the world by analysing how in Russia, surrogacy is unapologetically seen as an economic transaction, or in the words of the surrogates, a 'business arrangement', which may lead to a good (working) relationship between the involved parties but is not expected to last beyond the birth of the child. The gestational 'surrogate mothers' regarded themselves as workers in relation to the surrogacy child, not mothers. For this reason, I have introduced the term 'surrogacy worker' (Weis, 2013). Throughout the book, I am using the term 'surrogacy worker' in my analysis, and *surmama,* the local vernacular for 'surrogate mother', when replicating direct and indirect quotes from interviews and ethnographic observations. Further, I analyse reproductive migration patterns in form of (temporary) migration or regular (long-distance) commuting for surrogacy work by surrogacy workers in Russia, and their inherent stratifications, as well as the ethnic stratifications among surrogacy workers in Russia.

In doing this, I further reinforce the argument that there is not one way of doing surrogacy, but that surrogacy practices are socially culturally and politically embedded and need to be understood and analysed by taking their distinctive differences in account (König, 2018; Smietana, Rudrappa, & Weis, 2021).

Notes on Methods, Sample and Recruitment

This book is based on two ethnographic fieldwork periods in Russia (from September 2011 to January 2012, and from August 2014 to May 2015), and a cyberethnographic follow-up study (from January 2019 until March 2021).[9] Primarily, my research was conducted in St. Petersburg and its surroundings; however, I also undertook research trips to Moscow, the Republic of Karelia and Minsk, Belarus, and conducted online video or phone interviews with surrogacy workers in other part of Russia and in the Ukraine, when travelling to meet in person was not possible. Over eight years of research, I have collected a rich data set consisting of recorded and verbatim transcribed interviews; ethnographic fieldnotes of ethnographic interviews; participant observations in fertility clinics, maternity wards, gynaecological units, surrogacy agencies' premises and in surrogacy workers' homes and provided accommodation; online and newspaper surrogacy advertisements by agencies and individuals; cyberethnographic observations on agency and clinical websites; brochures and leaflets; discussions on surrogacy in openly accessible online forums; media reports; laws and regulations; surrogacy contracts; public statements by politicians and representatives of the Russian Orthodox Church and personal reflections over my role and own emotions in the fieldwork process. I have recorded and verbatim transcribed 37 interviews with 28 surrogacy workers and took ethnographic fieldnotes of conversations with a further seven surrogacy workers without recording interviews. There are several reasons why I could not record interviews with all the surrogacy workers who gave their consent to participate in my research. In some cases, I met surrogacy workers during or after visits at the IVF clinic, but situational and time constraints, such as the lack of a private room available at the clinic for an interview, or an agency driver waiting to return the surrogacy worker to her accommodation,

---

[9]The research from September 2011 to January 2012 received ethical approval from Utrecht University. The research from August 2014 to May 2015 and from January 2019 to March 2021 received ethical approval from De Montfort University (reference number 1384 and 3228).

impeded the opportunity to conduct an interview. In some cases, women preferred to withdraw their participation after finding out that their embryo transfers failed. In other cases, surrogacy workers consented to engage in conversation and provided interviews but preferred me to take notes rather than recording the interview. I also interviewed eight client parents, 13 agency staff including directors, managers, legal advisers and chaperones, and 17 medical staff, including IVF experts, endocrinologists, nurses, psychologists and obstetricians.

The sample of the surrogacy workers includes 39 surrogacy workers who carried between one and four surrogacy pregnancies, including twins and in one case triplets, and women who experienced miscarriages and failed embryo transfers. The sample includes women were local to St. Petersburg, as well as reproductive migrants or commuters, who moved or travelled to St. Petersburg on a regular basis for their surrogacy arrangements (see Chapter 4). Some of the migrant and commuting surrogacy worker were from different parts of Russia, others came from the Ukraine, Moldova, Belarus and Uzbekistan. The surrogacy workers were between 19 and 36 years old at the time of their participation in the research, and all of them had children of their own. In six cases, I was able to conduct research with surrogacy workers and client parents over a period of several months, collecting several follow-up interviews, joining them for medical appointments and exchanging information and updates between visits and interviews. In four cases, both surrogacy workers and client parents who were in a surrogacy arrangement together participated in my research, each being aware of the other's participation. The sample does not include women who were rejected on medical or psychological grounds or changed their mind. The reason for this shortcoming was the challenge of finding these women.

All client parents in my sample were Russian citizens; eight were living in St. Petersburg at time of the research, and one couple was living in Kazakhstan but sought treatment in St. Petersburg. Of the five couples that went through surrogacy, I met only two of the husbands in person, but was unable to record interviews with them as they were not interested in this level of participation. Two of the client mothers in turn participated over several months, one of whom provided interviews during her first and after her second surrogacy pregnancy. One client mother's husband was working abroad at the time of her surrogacy attempts and was unaware of his wife's intention but believed that his wife was undergoing her own IVF treatment, and the ultrasound pictures she sent were hers. This client mother, Evgenya, had lost her uterus following a complicated birth in her early 50s which led an emergency hysterectomy. On the advice of her (male) doctor, she never told her husband about the hysterectomy, scared to be abandoned over her deficiency of infertility. Finally, my sample also included two homosexual men, one of whom had already become a dad through surrogacy, while the other was interested in the option. See Appendix 1 for a detailed list of participants. When preparing for this pioneering empirical work on surrogacy in Russia, I chose to conduct an ethnography with the intention of mapping my research field and identifying the relevant actors and potential participants as part of the data collection. The person I was when I entered my research site in September 2012 – a young woman in her mid-twenties, a master's student from a Dutch university with the research endorsement of my local host institution, a foreigner with clumsy grammar, initially with no contacts to any doctors, agents, surrogacy workers or client parents – shaped my 'entry into the field' significantly.[10] Negotiating access to research sites, locating gatekeepers and standing my – ethical – ground as a young woman *and* an empirical researcher was a challenge. (For a detailed discussion on the ethical challenges of negotiating access and authority when recruiting participants through institutional gatekeepers, see Weis, 2017, 2019.) When preparing for my first research visit to Russia, I had rejected the option to contact clinics in advance as I perceived that a research request would easily be dismissed by a secretary before it ever reached a doctor or someone in the clinic management. Instead, I began visiting clinics that listed surrogacy services on their websites as soon as I arrived in St. Petersburg. To my initial despair, my early attempts at speaking to medical or management staff in the clinics were intercepted at the reception desk. After several unsuccessful attempts, I tried the following: I switched to enquiring about surrogacy services in English. In many cases, reception staff were unable to respond in English. Instead of asking me to leave, some called for someone with a better command of English, who in several cases were medical staff who took an interest in my research endeavour. Subsequently, they offered support in recruiting participant surrogacy workers and client parents, and endorsed my research to colleagues in other clinics. In another instance, I kept returning to the same clinic at different times, hoping for different front desk staff who hadn't yet sent me away. Returning a fourth time, the very doctor I was trying to see and speak to walked past just as I said his name. He stopped and enquired what the matter was about. He became interested in my research project at once and promptly invited me to his office to discuss it further.[11] Returning for my second research visit (Weis, 2017) and during my cyberethnographic follow-up study, I could draw on existing support from medical staff and expanded my research to newly opened clinics.

I attempted to make first contact with commercial surrogacy agencies in a similar manner, but recruiting agency staff for interviews was difficult and more difficult still to negotiate gatekeeping towards surrogacy workers. My requests to speak to surrogacy workers were often dismissed, the women were labelled as 'uneducated' and their recruitment for research futile. Agencies preferred and offered therefore instead to 'answer on their behalf'. After struggling to convince agencies, the purpose of anthropological research and importance of speaking to individual surrogacy workers, I was finally invited to join the manager of one of St. Petersburg's largest agencies in overseeing four of their workers' medical

---

[10]The Netherlands Institute of St. Petersburg awarded me a visiting research scholarship in 2012 Thank you again for you support, and your faith in my skills to deliver this research.
[11]During our first conversation, he then had the reception staff who nearly succeeded in sending me away serve me coffee. While I felt slightly uncomfortable with this situation, we soon built a friendly working relationship as I visited the clinic regularly. Even two years later, when I returned for my PhD research (Weis, 2017), she immediately recognised me and called to announce my arrival to the doctor before I had finished changing out of my coat and covering my shoes with the provided blue sterile plastic covers.

appointments. After having explained the principle of informed voluntary consent that was guiding my research, I had – naively – expected that the women attending the appointment that I was invited to were informed and had consented. On that day, Malvina, the manager, welcomed me to sit with her through the routine check of four pregnant surrogacy workers. I was assigned a chair in the corner from where I could see the desk of the doctor and the examination bed. The chair for the surrogacy workers stood sideways in front of the doctor's desk, so that each surrogacy worker was surrounded by the doctor to her right, Malvina in front, and me with some distance, to her left. Routinely questioning four surrogacy workers in a row about their pregnancies and examining them physically (which involved transvaginal checks of their cervixes in two cases), Malvina made no effort to introduce me or give me chance to speak. Realising quickly that these women had not been asked for their consent to my presence and not been informed about my intension, I focused my note-taking on the doctor and Malvina, and on Malvina's attitude and conduct with the women in her care.[12] Following this incident, I decided to not risk complying with agencies' violation of surrogacy workers' informed consent and desisted from asking surrogacy agencies to act as gatekeepers. Even though surrogacy workers are as much 'savvy participants' (Nahman, 2008, p. 67) in Russia's neoliberal reproductive economy as the Romanian egg sellers described by Michal Nahman, surrogacy workers' dependence on the goodwill of their agencies, or their imagined dependence on the gatekeeping clinicians because of their prestige and rank, could constitute the risk of compromising their voluntary informed consent (Weis, 2019). Instead, I refocused my recruitment of surrogacy workers and client parents on posting recruitment calls on social media and forums, and utilised responding to advertisements and snowball sampling. While this recruitment route was tedious work, it guaranteed that my participants gave voluntary and informed consent.[13] See Appendix 2 for selected examples detailing meeting and recruiting surrogacy workers, establishing a research relationship and reflections of positionality. To further address this inevitable power imbalance, I took the feminist position of weighing the stories of the surrogacy workers over the accounts of client parents, agency staff and clinicians. That means, when doctors discarded surrogacy workers' concerns as foolish, and when agency staff dismissed them as uneducated and ignorant, I maintain: this is their story. They are the experts in their own experiences and opinions, their feelings and their lives, and throughout my

---

[12]I have chosen to report these observations to illustrate the power imbalance in surrogacy arrangements. Yet, I do so without giving any description of the surrogacy workers involved as they have not consented to be involved in this research. In retrospect I asked myself many times if I should have left the room, but experiencing this situation at the onset of my MSc research, I feared loosing my hard-gained access.

[13]The research sample with regards to surrogacy workers in direct arrangements or in agency arrangements nevertheless is balanced; in some cases, surrogacy workers in agency arrangements responded to my social media recruitment posts, and in other instances, women had experience with both kinds of arrangements.

research and in this book, I respect and acknowledge their authority to narrate their experience (see also Davis, 2019).

Emotions 'in the Field'

While positivist research paradigms reject emotions in research as distortion, I position myself along other feminist qualitative researchers to argue for paying explicit attention to our own emotions and to use emotions that are stirred up in the research process and, thus, in the production of knowledge. Going into emotions rather than away from them when conducting research adds to our understanding, analysis and interpretation (see also Holland, 2007; Jaggar, 1989; Watts, 2008). Encountering, stirring up and being affected by emotions is inevitable in research (Jaggar, 1989), and I agree with Hoffmann (2007, p. 322), who states that 'when researchers act without awareness of their own emotions and the emotional labour they perform in the field, they will be more influenced by their emotions rather than less'. As qualitative researchers, and ethnographers immersed in the field in particular, we engage in both emotion work and emotional labour in managing everyday (research) interactions. Emotion work, as defined by Hochschild (1979), is one's efforts to change emotions in degree or quality towards inside, thus managing our own emotions as triggered by what we see, hear, feel, perceive, smell and see when we conduct research. Emotional labour is 'the management of feeling to create a publicly observable facial and bodily display' (Hochschild, 2003, p. 7). It is the labour researchers perform when engaging with research participants. In this research, working with (my) emotions was a significant research tool that made my research more robust and credible rather than undermining it.

A common argument against the use of emotion and bringing the researcher's subjectivity into research is the fear of bias (Campbell & Wasco, 2000). However, I content that contrary to that claim, engaging with my emotions significantly prevented bias in my research. Engaging with the emotions triggered by this research, feeling empathy with participants, feeling frustration and anger over power inequalities, power abuses and mistreatment, feeling excitement and grief, as well as suspicion, guided me to further questions and, thus, to deeper understanding. Recognising the potential of emotions means '[attending to discordant emotions] seriously and respectfully' (Jaggar, 1989, p. 169). An example is the interview with surrogacy worker Mila (Chapter 3, p. 68). Asking her about her satisfaction over the communication between her and her client parents, I *sensed* a dissonance between what she said and what her meta-communication expressed. As Ahmed (2017, p. 22) writes, 'a sensation is not an organized or intentional response to something. And that is why sensation matters: you are left with an impression that is not clear or distinct'. In this situation as in many others, I was left with an impression of being at the verge of discovering a new lead, a new question or an insight that would take me nearer to getting a complete picture.

Engaging in emotional labour and emotion work is, as the term implies, work. Conducting sensitive research is emotionally challenging. Acknowledging my personal experiences of distress, anger, sorrow, frustration or apprehension about a situation prompted me to reflect; understanding their genesis enabled me to build up resilience and face situations that could cause such emotions afresh instead of stepping back and, thus, applying a self-censorship onto my research. Such situations included attending appointments for pregnancies classed as high risk, witnessing the diagnosis of miscarriages, emotionally caring for intending parents and surrogacy workers after a miscarriage or a failed embryo transfer and addressing the experiences of abuse in interviews. For an account of how I navigated my personal emotional journey, including my very personal lessons on learning and applying self-care, see Appendix 3. Thus, emotions are a critical and valuable tool in empirical research: when we are engaging with emotions coming up during the course of research, and when we reflect upon causes and causalities, far from undermining our credibility, we are making our research more credible and robust.

Organisation of the Book

The book consists of five chapters. In Chapter 2, I analyse how women become surrogacy workers in Russia. I illustrate how surrogacy workers understand gestational surrogacy as moral and as work, and how they organise their social lives in order to become surrogacy workers. I complement these accounts with an analysis of the expectations and views of commercial surrogacy agencies, fertility doctors and client parents, and identify racialised imaginaries that drive their preferences. In Chapter 3, I focus on the relationships between surrogacy workers and client parents, and in particular, relational work performed by surrogacy workers which they understand as part of their tasks as surrogates. I show how surrogacy workers' perception of the relational work constituting parts of their surrogacy work is embedded in the Russian cultural framing of surrogacy as an economic arrangement and encourages them to anticipate a transient relationship with their client parents. In Chapter 4, I take a closer look at the geographic and geopolitical aspects of the social organisation of Russian surrogacy. I trace surrogacy workers' migration or commuting patterns to and within Russia and how this differentiates the practise of surrogacy in Russia from the social and geographical organisation of surrogacy elsewhere. In this chapter, I explore how surrogacy workers experience the resulting geographic and geo-political stratifications of their migration and commuting realities for their commissioned pregnancies. In Chapter 5, I explore the impact of the novel coronavirus COVID-19 on the practice of commercial surrogacy in Russia, the growing resistance to queer family building, and challenges and potential changes to the current liberal policy context. In the conclusion, I sum up my arguments to demonstrate how the practice of surrogacy in Russia differs from surrogacy practices elsewhere, and close with thoughts on the future of surrogacy, not only in Russia.

Chapter 2

Becoming a Surrogacy Worker

> I decided to be a surmama to solve my financial problems.
> [Surrogate motherhood] is an opportunity to receive the biggest
> possible amount of money in the shortest possible amount of time.
> (…) I am a single mother. I was living with my parents and I
> needed to find a place of my own. So, I went online, I simply
> wanted to know how much I could make. (…) But before this idea
> turned into a solid intention, I considered all the possible moral
> aspects thoroughly, I did that for over half a year. I asked myself:
> Can I go for this? Can I tell my mother about this? Can I tell my
> friends about this?
>
> (Diana, surrogacy worker in St Petersburg, May 2015)

In this chapter, I analyse how women became surrogacy workers in St
Petersburg. I illustrate how current and former surrogacy workers understand the
implications of gestational surrogacy and how they frame the reproductive labour
of surrogacy as a morally appropriate and as a form of work. Further I show how
they organised becoming surrogacy workers. I then complement these accounts
with an analysis of the expectations and views of local surrogacy agencies, fertility
doctors and client parents, identifying the (racial) imaginaries of who and what
constitutes an ideal surrogacy worker, and how these imaginaries impact on who
is able to become a surrogacy worker in Russia.

Surrogacy (as Work) in Russia

> [Surrogacy], for me, this is work. I basically don't see anything else
> in it.
>
> (Anna, two-time surrogacy worker, December 2014)

Awareness of Surrogacy

The Russian public is aware of the practice and implications of surrogate
motherhood, both as an optional fertility treatment for those who can afford, and

Surrogacy in Russia, 23–53
Copyright © 2021 Christina Weis
Published under exclusive licence by Emerald Publishing Limited
doi:10.1108/978-1-83982-896-620211006

as 'a job of a certain sort' with a promising earning for healthy fertile women who are already mothers. This general awareness comprises the knowledge that only gestational surrogacy is legal in Russia, whereby a surrogacy worker becomes pregnant with an embryo conceived from the client mother's or a donor's egg, and therefore shares no genetic link to the child she gestates.

Surrogacy arrangements by Russian celebrities, and custodial or financial disputes in arrangements gone awry, have also contributed to the awareness of surrogacy in Russia.[1] Singer Alla Pugachova and her husband Maxim Galkin, who became parents of twins through surrogacy in September 2013 are one example. In another instance, surrogacy worker Ira got interested in surrogacy when watching a talk show discussing an arrangement in which the surrogacy worker and the client parents fell out over money. She said:

> On that talk show, there was a girl who got herself in trouble. She gave birth and then she wanted more money, something along those lines. And that's when I got the idea to become a surrogate mother myself and then I started to talk about it with my parents.
>
> (Ira, surrogacy worker, February 2015)

---

[1]Two examples of high-profile surrogacy court cases in Russia are Mirimskaya vs. Bezpyataya, and Frolov vs. Suzdaleva bond (Bondar', 2017; Kozkina, 2018). In November 2015, Mirimskaya hired Bezpyataya for a surrogacy arrangement for a child with her second husband; the marriage broke down during the arrangement and ended in a divorce before the child's birth. A few days before the birth, Bezpyataya suddenly disappeared. It turned out that she was paid by Mirimskaya's second ex-husband to deliver secretly, register the child as her own, and leave for Cyprus. Mirimskaya filed a lawsuit against Bezpyataya and won; the court established Mirimskaya to be the biological and legal mother and the contract as valid. In Frolov vs. Suzdaleva, in May 2017, the Frolovs hired Suzdaleva to carry their surrogacy pregnancy. Suzdaleva got pregnant with twins and claimed double the amount of the compensation stated in the contract. It is unclear from media coverage if the contract stipulated whether she should only carry one child, or a higher sum for twins in case. The Frolovs refused to increase the pay. Suzdaleva subsequently went hiding, gave birth to the twins 'secretly' and refused to relinquish the twins. She took them home and gave them her own chosen names. She claimed that the Frolovs were unfit to be parents. The Frolovs sued Suzdaleva. In February 2017, the St Petersburg court ruled that the birth certificate stating Suzdaleva the mother is void and that the Frolovs are the rightful parents. However, while the ruling established parenthood, it did not include the transfer of the children, and Suzdaleva refused to give the children to the Frolovs. In March 2017, the Frolovs filed the next lawsuit to transfer the children – 11 months after the birth. Suzdaleva's lawyer argued that the children knew no other parents and that it would be in the best interest of the children to be the 'familiar mother'. In May 2017, the Frolovs won their case.
After another few weeks, the Frolovs won the next case and the children were handed to them and given new names.

Fig. 2.1.   Newspaper Advertisement by a Commercial Agency
Inviting Women to become Surrogates and Egg Donors.
Source: Author, 01/10/2012.
*Translation: We invite women with children as egg donors (22−30 years), as
surrogate mothers (22−35 years). Sperm donors 20−30 years. Tel. 767-06-xx.*

Приглашаем суррогатных мам!
Российская сеть клиник «Центр ЭКО» и компания «Свитчайлд» приглашает женщин в возрасте до 35 лет
стать суррогатными мамами для бездетных семей.
Благородная работа суррогатной мамы гарантирует самое высокое в России вознаграждение до 1 500 000
рублей!
Пожалуйста, заполните анкету и наш менеджер свяжется с Вами в удобное для вас время.

Fig. 2.2.   Online Advertisement by a Commercial Agency Inviting
Women to become Surrogates.
Source of text: Online screenshot, 25/04/2015
*Translation: 'We are offering women the opportunity to become surrogate
mothers! The Russian clinic network "IVF Centre" and the company
"Sweetchild" invite women up to the age of 35 years to become surrogate
mothers for childless families. The precious work of a surrogate mother
guarantees the highest possible reward in Russia of up to 1,500,000₽! Please,
fill in the questionnaire and our manager will get in touch with you at a time
convenient for you'.[2]*
Source of image: Drawing of the original image by author.

Ira made clear to me that she was not worried about herself 'getting into
trouble' and that she was aware how media oftentimes exploited such cases for
audience entertainment.

---

[2]1,500,000₽ equalled about £19,000 at the time of the advertisement in April 2015.

Besides regular tabloid media coverage, advertisements seeking surrogacy workers are frequently placed among employment ads online and in newspapers (Figs. 2.1 and 2.2).[3] In the context of such everyday confrontations with surrogacy – here presented as a promising work opportunity, there dismissed as immoral and dangerous – I ask how some women decide to become surrogacy workers, while others do not, to understand what is important to them in their decision-making processes.

For most surrogacy workers who I met, the media coverage on commercial surrogacy and online or newspaper advertisements aroused their initial curiosity. From there they turned to the Internet, where a Yandex search for 'surrogate mother' and 'St Petersburg' directed them to the websites of commercial agencies and clinics.[4] On online forums on in/fertility they thoroughly informed themselves on the medical implications in order to reassure themselves that the child would not be genetically theirs, which they regarded as important. 'I didn't exactly search for surrogacy – you stumble across a million references online', commented first-time surrogacy worker Olesya, and Ilya, who carried three pregnancies over the course of five years couldn't remember where that idea came from. She said 'I think, I watched something, or read something about it somewhere. And then, once I was interested, I started (...) collecting information. I saw application forms and contacted clinics'.

Only one woman reported that she was not aware of the commercial practice of surrogacy until her acquaintance Nadzeya told her about it as part of a successful attempt to recruit her. Nadzeya, a Belarusian citizen, had come to St Petersburg for surrogacy. She had initially kept her activity hidden and invented a different job as her reason to temporarily move to St Petersburg. But upon successfully completing the surrogacy arrangement, and encouraged by her agency to introduce further women for a bonus of 10,000₽ [£166] for each woman who got pregnant, upon her return home, she singled out women among her acquaintances whom she thought would be interested. Though recruitment via current or past surrogacy workers exists in Russia, it remains a marginal entry route into surrogacy. By comparison to India, where empirical scholarship suggests that the majority of women are recruited by former surrogacy workers as well as by women specialised in working as recruiters and brokers (Pande, 2014b; Rudrappa, 2015), women in Russia are much more proactive in seeking and entering surrogacy arrangements, and are very well informed about medical procedures involved.

---

[3]For an analysis of the presentation of surrogacy in a Russian tabloid, see the contributions by Olga Tkach, Olga Brednikova and Nadya Nartova in de Jong's and Tkach's (2009) edited volume 'Making bodies, persons and families: normalising reproductive technologies in Russia, Switzerland and Germany'.
[4]Russian online search engine.

Motivation: Surrogacy Gestation as Work

Who becomes a surrogacy worker? What entices women to come forward and offer their gestational services to strangers via agencies or upon making contact with client parents online? The surrogacy workers I met in St Petersburg were typically employed in unskilled or semi-skilled service jobs, such as receptionists or in sales, or stay-at-home mothers. Even though about half of them had a higher educational degree, only a few were working in an area related to their university or professional training. Half of the women were single mothers juggling childcare whilst job seeking or employed in multiple occupations. With the disappearance of state-subsidised childcare after the dissolution of the Soviet Union, paid care services are available only to those who can afford it (Zdravomyslova & Tkach, 2016). In addition, in Russia, women are disproportionately more likely to be made redundant or to have more difficulty finding new employment than men (Cockerham, 2007, p. 459). For instance, in Bashkortostan where many women had travelled from to come to St Petersburg as surrogacy workers during the time period of data collection (2012–2015), more than 60% of the registered unemployed were women (Delogazeta, 2012).[5] Nursing and child-rearing are primarily seen as women's tasks (Mezentseva, 2005), and many surrogacy workers' employment was episodic as they took responsibility for child-rearing. In addition to limited access to employment, women in Russia experience wage discrimination across the labour market, from manual to high-skilled labour (Mezentseva, 2005; Zakirova, 2014). As a consequence, many women in my sample, regardless of whether they were in a relationship and had a second source of income to support themselves and their families, dealt with employment and income insecurity. Single mothers in particular had to juggle sourcing affordable childcare, maintaining and finding multiple occupations to cover rent and living expenses, and substituting income loss when arranged jobs did not pay out salaries.

Becoming a surrogacy worker was thus a strategy intended to resolve this income insecurity, even if only temporarily, by doing what these women felt confident in and had experience in doing: carrying a pregnancy to term. Furthermore, it appeared to be a relatively 'easy' job. They could be pregnant for their client parents whilst working and caring for their own children as they had done in their previous own pregnancies. Finally, the final compensation of between 700,000 and 1,000,000 Roubles, depending on individual arrangements (as I will elaborate further in this book), often exceeded their annual earnings. However, surrogacy work could also add to women's histories of precarious and episodic employment. Agencies and client parents frequently instructed surrogacy workers when employed elsewhere to quit their jobs in order to reduce their commitments to be more available to meet the demands of agencies and client parents. Such requests added to their disrupted working lives and deprived women of their right to paid maternity leave and pay. If hiding their surrogacy

---

[5]The Republic of Bashkortostan, also known as Bashkiria, is located between the southern Ural Mountains and the Volga River.

period, blank spots were generated in their employment history, making these workers far less employable. Such work-life disruptions were particularly frequent when surrogacy workers decided to repeat surrogacy after a mandatory year of rest but needed to cover the interim months with employment.

Surrogacy work itself is unpredictable and precarious. IVF treatments have a low success rate of just over 30% for women under the age of 35 (HFEA, 2020). IVF pregnancies have a higher risk of early miscarriage in the first trimester (Isakova, Korsak, & Gromyko, 2001; Sunkara, Khalaf, Maheshwari, Seed, & Coomarasamy, 2014). They also have a higher risk of multiple pregnancies as in Russia, at the time of data collection, often two or more embryos are transferred to increase the chances of success (RAHR, 2015), which can lead to complications during the pregnancy and often end with elective Caesarean sections in surrogacy arrangements. It is important to note here that it is not the surrogacy workers who may elect to have a Caesarean section, or choose to give birth vaginally: the choice lies solely with the client parents and agencies. It is common practice to compensate surrogacy workers an additional sum if a Caesarean section was undertaken, in order to compensate for the loss of future surrogacy work, as most doctors would refuse to work with a surrogacy worker with a uterus that had been scarred by a Caesarean section.

Further factors that render surrogacy work unpredictable and precarious are the requirement to comply completely with doctors', agencies' and client parents' treatment and timing preferences from the embryo transfer until the birth. After having the experience of carrying a twin pregnancy resulting from an embryo transfer with two embryos, Daria was exclusively searching for new client parents who would agree to a single embryo transfer. '[A twin pregnancy] takes a lot. A lot! It is difficult!' – 'I suppose it is difficult to find bio parents who will agree on a single embryo transfer?', I commented, to which Daria replied, 'Well, yes. They will still transfer two. But you know, they keep on saying to not worry, that transferring two wouldn't mean that two will survive'. Still, she was hoping to find a couple who would respect her request. In addition, while they are carrying a surrogate pregnancy, women are not allowed to seek other medical procedures. As a consequence, surrogacy worker Anna lost two molars in her first commissioned pregnancy.

> After the 20th week the first one started to loosen and there was nothing I was allowed to do about it. Give birth, that's it. And then it was too late. I thought, damn it, I am 30 and I am losing teeth! And my grandmother scolded me that I am wasting my health.
> (Anna, two-time surrogacy worker, December 2014)

When I asked Anna, who was pregnant with her second surrogacy pregnancy when I met her, how she saw surrogacy and her role, my question surprised her. She answered without batting an eye: 'This is my work'. When I probed further 'So when someone discovers for the first time that you are a *surmama*, how do you explain what you are doing?' Anna reiterated 'That I work. For me, this is work. I basically don't see anything else in it'. For her, losing two teeth was a malady. She perceived it as an occupational hazard that comes with the job. Daria agreed with Anna when she explained:

> Well, I think [choosing surrogacy] for me was as it is for all of us. It is the very same question: the financial question. {She laughs.} [I do it] for the money. [Surrogacy] is a job of a certain sort.
>
> (Daria, surrogacy worker, November 2014)

The women's evaluation of commercial surrogacy as a form of work did not conflict with their identity of being a surrogate *mother*, a *surmama*. In Soviet Russia, a woman's role was defined as a worker mother, whose duty it was to work and to produce future generations of workers. In return for their services of motherhood and reproduction to the state, mothers received money and state-subsidised services (Issoupova, 2012). In post-Soviet Russia, subsidised childcare was one of the first casualties of the new system. It forced those women out of employment who could not rely on family-supported childcare, or for whom high childcare costs made employment no longer feasible (Bridger, Pinnick, & Kay, 1996). Within this context, surrogacy became an opportunity to earn money in their capacity as mothers: after having worked as mothers for the Soviet state in exchange for services and benefits, women now worked as gestational mothers in the privatised market of commercial surrogacy. Consequently, Russia's *surmamas* embraced their dual identity of workers and mothers, and workers as mothers, instead of seeing being a worker or a mother as dichotomous. The examples of Anna's and Daria's conception of surrogacy as work and their avid description of surrogacy as work rather than a gift, show that surrogacy workers in Russia unlike surrogates in the US and the UK do not seek to obscure and disclaim their surrogacy labour (Jacobson, 2016; Smietana, 2017). Furthermore, as the monthly allowance was equal to or exceeded their monthly income, the women perceived it as their salary, which reinforced the notion that carrying a surrogacy pregnancy is work.

Philanthropic motives fed into some women's decisions, as Gul'nur, a mother of two, for instance explained:

> I dearly love my children, and because of them I decided to take that step. I consider it only moral that with my action I can make one family happy and make the life of my family a bit easier.
>
> (Gul'nur, surrogacy worker, January 2015).

Yet still, weighing in the benefits for her family, Gul'nur's motivation cannot be described as altruistic. In addition, Gul'nur experienced easy pregnancies with her own children and, considering her family complete, surrogacy became a convenient way to earn much-needed extra money. Philanthropic motivations and financial interests are not mutually exclusive. Classifying women's motives into one category or another is misleading and fails to do justice to those women who want to help, yet whose financial situations do not allow them to be selfless.

Over the course of 15 months of ethnographic fieldwork, I met no surrogacy worker who would still have opted for surrogacy work, if she had seen an alternative that was as profitable but less precarious (given the uncertainty of a successful embryo transfer and maintaining the pregnancy), less invasive (hormones, control checks, supervision by agency and/or client parents), had less of an impact on intimate, family and social life, and less potentially harmful (complications or miscarriage) or even lethal. The social stratifications between the women who considered carrying a pregnancy for money and those for whom the demands and risks outweighed the potential gains are undisputable. None of the women in my research sample would have opted for surrogacy work if their material situation had been better. In Russia, turning to surrogacy was a choice embedded in the women's economic situation, and meant for the surrogacy workers, a form of work. Furthermore, as noted in analyses of surrogacy practices elsewhere (Majumdar, 2017; Rudrappa, 2015; Twine, 2015), there is clear stratification between the women offering the gestational labour and the women and men purchasing it.

Drawing and extending on Bourdieu's (1986) theory of the convertibility of capital further illuminates surrogacy workers' rationale. Bourdieu (1986, p. 241) describes capital as accumulated labour and lists social, cultural and economic capital as resources which individuals can draw upon when negotiating social and economic relationships. I add reproductive capital, which I define as an individual's fertility, the possession of viable and healthy gametes and, in the case of cis women, their ability to conceive, gestate, give birth and breastfeed, to this set of forms of capitals (see also Hudson, 2008, p. 271 for her earlier use of reproductive capital). Surrogacy workers possess the reproductive capital that client parents need to achieve parenthood: they are healthy, fertile and young. By engaging in surrogacy work and providing their uterus for surrogacy gestation, they are able to convert their reproductive capital into economic capital.

'*And So I Asked Myself: Can I Do This?*'

The question 'Can I do this?' – that is, carry someone else's child in return for financial compensation and then part with it immediately after birth without wavering – is the first question women reported asking themselves when they considered becoming surrogacy workers. Their accounts revealed the binary nature of the principle in question. Firstly, could their personal and moral understanding of motherhood be compatible with birthing another person's child and parting with it, for money? Secondly, aware that they couldn't make such a decision in a vacuum, but having to consider their immediate social surroundings they asked themselves: who could they confide in, whether to keep their surrogacy work secret, and how to organise childcare and arrange their absence from home and family (when necessary).

'**Can I Give away the Child?**': Surrogacy Workers' Perception of Their Relationship to the Surrogate Child

Two questions intrinsically linked to 'Can I do this?' were 'Am I morally prepared?' and 'Will I be able to give away the child?'. Dasha's account illustrates.

Dasha: I think I heard about it on TV. And I got interested and started to search for it. That was about half a year ago. I have a small child.

(Continued)

> He is one year and one month old. And I started collecting information and preparing myself morally – I told my husband. We have some problems with our living situation. And so we decided to try [surrogacy]. We gathered more information, waited a bit until my child was a bit older and then I put an advertisement [online].

Christina: How did you prepare yourself morally? How did you do that?

Dasha: Well, I know that this child is not mine, I will only carry him. And when I give birth, I will give him away. Morally...? Well, [pauses] that it is not my child.

December 2012

Considering the medical facts and the local 'social construction of natural facts' (Strathern, 1992, p. 17), Dasha, like the other surrogacy workers I met in St Petersburg, had come to the understanding that they were not giving *their* child away because the child would not be conceived using their eggs. The accounts of surrogacy workers in Russia showed that their understanding differed significantly from that of Indian and Vietnamese surrogates who gave the gestational link paramount importance and spoke of surrogate children as *their* children whom they loved and much missed after they were given away (Hibino, 2015; Rudrappa, 2015, p. 85).[6] Instead, in a similar way to the framing of the US-American surrogates who relinquished the 'ownership of the child' even when engaging in genetic surrogacy arrangements where the child is genetically related to them (Ragoné, 1996), surrogacy workers in Russia relinquished their 'ownership' of the surrogate children through the client parents' provision of their genes and/or their intention to raise the child.

Surrogacy workers further enhanced their understanding of this 'genetic essentialism' (Cussins, 1998, p. 48) by drawing on and emphasising the perceived otherness of the unborn to their body: 'I am not the genetic mother, the boy is not my genetic child' (surrogacy worker Alexandra). Some surrogacy workers explained that they physically perceived the genetic otherness from the moment of conception: some suffered badly from morning sickness during their surrogacy pregnancies but symptom free whilst pregnant with 'their own' children, others felt it the other way around. Asenka for instance recalled:

> I carried my own [child] so much more easily. I did not have morning sickness as I did during the surrogacy pregnancies. I was literally dying the first three months, right after the implant [the embryo transfer], it was clear that I was pregnant, I felt really bad. Those three months, the first time [first surrogacy pregnancy] and

---

[6]Surrogacy workers in Russia were on the one hand Russian women, but also Ukrainian, Moldovan, Belarusian and from the Central Asian Republics.

the second I didn't eat anything. I lived on an apple a day, because eating was impossible. I was chucking up my guts, feeling so nauseous was tough.

(Asenka, surrogacy worker, August 2014)

Furthermore, the surrogacy workers in Russia described the surrogacy children they carried with the adjective *chuzhoy*, which translates to 'someone else's', 'to someone else belonging', 'foreign', 'alien' and 'other.' The translation of course is context-sensitive, yet listing the spectrum of possible translations gives a non-Russian speaker an understanding of the significance of relating to the surrogate child as *chuzhoy*. Three-time surrogacy worker Rada, for instance, narrated a conversation she had with her husband about how they considered people's assumptions that surrogacy workers would claim the child as their own as unfounded and concluded:

I was morally prepared. I knew it was someone else's [*chuzhoy*] child. I didn't even question that. Why would I take someone else's [*chuzhoy*] baby home?! I *knew* he belongs to someone else [*chuzhoy*]. And my husband – my husband loves children, but that one belongs to someone else. If we wanted another child, we could make *our own*. [emphasis hers]

(Rada, surrogacy worker, November 2012)

In a similar vein, Lyubov recalled how her husband referred to the foetus as 'our intruder [nash okkupant]'. With 'our' he denoted his acceptance and embraced the situation, with 'intruder' he clearly demarcated who was and who wasn't included in his family emphasised the temporality of his acceptance of the child. Surrogacy worker Diana further used the metaphor of 'trying to grow oats in a rice field' to describe how she felt about the surrogacy pregnancy compared to her previous pregnancy with her daughter. 'They put a seed and you don't know whether it will grow or not, and if it will grow, how it will grow'. Because 'nothing of that seed [the embryo]' came from her, Diana found the idea of hosting and nurturing this '*chuzhoy* being' so bizarre that she said that she was even surprised to have birthed 'an absolutely healthy baby, a chubby cherub'. Trying to make sense of the success, she, like other surrogacy workers, pointed out that the success hinged entirely on the rigorous medical protocol and hormone supplements that they followed during the first trimester. In Ilya's words,

In fact, nothing is up to us. Well, we swallow pills – besides that, nothing depends on us. They prepare their endometrium for the transfer, then the embryo is transferred. Then we wait. We wait. First for the hCG [the pregnancy test], for the next screening....

(Ilya, surrogacy worker, November 2014)

Such explanations echoed the explanations agency staff gave to them as well as to me and the client parents: with the help of the synthetic hormones, doctors create the required conditions. If it wasn't for the hormones and the doctors' expertise, the body would detect the embryo as a foreign object and signal 'Get rid of it!' But with the help of modern medicine and the doctors' expertise, the body is tricked and keeps it. While inaccurate from a medical point of view, such narratives were powerful and purposeful metaphors: they reassured surrogacy workers that surrogacy pregnancies are different and entirely artificial, and their success has almost no relationship to the surrogacy workers' contribution. Teman (2010, p. 278) describes how, as a consequence of the medical intervention required to achieve and maintain an IVF pregnancy, surrogacy workers' 'bodily systems [were] being overridden and medically managed to the hilt'. But surrogacy workers welcomed, internalised and instrumentalised this very experience of medicalisation to underline the missing connection between their body and that of the baby they 'produce' from the beginning of the pregnancy.

Shortly before her delivery of her first surrogacy child, Rada received another strong and unexpected confirmation of her notion that she 'had nothing to do' with the children she carried as a surrogacy worker. At her last monitoring appointment, her doctor was pleased to inform her that the baby had turned into the optimal vertex foetal birth position. Having delivered all three of her own children in breech, she was taken aback that the surrogacy baby had turned. While the doctor congratulated her on her 'good fortune', for Rada the surrogacy baby's 'otherness' to her body was the only reasonable explanation.

Surrogacy workers' descriptions of their relationship to these '*chuzhoy*' children delineate two notions. First, based on their medical knowledge of gestational surrogacy and IVF, surrogacy workers regarded the child as 'not theirs' because they do not pass on any of their genes, but merely nourished the child. Second, the necessity of artificially maintaining the pregnancy through administering synthetic hormones supported their perception: the growing life inside them was 'foreign' to their bodies. That led to the understanding was that they were not giving the child *away*, but *back* to those to whom it belongs, the client parents: the owners of the gametes, and the individuals who intended to parent the child.

Being and Staying 'Morally Prepared': Surrogacy Workers Challenging the Assumptions of Motherhood

> I maintain – and say it to all of them: you need to prepare yourself mentally [to become a *surmama*]. Without moral preparation, without psychological preparation, I think not everyone can do it.
> (Asenka, surrogacy worker, August 2014)

While 'moral' is basically defined as 'of or relating to human character or behaviour considered as good or bad (...) [,] the distinction between right and wrong, or good and evil, in relation to the actions, desires, or character of responsible human beings' (Oxford Dictionary, 2017), Cassaniti and Hickman (2014, p. 258) remind us that 'real moral action can only take place when a particular social actor is free to consciously choose a moral stance'. None of the surrogacy workers in my sample had been coerced into surrogacy, and, despite finding themselves in financially precarious situations, they approached compensated surrogacy gestation as a form of work. It is therefore reasonable to assume that they choose their moral stance consciously and freely. In this section, I show that being 'morally prepared' to be a surrogacy worker encapsulates two meanings for the women. First, surrogacy workers regarded surrogacy as doing the right thing, and secondly, by referring to themselves as being morally prepared, they referred to their intent of acting upon their decision to *surrogatemother* and not to change their mind about relinquishing the child.

A public opinion survey by the Russian Public Opinion Research Centre (WCIOM, 2013) reported a divide in Russian society over whether commercial surrogacy should be considered acceptable, with only a minority considering it commendable and a quarter of the participants considering surrogacy as 'morally intolerable'. According to Hochschild (1979, p. 563), a society's social guideline '[directs] how we want to try to feel'. In light of divided public opinion and the condemnation of surrogacy by the Russian Orthodox Church and many conservative politicians, surrogacy workers did not make their choice lightly, but only after considerable reflection. Thus, fully agreeing with and supporting the notion that surrogacy is morally sound as they were not giving their child away but supporting someone else in having their own child, they did not feel a dissonance between what they were doing and how they felt about their actions. Based on that, they were prepared to confront critical voices and defend their decision to be surrogacy workers. Three-time surrogacy worker Rada gave the following example how she reprimanded her mother-in-law for repeated critique over 'giving her own child away' by reminding her of her previous abortions and choice to end life while she, through surrogacy, created life.

> When I was preparing for the first time, when my mother-in-law said: 'What! To carry a child for 9 months and then give it away! What?!' And I said, 'And what about when you went to get your abortions?' She went to get an abortion five times. There used to be less means of contraception then. She said, 'That is different'. And I said. 'What is the difference?' Five times she killed her own [child] – And that was it. She stopped talking to me about this topic.
>
> (Rada, surrogacy worker, November 2012)

Thus, on the basis that they felt surrogacy was morally sound, the surrogacy workers in my sample felt 'free of personal conflicts' and therefore 'morally prepared' to enter surrogacy arrangements.[7]

'Being morally prepared', however, carried a second meaning for surrogacy workers: to be ready to act upon the decision to hand the child to the client

---

[7] I avoided asking surrogacy workers *why* they became surrogacy workers and descriptively asked *how* instead. I further desisted from asking suggestive questions, such as whether they considered surrogacy to be moral. The discourse of morality was initiated by the surrogacy workers.

parents. That means, throughout their pregnancy, surrogacy workers had to work on their emotions to be able to act upon their intentions and not unintentionally form an emotional attachment to the child.

By doing so, they rebut opponents of surrogacy who call into question whether surrogacy contracts should be enforceable as women are not yet pregnant when signing surrogacy contracts and incapable of predicting a change in their emotional or mental state (see, for instance, Shanley, 1993 and Leissner, 2012). Such argument suggests that maternal bonding '[arises] naturally and inevitably out of the embodied experience of pregnancy' (Dow, 2017, p. 7) and as such '[comes] dangerously close to biological determinism' (Anleu, 1990, p. 65). These normative expectations about the nature of motherhood have already been challenged by numerous accounts of surrogates across the globe that report of no or minor regrets over their surrogacy experience or postpartum distress (Ragoné, 1994; Teman, 2010; van den Akker, 2003).

In order to maintain the necessary detachment and to perform their work, surrogacy workers asserted that one needed to be absolutely ready to relinquish the child. The women in my sample agreed that they would advise anyone who wasn't feeling 100% certain that they were able to relinquish the child to stop considering becoming a surrogacy worker.

The following excerpt from a conversation with two surrogacy workers living in shared accommodation, both pregnant with their second surrogacy pregnancy illustrates their understanding of 'morally prepared':

Mila: We are prepared for it. We are prepared to do this, because [the child] is not ours. It is work.

Yuliana: When I gave birth, [the doctors] told me that everything is fine, [the twins] are healthy. That was all that was important to me. Later, the parents (...) showed me pictures of the children. I looked at them, 'well nice, children'. {Her voice, as she recalls her reaction, reflects no affection or interest.} That was it. That was three or four months after I had given birth.

Christina: And you haven't given them any further thought?

Yuliana: Absolutely not. We didn't come here to think much about them. You need to take this step already fully prepared.

Mila: Yes, already fully prepared and ready.

Yuliana: If you have any doubts, like 'maybe I won't be able to give them away' then it would be better not to do this. For real. Because then you don't know what will happen to you during the pregnancy.

September 2014

In a different conversation, surrogacy worker Asenka's response was in agreement; she concluded with 'You need to be morally prepared – if you are not morally prepared, don't even go there!'

For surrogacy workers, 'being prepared' also meant being prepared to fight potentially developing feelings for the child during the pregnancy. Thus, *being prepared* is not a completed process of *having prepared oneself*, but an ongoing process of being prepared to continuously manage one's own emotions, to perform 'emotion work' (Hochschild, 1979). Hochschild (1979, p. 561) defines emotion work as 'the act of trying to change in degree or quality an emotion or feeling (...) [by] evoking or shaping, as well as suppressing, feeling in oneself'.[8] Hochschild (1979, p. 561) further emphasised that '"emotion work" refers to the effort – the act of trying – and not the outcome'. Individuals prompted to perform emotion work set up an emotion-work system (Hochschild, 1979, p. 562). Over the course of my research, I learnt about four such emotion-work systems put in place by surrogacy workers.

One strategy to keep detachment intact was to focus their attention on their own biological children. For instance, whenever Asenka felt the risk of becoming emotionally attached, she reminded herself 'I know why I am doing this, (...) I have my own [child] to raise and clothe'. A second common emotion-work system employed to maintain detachment was to talk to the child. Alexandra repeated time and time again to the in utero child 'I am not your mother' and 'others are waiting for you'. By addressing the child, she introduced the approaching reality of separation into her own awareness. She was well within her first surrogacy pregnancy when she shared with me her worries that she could anticipate her eventual reaction, despite having already made up her mind. 'Maybe I will cry. Maybe I will feel sorry. Yet I have understood it. He is not mine. Others are waiting for him'. She explained that it felt morally wrong to even think of depriving the client parents of their long-desired child. In addition, she would not have the financial means to fight to keep the boy and raise him along with her two children.

A third approach was only available to surrogacy workers who had a personal relationship with their client parents. Two women explained how the relationship with client parents helped them in the detachment process: interaction with the recipients served as a constant reminder that these people had been waiting and intending to be the parents for a long time. In all the arrangements in which the client parents were in personal contact with their surrogacy worker, the parents permitted them to see, hold and part from the child after delivery. This opportunity to consciously part from the child and see the unity of the newly created family gave surrogacy workers a feeling of satisfaction and closure.[9] It confirmed their role as not-parents, but the *means* through which the client parents became parents.

A fourth variation of the emotion-work system which was also fully endorsed by the commercial surrogacy agencies appropriated the medicalisation of the surrogacy pregnancy to maintain detachment. The intensive medicalisation and

---

[8]Hochschild distinguishes between *emotion* and *feeling*: '"Emotion" denotes a state of being overcome that "feeling" does not' (Hochschild, 1979, p. 551).
[9]In some occasions, surrogacy workers shared how blessing the child helped them in letting go and moving on.

supervision of their surrogacy pregnancies in high-end, private medical centres, often luxuriously designed, was a core instrument in reinforcing surrogacy workers' role as workers in the reproductive assembly line, as it impressed and intimidated many. Being inculcated by agencies and medical staff that nothing of the commissioned pregnancy is theirs, but that it is created and maintained through the highest medical expertise, had the desired effect on the pregnant women. It ensured that they disconnected from their intuitive knowledge of their bodies and their pregnancies to surrender all control and authority to the medical experts and the agency staff.[10] Mila's experience of foetal movement during her first surrogacy pregnancy illustrates how the technocratic medical care and the medicalisation of the pregnant body aids the emotion-work system.

> In my own pregnancy, I carried [my child] into the 40th week and time was flying! And I was not bothered by anything. This second one worried me of course. The *programme* [surrogacy], I obviously mean. It made me feel bad. And whenever something happened, I freaked out.

She re-enacted a phone call with Eliza, the agency's manager, in a theatrical performance.

> 'Eliza! He [the foetus] is not moving! Is that OK?' {Imitating Eliza's voice:} 'It is still early, that is fine. But go to see Sasha [the agency's gynaecologist] and she will have a look.' - And then the moving started! He was quite kickin' and dancin' in there, and again I called Eliza. 'Eliza! But is it ok that he is moving so much!?' {Imitating Eliza's voice:} 'That is fine, Mila. But go and see Sasha and you will see.'

Mila herself paused and laughed. Then she got serious again and continued.

> You are more cautious [prislushivaeshsya]. With your own, you don't monitor it like that, you keep going and going and going. But here you pay close attention to whether he is moving, and about this and that, and you constantly ask yourself: What is necessary? What do I need to do? And that every day!
>
> (Mila, surrogacy worker, September 2014)

Though she explained that she paid closer attention to foetal movements during the surrogacy pregnancy, she did not engage with her intuition and embodied knowledge as she did before. When she noticed her daughter's movements in her

---

[10]A third effect of this technocratic approach (Davis-Floyd, 2001) is that embryos and foetuses are elevated to personhood on their own, whereas the women who enable the existence of these very babies disappear as non-persons (see also Rudrappa, 2015, pp. 126–142).

first pregnancy, she *felt* that she was well, and this gave her peace of mind. In the commissioned pregnancy, the worry of failing to perform her duties as a surrogacy worker, the fear of missing a sign of foetal distress or miscarrying, stopped her from engaging with the pregnancy and so she surrendered the interpretation and care to the denoted expert. Assuming the role of a diligent worker, she paid close attention to any foetal movement and signs of the pregnancy but severed her emotional engagement, blocking her embodied, intuitive knowledge. Mila's response to the foetal movements shows how the surrogate child becomes a product of work, consisting of diligent adherence to the medicalised care provided by medical experts. The surrogacy worker overwrites her role as a mother with that of a worker, aided by the medicalisation and the agency's encouragement to seek external advice rather than rely on her own experience and intuition. 'Emotion work can be done by the self upon the self, by the self upon others, and by others upon oneself' (Hochschild, 1979, p. 562), all as part of or consequence of an emotion-work system put in place. Mila adjusted how she felt to how she should feel, aided by the efforts of the agency and medical staff.

All these different approaches of preparing oneself to stay morally prepared, manage emotions by suppressing, transferring or deferring them, or by embracing a model of technocratic pregnancy care were known to each surrogacy worker and were reflected in their parlance. Like Mila in the recent example, surrogacy workers spoke of pregnancies with their own children as '*my pregnancy*' and disowned commissioned pregnancies by referring to them as '*this/that pregnancy*' (see also Fisher & Hoskins, 2013, p. 509).

Thus, to become a surrogacy worker, the women agreed that one needed to be 'morally prepared', which referred to two things. First, surrogacy workers perceived gestational surrogacy as a morally right act, in line with their own principles. Second, to perform the work of surrogacy, being morally prepared meant to act upon their decision to carry a child for someone else with the sole intention of handing the child to the expectant client parents as agreed upon beforehand. In order to do so, surrogacy workers constructed different emotion-work systems. Their capacity to act on their decision and counter potential attachment shows that 'being morally prepared' is a process throughout the surrogacy arrangement and challenges the normative assumption that women bond with the child during gestation.

Organising becoming a Surrogacy Worker

Once intending surrogacy workers had settled the questions concerning their own perception of surrogacy, the next questions to settle concerned their immediate familial and social surroundings. The first people they gauged or discussed these matters with were the people they lived with and very often depended on for collaboration and support during the arrangement, in particular concerning childcare: partners and parents.

In general, surrogacy workers felt there was a generational divide between themselves and their parents' education and upbringing, and therefore also in the perception of surrogacy (see also Khvorostyanov & Yeshua-Katz, 2020). In order to get a sense of whether to inform their parents and expect support, or spare them both the worry, some women tested the water with probes to evaluate their reactions. Dasha, who I met on the day of her embryo transfer, decided against telling her parents for the time being, despite the fact that she lived with them, along with her young son and husband. She initially approached the topic with her mother by commenting on the case of a Russian celebrity having children through surrogacy. 'I told my mother about it: "look, this is surrogate motherhood..." and my mother answered, appalled: "Fuh, such a nonsense!!"' She therefore chose to keep her surrogacy pregnancy to herself.

> I don't know how people will react... In general, people are not informed, and they know little about this. They got all what they know from TV where [surrogacy] is considered to be bad. That the women are selling their own body. [The image of surrogacy] is negative, and I don't want it to affect my own family, and my child, therefore I don't want that somebody knows about it. (...) I keep it secret. Only my husband knows about it. Even my mother doesn't know, unfortunately. (...) in the last months I will go to live close to the bio-parents. They have their own house, and I will live there with my little child. He will then almost turn two. That is so that nobody sees it, the pregnancy.
>
> (Dasha, surrogacy worker, December 2012)

Temporarily leaving family and friends in order to conceal the surrogacy pregnancy and pretending to take up employment in another city was a common strategy to manage surrogacy work (see chapter 4 for in-depth analysis).

Ira, along with other women in the sample, actively sought advice and support from their parents. For her, parental support was paramount. After educating herself about the whole process of gestational surrogacy online, she shared the idea, the medical facts and the financial prospects with her parents. '[And then] we decided that I will go for it'. Her family's full support was paramount, as reflected in her choice of words 'we decided'.

Married women generally shared their ideas and intentions first with their husbands, not least because Russian Federal Law № 323 requires married women to provide their husbands' written consent to become surrogacy workers. While I did not speak to surrogacy workers' husbands, the overall idea that I could gather from surrogacy workers' stories was that their husbands objected at first, but in the end, conceded.[11] A conversation with Yuliana, Mila and Marcella, on how they won their husbands' approval, illustrates this clearly. All three women had come to St Petersburg for surrogacy and had left their child

---

[11]As mentioned earlier, I only interviewed women who became surrogacy workers, thus who had obtained their husbands' consent. I am not able to gauge how many women did not succeed in obtaining consent and permission in comparison to those whose husband interfered with their plans.

in care with their partner or parents. Yuliana, originally from Ukraine, recounted how her husband initially strongly opposed her plans. 'Why?' She repeated my question with amusement. 'I am his wife. I am his property!' Yuliana perceived herself as *given* to her husband in marriage, no longer bearing her father's last name but her husband's name from then on. Following this patriarchal gender ideology, a child resulting from her reproductive labour should belong to her husband. Yet, with gestational surrogacy, the child carried none of her or her husband's genes and she both recognised and questioned these cultural and social norms. Highlighting the surrogacy child's lack of genetic relatedness to her husband, along with the financial opportunities to provide more for their own children than her husband was able, she concluded with 'he became resigned. (...) It took me a long time to win him round and he only signed the permission on the evening my train left'.[12] Beginning her narration with a solemn countenance, she had joked over her final victory. Mila and Marcella joined in with affirming giggles, and then all three women goaded each other into recalling their husbands' initial objections to surrogacy or them leaving to travel to Russia, their attempts at protesting and their own winning responses. It was obvious that they found mutual acknowledgement and delight in having shown their husbands that, despite being required to gain a signature showing their husband's consent, they were really the ones in charge. As sociologist Kiblitskaya (2000, p. 69) remarks on the increase of married female breadwinners in Russia: 'In many instances, the survival of the family in post-Soviet Russia depends on the woman's ability to find work' (see also Ashwin & Lytkina, 2004).

Unwed or divorced surrogacy workers obviously did not need to provide anybody else's consent to go about their plans. However, reaching a mutual agreement with a current partner was nevertheless necessary for the sake of the relationship. Three-time surrogacy worker Ilya had been cohabitating with her partner Viktor, stepfather to her son, for many years before getting married. When she decided to work as a surrogate for the first time, she and Viktor were not yet married, so she – and here she was not apologetic – did not need his permission. 'The first [commissioned pregnancy] was not pleasant for [him]. He had no clue what to expect, and nothing was needed of him'. With the latter, Ilya referred to neither needing Viktor's permission nor his contribution. She got pregnant from a test tube embryo, and during the pregnancy, all the decisions and instructions came from the client parents, the doctors and/or Ilya. Viktor was relegated to the role of passive onlooker for nine months. What made the experience even more unpleasant and awkward for him, as Ilya conceded, was that Viktor strongly desired a biological child with Ilya. Instead, while his friends all

---

[12]That Yuliana had already purchased her tickets for the almost 24-hour train journey to St Petersburg for her first surrogacy pregnancy days before she had her husband's signature on the paperwork also suggests that she felt confident about going.

transitioned into fatherhood with children of their own, he intimately experienced three pregnancies that would not take him over that threshold and he only remained the stepfather of Ilya's teenage son. By the time Ilya prepared for her second surrogacy pregnancy, they were already married and Viktor opposed her plans. He could have refused to give his permission, but finally, he gave in. 'When I prepared for the third time, he already understood that it is utterly senseless [to contradict me]. I didn't ask him his opinion... I planned it', Ilya recounted her third surrogacy pregnancy. She admitted that she was aware of Viktor's unease about her commissioning out her womb and stalling him from fulfilling his wish to father a child with her. Ilya, however, rejected the idea of returning to swaddling and cradling an infant just as her son was about to finish school and move out of the house. She anticipated the new independence and prospects of realising her career ambitions of opening a small business. The remaining money after having bought an apartment was going to be her starting capital.[13]

Obtaining the husbands' written consent, as stipulated by law, could pose a significant obstacle to women's plans to become surrogacy workers. However, in a similar vein to the above examples, in all the accounts of the married surrogacy workers I interviewed, it took only a matter of time and the art of persuasion to win their husbands' consent. The pragmatic reason, that of the prospect of earning much-needed money, rarely had a stronger counter-argument. Married surrogacy workers referred to the required consent signature as a mere formality and a bureaucratic hurdle rather than a real obstacle. Their experience contrasts starkly with accounts of coercion in India, where researchers have collected reports of women who had been forced into surrogacy by husbands and in-laws (Deomampo, 2013b; Pande, 2014b).

Who Is Desired to Be a Surrogacy Worker?

Not long ago we had a couple who requested to view their preferred [surrogate] candidate naked, to inspect her body and ensure that she was healthy and without any mistakes and things like tattoos.[14]
(Nikita, lawyer for a surrogacy agency; field notes October 2012)

Selecting a Docile, Healthy and 'Poor, but Not Too Poor' Worker Mother

Surrogacy workers' self-assessment of their ability to become surrogacy workers is crucial, but equally important are the imaginaries and the suitability assessments of commercial surrogacy agencies and client parents.

---

[13]A year later, Ilya had opened a pet shop with the earnings from her final surrogacy arrangement.
[14]Nikita preferred to not provide details on how his agency responded to the request.

In 2015, a large Moscow-based surrogacy agency that recruited women from all over Russia stated that they accepted only 10 out of 700 women who expressed interest in becoming a surrogacy worker into their programme to match with client parents. Besides selecting women on their age and medical records, agency owners in St Petersburg and Moscow had a distinct idea of the ideal candidate: A surrogacy worker should be 'financially motivated' and 'business oriented', or in other words, 'poor, but not too poor', and finally, she should be docile.

Unlike in the UK and US, where the notion of altruism prevails in the surrogacy discourse and surrogacy workers describe their surrogacy gestation despite the financial compensation as a 'labour of love' and a priceless gift (Berend, 2016a, 2016b; Jacobson, 2016; Ragoné, 1999), within the cultural framing of surrogacy as a business arrangement in Russia, those involved renounce metaphors that veil or distract from the transactional core of commercial surrogacy. In a similar vein to the way surrogacy workers like Daria called surrogacy 'a job of certain sorts', agency owner Veronica explained matter-of-factly:

> Of course, their main motivation to come here is to earn money, because these women have their own children, and their material prosperity can be quite low, and therefore [surrogacy] is one possibility to earn money at this difficult period in their life. Take Yuliya's case for example. [Yuliya, 24 years old, is a single mother.] She is in quite a difficult situation. She is divorced but still living with her ex-mother-in-law because she cannot afford to move out. Her son is very hyper-active and to assume that she is thinking of keeping this child as a second child – that is nonsense. That is impossible. She doesn't need that child. She needs money. Therefore, I am simply 100% convinced that she doesn't want to keep it. (…) If we believe that they need money, then we invite them to work with us.
>
> (Veronica, agency owner, September 2012)

The notion of a primarily financial motivation being the most appropriate is also reflected in agency's marketing and recruitment strategies on their social media feeds. The image below depicts a surrogacy worker having received her final compensation after returning from the maternity ward (Fig. 2.3). The first line of the caption reads:

> What should a surrogate mother do with the payments? The amount is rather large! Even though they say that money is not the most important, [icon of monkey covering its eyes] it lets you live as you want, and just spend time with the most important [people in your life]: yourself and your family! [family icon]

Grigory, owner of the high-end surrogacy agency 'Surrogacy Exclusive', further added that a surrogacy worker neither needed to be or needed to pretend to be altruistic. Instead, she needed to convince him of the opposite: her monetary incentives.

Fig. 2.3.   Social Media Post Advertising Surrogacy and Final Compensation. *Source:* Instagram; image anonymised by account holder.

[Surrogacy] is a paid service. And of course, it's work (…) it's a job – one of the most responsible jobs in the world and of course the surrogate should get an appropriate remuneration. (…) [The ideal surrogate mother desires] to help childless people to become parents. And of course, she should not be altruistic. She should wish to get money for herself, for her family, for her own children. (…) It creates motivation.

(Grigory, owner of a surrogacy agency, August 2014)

For agencies, financially dire situations guarantee that the surrogacy worker wouldn't break the contractual agreement and attempt to keep the child. Federal Law No. 323 stipulates that the woman who has given birth is the legal mother.[15] Therefore, a stable, yet financially pressing situation serves both the agencies and the client parents as a reassurance of their surrogacy worker's suitability.

Another preference in the selection process for agencies is the surrogacy worker's education and intellectual competence, and docile character attributes. Whilst spending time on agency and medical premises, I observed interactions between agency staff, client parents and surrogacy workers. My ethnographic

---

[15]In the past couple of years a few legal disputes over parental rights to a surrogacy-born child have ended with the court granting the parental right to the client parents, such as Mirimskaya vs Bezpyataya (November 2015) and Frolov vs Suzdaleva (May 2017). These cases now serve as precedents.

observations revealed how agency staff preferred the less educated candidates over the higher educated ones. Intellect and education were not regarded as necessary to fulfil the task of 'only being the carrier', and furthermore, less educated women were perceived to more likely submit themselves to the agency's guidance without questioning either instructions or authority.

Pawel, a young homosexual man who considered surrogacy as his route to parenthood, was told by his agency consultant not to waste time choosing a surrogacy worker. He was to cede the choice to the agency and focus instead on choosing the right egg provider. He recalled the consultation with Aliza, the agency owner:

> [She said that] with surrogates nothing like the education or their look influences your baby. The donors are usually different, with a different social status. They are usually from good families, with good education, with good looks and appearance. The surrogate mothers, {imitates Eliza's voice} 'according to my experience, the dumber, the better'. – And she laughed. And then she told me that when girls with high education go into surrogate programmes, they overthink. And the process gets more difficult. But a stupid girl from a village – {he pauses and then again imitates the mocking tone in Eliza's voice imitating a fictional girl from a village} 'I will be ok, everything will be fine'. (...) [She reassured me that] with [one like] her everything will be fine. She immediately gets pregnant, carries easily and gives birth easily. Because they don't think about the potential problems by default. (...) For such girls, surrogacy is a lifestyle. They come back to them every year. They give birth to three or four children.
> (Pawel, intending client father, January 2013)

Furthermore, agencies preferred to recruit women who were completely new to surrogacy or continued working with previous experienced workers trained already by agency criteria: to be docile and adhere to the agencies' rules and expectations. Experienced surrogacy worker Rada, who had arranged all three of her surrogacy arrangements directly with the client parents, chuckled as she recalled how she once called a surrogacy agency to enquire about their payment for someone with experience. Once she clarified that her experience came from direct arrangements, she was told that there was no current demand for surrogacy workers.

Not all client parents felt comfortable with the work ethos and practices of commercial surrogacy agencies, and some simply felt confident enough to manage their surrogacy arrangements, from the selection of their surrogacy worker, to taking care of all legal matters on their own. When choosing a direct arrangement, client parents were keen to enter into conversations with their surrogacy worker, in person or over the phone or by Skype if the distance demanded, to feel a personal connection and to address with ease any sensitive questions, such as their respective stance on abortion and Caesarean section. Client parents were equally keen to know that their surrogacy worker lived in decent conditions. When the woman who responded to client mother Yana's advertisement disclosed that she and her son shared a room in a kommunalka, Yana immediately crossed her off her list. For Yana, a kommunalka, a relic of the early Soviet period when large apartments were divided up into rooms each occupied by one family, evoked the image of a cramped and unhygienic space and therefore not the place and conditions in which she wanted a woman who was gestating her child. She therefore dropped the candidate upon finding out. Client mother Katharina in turn visited the home of her surrogacy worker Inna prior to signing the contract to ensure that the home was well taken care of and Inna took care of her nutrition.

> I saw what was there, and it is good food. There are no sausages or such things. Meat is meat, and there are vegetables – and she is eager to prepare good food for the family, and they don't go for fast food and so on.
> (Katarina, client mother, October 2012)

These choices confirm that surrogacy workers were not recruited from the poorest social class, despite the frequent, ignorant claims that bring surrogacy into disrepute. The life and health circumstances of women living in poverty, without sufficient heating during a winter that can last six months or without sufficient food, were considered too precarious for client parents. It is hardly surprising that they did not feel comfortable in entrusting their babies to women living in poverty. Most surrogacy workers in Russia have living conditions that are stable, yet which have room for improvement.

Once client parents or agencies have selected their preferred candidate, they need to seek approval of their embryologist. Dr Nikolai, an IVF expert with a decade of facilitating embryo transfers for surrogacy arrangements, shared his experiences and personal frustration with some intending surrogacy workers as he explained his approach of selecting candidates he considered suitable.

> When I am not satisfied with something (...) we exchange the surrogate mother. (...) It's not as if a woman decides to be a surrogate and so she can be one. (...) I need results; [I am not satisfied with] only implementing the procedure. (...) Russian women approach [surrogacy] as if they were part of a production line: in August she has an abortion, in September she donates her eggs, and now [in October] she comes for stimulation [for surrogacy]. And she hides her previous involvements! And sometimes they even work in multiple jobs, running from 'A' to 'B' while getting the stimulation shots!! That way I don't get the results I want. That is ongoing commercialization for you.
> (Dr Nikolai, embryologist, October 2014)

Dr Nikolai's account again reflects how surrogacy workers understand surrogacy as a 'job of a certain sort', and often come to surrogacy as well as egg provision incentivised by financial needs. Being approved by the doctor of the client parents or the agency is the last hurdle women have to overcome to become a surrogacy worker, after first having made up their own mind and then having been selected by an agency or client parents.

Racialized Imaginaries

Even when a woman comes from the right socioeconomic stratum, is healthy and fertile, appears docile, is financially motivated and business oriented, and presents herself as a loving, caring mother to her own children, she may not yet be considered an ideal surrogacy worker in Russia. Like any other market in reproductive services in any part of the world (Culley, Hudson, & Van Rooij, 2012; Deomampo, 2013a, 2013b; Ragoné, 2000; Speier, 2016; Twine, 2017), racialised imaginaries shape the Russian surrogacy market. In this last section on how women become surrogacy workers in Russia I therefore analyse the racialized imaginaries that shape the practice of surrogacy. To show how the practice of commercial gestational surrogacy in Russia has developed its distinct own 'reproduction of whiteness' (Speier, 2016) requires an explanation of how 'Russianness' in post-Soviet Russia – being *russkiy*, ethnic Russian, rather than *rossiskiy*, a Russian citizen – has become a synonym for 'whiteness' (Zakharov, 2015).

At the time of the Soviet Union, internationalism, egalitarianism and the friendship of peoples were key doctrines of the Soviet ideology, alongside a fierce suppression of manifestations of nationalism. It was the Soviet state's aim 'to seek out the remotest and tiniest communities and make them their "own" [*svoy*], a word which also implies making them less strange or alien' (Vitebsky, 2005, p. 47). In this context, Russianness was regarded the ideal. As the historian Yuri Slezkine (2000, p. 231) writes, 'Russianness was assumed (...) to be equal to [Soviet] modernity'. Furthermore, 'the Soviet multinational state was built on the assumption that non-Russians were, on the whole, more backward than Russians' (Slezkine, 2000, p. 229), and needed to catch up (see also Michaels, 2000). To illustrate this point, during the Soviet era, the terms *malye narody Severa* [small peoples of the North] were used to refer specifically to the indigenous, often nomadic population living north of the Arctic circle, and *otstalye narody* [backward people] was a term in common currency for the non-Russian population within the Soviet territory in general (Martin, 2001).

Glasnost in the 1980s and the subsequent dissolution of the Soviet Union paved the way for new nationalist discourses and an expression of nationalist sentiments in Russia (Pachenkov, 2010; Sevortian, 2009) and revived Russia's desires to guard one's own nation against immigration and foreign infiltration. Those formerly appropriated and made *svoy* were to become strange and alien again. As Sevortian (2009, p. 21) put it, 'to an extent it was predictable that some form of ethnic based nationalism should have replaced the composite Soviet identity'. Marger (2015, pp. 28–29) contends that '[today's ethnic] stratification is not random, (...) [it] is legitimized by an ideology that justifies the resultant inequality'.

In the general population of Russia, *russkiy* Russians make up the majority, and many other ethnic groups were differentiated and ethnicised as non-Russian and merged into a generalised category of the 'black' other (Zakharov, 2015,

p. 157). Racialised categories were more clearly demarcated: 'white' includes ethnic Russians, and may include the other east Slavic ethnic groups of Belarusians and Ukrainians, whereas '"black" includes people of Asian descent as well as those from the Caucasian republics or Africa. Black is not a question of pigmentation; rather it is a cultural category' (Zakharov, 2015, p. 62). These terms and categorisations are also applied in and shape the markets in surrogacy in Russia: 'white' Russian client parents, who represent the majority of client parents in Russia, avoided reproducing (their) whiteness through the reproductive labour of 'black' – visibly minority ethnic Central Asian or Russian – women. Instead, the ethnic stratifications in Russia's markets in surrogacy unfold along different markers. 'Black' women are coded as undesired and consequentially disqualified to reproduce for 'white' client parents. Russian/'white' client parents reproduce their whiteness by employing the gestational labour of 'white', Slavic surrogacy workers.

Client parents expressed their main concerns about Central Asian women as surrogacy workers as being their cultural and religious 'otherness', which they saw as being expressed in different hygiene standards and excessive submissiveness to their husbands, and controversially, also in sexual promiscuity, all of which presented a threat to the baby *in utero*.[16]

Client mother Nadezhda categorically ruled out the option of employing Central Asian women. To defend her position, she pointed out the high rates of

---

[16]Addressing ethnic/racial preferences in their choice of surrogacy workers in interviews with client parents was methodologically and emotionally challenging. When something or someone is absent, such as in this case the option of hiring a Central Asian surrogacy worker, it rarely comes up naturally in conversation. To understand what causes the absence, I needed to address this absence explicitly. The client parents that harboured resentment against Central Asian surrogacy workers did not consider themselves racist. Consequently, my introduction of the topic and my questions on the reasons of their choices to not hire or consider a Central Asian surrogacy worker affronted them and caused discomfort. I had to manage these situations carefully to maintain good research relationships in order to understand what was going on. Other client parents in turn were confident in the accuracy of their assessment that Central Asian women were unsuitable, which caused me moral yuck reactions. I struggled to not counter their remarks, but I tried to remain open and empathetic to their experiences of loss, hope and grief as people struggling with infertility. Again, in order to understand what was going on, I had to encourage them to continue in more detail. In order to manage these interview situation, I reminded myself that my role as a researcher is to listen to *their* story, and not argue with them (see also Blee, 1998), but I felt uncomfortable and upset for not speaking up. One strategy of dealing with such upsetting fieldwork encounters was airing my frustration to friends and colleagues. On one particular day, when sharing an unpleasant interview experience with a colleague and recounting how my interview partner normalized an Uzbek surrogacy worker being denied housing on the basis of her ethnicity, to my dismay, my colleague replied: 'I have an apartment that I rent out and I would never take an "Eastern" woman – because it's another culture, they are different, and you don't know what they are doing. She might be cooking *plov* [Uzbek rice dish] on the floor, and I just don't want that'. Indeed, racialised imaginaries and racist resentments go deep.

crime and illegality reported among Central Asian labour migrants in Russia and continued 'I never ever considered such an option in the first place. (...) There are simply so many illegal Tajiks here (...).[17] [T]hose who come to us are not the best representatives of their nations'. Moreover, she described Central Asian women as having lower personal hygiene standards.[18] Her tone and body language revealed that she felt uncomfortable about voicing such sentiments out loud, and so she expressed her resentment in an implicit comparison.

> Towards a [surrogate mother] from Buryatia or Tatarstan or such, I have a slightly different attitude (...) they are clean [tchistoplotniye], they do not belong to a beggar nation [nishaya natsiya].[19]
>
> (Nadezhda, client mother, April 2015)

The meaning of *tchistoplotniye*, 'clean', is more complex in Russian than in English: beyond referring to all things related to (personal) hygiene, and how one maintains their person, the home and children, the meaning of *tchistoplotniye* extends to one's choice of language and expression as well as prudence in the choice of intimate partners. Referring to Central Asian women as not *tchistoplotniye*, client mothers on the one hand were apprehensive of potential infections of the reproductive tract, particularly infections caused through sexual intercourse, and hinted at sex work. On the other hand, they were referring to moral

---

[17]Besides 'black', another common slur to refer to people of Central Asian ethnicity is referring to them as 'Eastern' or 'Tajik', thus generalising them into monolithic categories. When people in Russia refer to an individual as 'Tajik', they did so in a way that is consciously derogatory. Of all five Central Asian republics, Tajikistan is economically the weakest, and Tajik migrants therefore are the most numerous group among Central Asian labour migrants in the Russian Federation (Ryazantsev, Pismennaya, Karabulatova, & Akramov, 2014). Referring to someone, or all Central Asian migrants as Tajiks is an ethnic slur that expresses that there is no significant difference among them, that 'they are all the same', and in particular, 'they are all the same poor'.
[18]Many Central Asian migrants in Russia are forced to live in substandard and crowded living conditions leading to poor sanitation. Reasons include a systematic discrimination on the housing market, substandard accommodation provided by employers and high living costs (King, Dudina, & Dubrovskaya 2020; Tkach & Brednikova, 2010). Several agency staff and client parents have grounded their opinion and apprehension in news reports on national television. One illustrative example is the comment by agency owner Veronica: 'Not long ago I watched a documentary on TV. They examined the trains that come into Moscow from the East, [bringing] the workers from Central Asia (...). Of course, everywhere one could find many nasty illnesses, which [the migrants] don't check up on and don't treat. They come here and you can't even imagine what they are bringing with them'. [Veronica, September 2014]
[19]The Republics of Tatarstan and Buryatia are federal subjects of the Russian Federation. The majority of the respective local population consists of ethnic minority groups. The Tatars are a Turk people, and Buryats are the largest indigenous group in Siberia and speak a Mongolic language.

notions, whereby they saw their own Russian culture as pure, a quality of being Russian, opposed to non-Russians, whose 'quality of the self' was opposed to this Russianness (Zakharov, 2015, pp. 64, 72). Yet, by naming regions of Russia with a high demographic rate of ethnic minority population, from where she would accept a non-Slavic surrogacy worker, it appears that Nadezhda tried to distance herself from being racist and instead base her aversion on the countries' development standard, for which surrogacy workers could not be held responsible.

Client mother Yana made no secret that she was not too keen on employing a Central Asian surrogacy worker. She had chosen Gulshanoy, an Uzbek woman, only after several attempts with Russian surrogacy workers had failed and her remaining budget was small. Aware of client parents' reservations, women from Central Asian republics, who live in Russia and want to become surrogacy workers, tend to significantly lower their financial expectations to compete with Slavic women. Gulshanoy, divorced and a mother of three, had come to St Petersburg for work and been brokered to Yana via an intermediary. Yana preferred to not share any details about this middle person and the arrangements she had with them. She took a liking to Gulshanoy and her apparent fertility, given her three children. Yana's doctor also approved of her and so Gulshanoy started the hormone treatment in preparation for the embryo transfer. Only then Yana did enquire and learn that Gulshanoy had found a new partner, also Uzbek, with whom she had moved in. Yana immediately annulled the agreement and requested Gulshanoy to stop the medication. She was eager to emphasise that there was nothing wrong with Gulshanoy. On the contrary, she stressed that Gulshanoy had made a proper and clean impression; it was her partner that posed the problem: 'Being Eastern like her (...) he needs sex'. Yana was convinced Gulshanoy would not be able to avoid sexual intercourse during the arrangement from preparation until birth, on which Yana insisted, on the advice of her doctor. Yana complemented her assumption of the obedient Eastern woman with the image of the oppressive Eastern man, who is driven by lust and/or instinct, incapable or unwilling to understand and control himself (Hoodfar, 1992; Varisco, 2007).

For client mother Anastasia, Central Asian surrogacy workers were only acceptable if they were single – and she added religious imaginaries to her racialised imaginaries. Anastasia chose Akmaral, her Muslim and Kazakh surrogacy worker, because she had previous experience,

> (...) and because she had no husband at that time. Had she been married and had three children instead of one, then I would not have taken her. Because among Muslims, women are not allowed to dispute their husbands. If the husband wants sex, the wife has no rights to refuse him, even if she is pregnant with my child, even if she is at a risk of miscarrying. More than that, regardless of her being pregnant, she is solely responsible for the household duties. Muslim men don't assume female duties. (...) All that exposes the pregnancy to risks.
>
> (Anastasia, client mother, October 2012)

Anastasia opposed surrogacy workers continuing sexual intercourse during the pregnancy. Such discomfort on the part of client parents is not limited to Central Asian women, but concerns client parents regardless of their surrogacy workers' ethnic identity. However, Anastasia's previous choice of married Russian and Ukrainian surrogacy workers implied the assumption that Slavic women follow this request conscientiously and, if necessary, oppose their husbands, whereas a Central Asian, Muslim woman would not. This view, held by Yana as well as other client mothers in my study, patronisingly sees Muslim women as victims unable to resist their husbands, and incapable of acting in a way which did not conform to their religious faith and follow their own moral judgement. Slavic women, by contrast, were seen as modern and emancipated enough to oppose their husbands (and these Slavic husbands to be willing and able to accept this restriction), and if Orthodox religious, capable of setting themselves above the Church's condemnation of surrogacy and able to follow their own moral judgement (Ivankiva, 2012).

Most Russian client parents in my sample and as reported by agency staff in my sample considered Central Asian women inadequate to work as their surrogacy workers. They listed surrogacy workers' attributed obedience to their husbands over their doctors a result of their cultural and religious upbringing. Crucially Central Asian women were disqualified on grounds that they would not be able to abstain from sexual intercourse and were regarded to have low hygiene standards. Consequentially, agencies preferred not to hire women of Central Asian ethnic origin even though many were considered to be ideal candidates for surrogacy due their fertile nature, docile culture and their 'distinct, distinguishable phenotypical appearance' (Veronica, agency owner), which would clearly mark them as not the parents. Veronica further elaborated her take on how Central Asian women's distinct difference was an advantage by means of the example of a pregnant Uzbek surrogacy worker.

> [She not only] has her own to children to take care of, she also has such a specific nationality – in this case I have a 100% guarantee that she doesn't need someone else's child, but more over that she won't keep a *Russian* child. [Emphasis in original].[20]
> (Veronica, agency owner, November 2012)

Ala, surrogacy worker coordinator in the large agency Happy Baby, made no secret out of her personal preference for hiring and working with Central Asian candidates. She explained:

> In my experience, they get pregnant easily and carry pregnancies excellently well. That seems to be in their genes. They all have large families, and from a medical point of view, everything goes smoothly with them. In patriarchal societies [like theirs] there is

---

[20]Veronica was conflating ethnicity with nationality.

more obedience and as a consequence, we have fewer problems with the Eastern girls [vostotchnye devotchki] [than we have with the Russians].

(Ala, surrogacy agency coordinator, September 2014)

However, in her experience, the majority of client parents are ethnic Russians, who prefer to hire ethnic Russian or another ethnic Slavic (Belarusian, Ukrainian) surrogacy workers. Hence, her agency, like other agencies in St Petersburg, responded to the ethnically marked demand with a selective, 'supply and demand' oriented recruitment.

We hardly, hardly ever accept such girls [Central Asian women], because the bio[logical] parents don't want them. The parents are foremost Russians, European Russians, and they don't want 'Eastern' [women].[21]

Dr Victoria, an IVF expert who is experienced in discussing the option of surrogacy with her patients, confirmed the reluctance towards Central Asian women by her Russian patients.

You ask why [they don't want Central Asian women]? Because surrogate mothers have to meet more demands. More demands [than an egg donor], and her social status needs to be higher. Long story short, it needs to be one of our Russian girls rather than a girl, a woman who has come from Central Asia. [Intending parents] look at her more in a more complicated manner, and it is more difficult to supervise her. The chance of women who come from Central Asia having infections is higher, and the law requires citizenship to be taken care of and to give birth, she needs the right to be in Russia.[22] For that reason, it is more likely a Russian woman [is chosen].

(Dr Victoria, embryologist, October 2019)

As a result, for Ala's agency, hiring Central Asian women is unprofitable: To enter a potential surrogacy worker into their database and to be ready for the medical procedures if client parents approve an offered candidate requires the surrogacy workers to have passed all medical health tests as required by the medical order. These test results expire after approximately three months, and

---

[21]With 'European Russians' she intended to forestall any misunderstanding in my side and make sure that I understood that she spoke of ethnic Russians [*russkiy*] rather than Russian citizens [*rossiskiy*].

[22]All citizens from countries of the former Soviet Union need to apply for a work permit and insurance to live and work in the Russian Federation. With a valid work permit, labour migrants are entitled to medical treatment. Dr Victoria's response, however, hints to the unregistered and therefore illegalised labour migrants in Russia.

with Russian client parents' reluctance, many agencies regard such monetary investment a waste of time.

However, in large agencies like hers, with client parents increasingly coming from abroad and occasionally being of Muslim faith and looking for a Muslim surrogate, they made exceptions, and Central Asian women were accepted.

> We only take 'Eastern' girls when the bio-parents ask for it, and (…) [this is only the case] when the bio[logical] parents themselves are Eastern. They prefer such girls, because among Slavic girls, rarely you find a Muslim among the Slavs. When the bio-parents are Muslims then it is critically important to them that their *surmama* is Muslim and then we are of course eager to find them one.
>
> (Ala, surrogacy agency coordinator, September 2014)

As a result of these racialised imaginaries, Central Asian women who sought to enter the market but could not 'wait' to be the 'lucky few' chosen by agencies, had to resort to the strategy of lowering their financial expectations, such as Gulshanoy did, to be competitive and to compensate for their racialised undesirability with a financial incentive. Thus, for Central Asian women to be able to convert their reproductive capital into economic capital, they had to discount their reproductive labour, despite the widespread stereotype of their hyper-fertility.

Conclusion

This chapter has addressed how women become surrogacy workers in Russia. It has compared surrogacy workers' points of views and analysed how they made their decision to become a *surmama*. It has discussed the perspectives of the client parents and commercial agencies and common patterns in considering women as suitable and desirable to perform this form of reproductive labour.

Knowledge about what surrogacy is, and that commercial, gestational surrogacy may be a 'certain kind of job' and way of making money, is widespread in Russia, not least because of the publicity of celebrities using surrogacy for their family building, and advertisements for surrogacy and gamete donation appearing prominently in the employment section of newspapers. Therefore, rather than being actively recruited, the majority of women who become surrogacy workers in Russia have stepped forward on their own initiative and applied to commercial agencies or uploaded their commercial offer to respective online platforms.

The women who did so did not take their decision lightly, but only after thorough consideration of their own moral disposition as well as their wider social circumstances in their role as mothers and partners. They spent time considering whether they felt capable and comfortable with the idea of becoming pregnant and then parting with the child. Understanding that for them a genetic bond carried more importance than a gestational link and that they therefore would not be *parting* from *their* child after delivery, but would instead be giving the client parents a child back that they had been caring for, they perceived their role as workers rather than mothers. Yet, they also anticipated that this moment of handing the child back might be challenging and therefore implemented various emotion-work systems (Hochschild, 1979) that supported them throughout the commissioned pregnancies so they did not falter in their decisions.

Secondly, they were aware that they couldn't make such a decision in a vacuum but needed to consider with whom they wanted to share their decision to become surrogacy workers, and who needed to know in order to support them with childcare for their own children.

Women made their choice to become a surrogacy worker based on their socioeconomic realities: many were single mothers and/or working several jobs to make ends meet, and while the compensation for a surrogacy pregnancy did not promise the end of their financial struggles, they promised a temporary relief. Furthermore, women made their decision taking into account their socio-political realities and the cultural framing of surrogacy in Russia: they were working mothers, and perceived surrogacy first and foremost as a job, rather than a calling or a gift, as surrogacy is described in the UK and US. They worked as 'surrogate mothers' to convert their reproductive capital into economic capital.

The next step in becoming a surrogacy worker is finding client parents, either directly, for so-called 'direct arrangements', or through commercial agencies. Here, women interested in becoming surrogacy workers underwent a selection process guided by the various expectations and racialised imaginaries of the agencies and client parents: besides being healthy, a desirable surrogacy worker was expected to display docility, a certain amount of financial need and monetary rather than altruistic inclinations. Furthermore, besides repeatedly emphasising that surrogacy workers are merely a vessel or incubator and their genetic set-up is irrelevant, racialised imaginaries in which 'Slavic' women are considered more desirable than Central Asian women ensured that Central Asian women were disadvantaged in the markets on surrogacy, unless they filled a niche request.

Chapter 3

Making the Relationship Work

> We have hardly anything in common. We are from different social
> classes. That is always the case. The *biomamas* and the *surmamas*
> are different: different age, different upbringing, different
> residential areas. (...) We accompany each other for these nine
> months. And then we part and do not meet again.
>
> (Inga, surrogacy worker, October 2012)

In this chapter, I focus on the relationships between surrogacy workers and
client parents, and, in particular, the efforts surrogacy workers make in navigating their surrogacy arrangements.[1] I argue that, for the relationship to work,
surrogacy workers perform relational work, which can be defined as 'the creative effort people make establishing, maintaining, negotiating, transforming and
terminating interpersonal relationships' (Zelizer, 2012, p. 149). This relational
work constitutes a substantial part of surrogacy workers' service for client
parents. Furthermore, the relational work itself and individuals' perception of it
as work are embedded in the cultural framing of surrogacy as an economic
arrangement. This encourages all actors involved in surrogacy arrangements to
perceive relational work as a given part of surrogacy workers' service. This, in
turn, also encourages surrogacy workers to anticipate a transient relationship
with their client parents, which ends with handing over the child after giving
birth.

The relationship between a surrogacy worker and her client parents has been a
long-standing interest in empirical surrogacy research. The overarching findings
of this research, which is based on surrogacy arrangements in Israel (Teman,
2010), United Kingdom (Imrie & Jadva, 2014; Jadva, Murray, Lycett, MacCallum, & Golombok, 2003), United States (Berend, 2016a, 2016b; Haylett, 2015;

---

[1] I acknowledge that both parties, the surrogacy workers and the client parents, are equally
involved in navigating through and working on the relationship. In this chapter, I focus on
the perspective of the surrogacy workers. For an analysis focussing on client/intending
parents' perspective and experience, see for instance Weis and Norton (2021), Smietana
(2017) and Teman (2010).

Surrogacy in Russia, 55–77
Copyright © 2021 Christina Weis
Published under exclusive licence by Emerald Publishing Limited
doi:10.1108/978-1-83982-896-620211008

Jacobson, 2016; Ragoné, 1994) and India (Deomampo, 2016; Pande, 2014b; Rudrappa, 2015), is the tendency among surrogacy workers to expect, seek and highly value the development of a relationship and to regard the achievement of a lasting bond as a marker of success and satisfaction (Berend, 2014, 2016b; Haylett, 2015; Imrie & Jadva, 2014; Teman, 2010). Moreover, forging a lasting bond is seen as a way to de-commercialise the contractual arrangement (Berend, 2016b; Haylett, 2015; Jacobson, 2016; Teman, 2010), or, in contrast, in India, as a strategy to obtain greater (material) gain, for example, in the form of additional gifts or money after the arrangement is concluded (Pande, 2014b). In this chapter, I engage with these findings on surrogacy relationships and contribute to the existing body of literature with insights from surrogacy arrangements in Russia, where relationships between surrogacy workers and client parents are seen as part of the work arrangement and are transient in their nature.

To identify the subtleties of surrogacy workers' agency in their surrogacy arrangements and relational work, and how these shape the relationship and arrangements, I draw on Sherry Ortner's (1997, 2006) concept of 'serious games', which Ortner developed from practice theory (Bourdieu, 1977; Giddens, 1984; Sahlins, 1981). For Ortner (1997, pp. 10–14), agency is a culturally constructed and socially embedded capacity to act. Thus, I conceptualise surrogacy arrangements as a 'game' that is played under certain rules and add that such games are taking place within a certain setting. The game is 'serious' as much is at stake, and surrogacy workers are active players who learn the rules. Knowing the rules they have agency to play in accordance with them, but may also challenge them or eventually even cheat. According to Ortner, the way individuals act is always socially embedded. They are 'involved in, and can never act outside of, the multiplicity of social relations in which they are enmeshed' (Ortner, 2006, p. 130). These social relations are characterised by inherent power inequalities, social and biological stratifications between surrogacy workers and client parents, the commodification of surrogacy workers' reproductive capital and the cultural framing of surrogacy as a business arrangement.

As discussed in Chapter 2 'Becoming a surrogacy worker' and addressed by Inga in the quote at the beginning of this chapter, surrogacy workers' and client parents' socio-economic realities are stratified. Client parents possess greater economic, social and cultural capital than the women they hire as gestational carriers, and based on their accumulated capital, they continue to have access to resources that the latter do not. Further, because surrogacy in Russia is framed as an economic transaction, surrogacy arrangements are perceived as a form of temporary employment. Therefore, surrogacy workers and client parents conceptualise their relationship in terms of a hierarchical 'employer–employee' relationship, based on and reinforcing the notion of surrogacy as work, and which shapes their interactions.[2]

The next contextual layer to consider is surrogacy workers' and client parents' varying degrees of reproductive capital, as described in the previous chapter. To recap, I define reproductive capital as an individual's fertility, the possession of viable and healthy gametes, and in the case of women, their ability to conceive, gestate, give birth and breastfeed. While surrogacy workers are rich in reproductive capital, client parents need to rely on surrogacy workers' reproductive capital in order to fill their own reproductive desires.[3] These varying degrees of reproductive capital lead to biological stratifications between surrogacy workers and client parents and intersect with social and economic stratification. When entering surrogacy arrangements to convert reproductive capital into economic, and economic capital into reproductive, Mitra and Schicktanz (2016, p. 8) point out that

> ...[intended parents], unlike the surrogates who feel very confident about their reproductive capacities, (...) feel extremely vulnerable and anxious during the whole procedure for not having any control over their attempted conception.

---

[2]Using the term 'employee' for a surrogacy worker in Russia is problematic, even though surrogacy workers commonly make sense of their role by referring to themselves as 'hired workers' and 'employees', and to client parents and agencies as 'employers'. Surrogacy worker Anyuta, for instance, explained, 'I am like a worker for [the parents] during the time of the pregnancy, because I need to fulfil their requests', whereas Ilya outlined how *surmamas* 'clearly perform duties, like in an employee-employer [relationship]'. However, the reality of the arrangement is that surrogacy workers do not have the legal status, rights and protection of employees. Working as a surrogate, they neither have fixed hours, work insurance or sick leave, nor bargaining rights, taxes or pension schemes. Instead, the social organisation of commercial surrogacy in Russia suggests that surrogacy workers are independent contractors. Self-employment in Russia is largely informal, and many agents do not register as legal employers in order to avoid taxation, yet while it is considered an indicator of being an employee to be provided with more working rights than an independent contractor, agencies and client parents face no regulations that limit their management of their surrogacy workers, including intrusion into their private lives. Surrogacy workers have fewer rights than independent contractors and little or no protection vis-à-vis their 'employers'. Yet, for surrogacy workers, framing surrogacy arrangements in employer–employee terms is their choice of words, and I, therefore, use the term to present their own voice.

[3]See also the work of Sara Lafuente-Funes (2020) on the bioeconomy of egg provision, who argues for a move away from the concept of egg 'donation' and instead towards an understanding of the reproductive labour of egg providers as the 'transference of reproductive capacity' (TRC). Lafuente-Funes (2020) argues that 'TRCs can involve eggs, sperm, uteruses, and biological processes such as pregnancy, gestation, and birth-giving. TRCs can take place through a mutual agreement or under coercion. TRCs can be paid or unpaid, can take place under the so-called *altruism with economic compensation* model, or within a relational context in which the different parties share a personal relationship'.

Therefore, client parents seek to control whatever *is* or *appears to be* in their power during the surrogacy arrangement, such as the timing of appointments, the surrogacy workers' diet, the supervision of the pregnancy, the selection of the medical professionals, and the location and arrangements for the birth, in an attempt to mitigate their powerlessness. By entering into contractual surrogacy arrangements with the notion of surrogacy as a paid service, surrogacy workers commodify their reproductive labour. Such commodification is 'rarely simply given, unambiguous or complete (...) [and] the question remains how the commodification (...) is understood and experienced by those involved in such relationships and processes' (Constable, 2009, p. 54).[4] Zelizer (2005, pp. 1–2) reminds us that intimacy and economic activity are closely intertwined, sustaining as well as complementing each other. Therefore,

> ...we should stop agonizing over whether or not money corrupts, but instead analyze what combinations of economic activity and intimate relations produce happier, more just, and more productive lives. It is not the mingling that should concern us, but how the mingling works.
>
> (Zelizer, 2005, p. 298)

In this chapter, I explore this mingling of the intimate and economic by conceptualising the social relations between surrogacy workers and client parents as serious games, pervaded by power and inequality in multiple ways (Ortner, 1997, p. 12), and the surrogacy workers as skilful, active players, no matter how constraining their circumstances (MacLeod, 1992). I trace how surrogacy workers' serious games develop, how they learn the rules and develop strategies, come to bend or break the rules and co-create new ones. I show how surrogacy workers' agency is complex, entailing acceptance, accommodation, ignorance and resistance – often simultaneously. Their agency is suited to their situation as well as their context and purposefully aimed at achieving their goals. The chapter is organised as follows. I begin by exploring how and with what kinds of expectations and intentions surrogacy workers choose direct or agency-mediated surrogacy arrangements. Next, I explore how the relationships develop during the pregnancy, and how they may differ in direct or agency-mediated arrangements. Finally, I close by describing the course the relationships may take after childbirth.

Doing the Groundwork: Choosing between a Direct or Agency-mediated Surrogacy Arrangement

The two most common options for client parents and surrogacy workers when entering a commercial surrogacy agreement are working with a commercial

---

[4] I draw on the Marxist definition of commodification described as 'the process of assigning market value to goods or services that previously existed outside the market' (Constable, 2009, p. 54).

surrogacy agency or *napryamuyu*, so-called direct arrangements. Commercial agencies select suitable surrogacy workers and mediate all communication until completion of the programme, whereas in a direct arrangement, client parents and surrogacy workers take all matters into their own hands.

Agency Arrangements

Surrogacy agencies in Russia are private commercial enterprises that select suitable surrogacy workers based on medical guidelines and their own psychological assessment criteria. They match them with client parents, provide client parents with legal guidance, supervise the pregnancies, provide a notary to obtain surrogacy workers' consent to hand the baby over after childbirth, administer the payment of the surrogacy workers and, finally, guide the client parents through establishing legal parenthood.[5]

Most agencies, especially larger ones that coordinate 20 surrogacy arrangements or more at the same time, prefer to inhibit direct contact between surrogacy workers and client parents. They argue that contact between the two parties may 'spoil' surrogacy workers as it may encourage them to take advantage of their client parents by claiming extra benefits possibly leading to jealousy among them. In the words of agency coordinator Ala, 'the more they are in touch [with their bio parents], the more capricious the surrogate mothers are'. For agencies, contact between surrogacy workers and client parents poses the risk of arousing emotions, and emotions pose the risk of making the economic arrangement messy. By managing surrogacy workers and client parents separately, agencies forestall contact in aid to obviate risk of mediating conflict. To client parents, the agency staff present the arrangement of no contact to the surrogacy worker as a favour and report it as being well-received by the client parents. According to Ala, 'if client parents were interested in contact, they would not have chosen an agency in the first

---

[5]Depending on the individual agency, two or three sets of contracts are concluded: between the agency and the client parents, between the agency and the surrogacy worker and, eventually, between the client parents and the surrogacy worker. The contract between the client parents and the agency covers the selection, provision and supervision of the surrogacy worker, arranging the delivery and the subsequent bureaucracy of recognising the client parents as legal parents. The surrogacy worker's employment contract is comparative to a contract for temporary work, more specifically, agency work. She is hired by the agency to be hired out to the selected client parents. Her contract includes compliance with three embryo transfers and submission to the agency's rules. If an embryo transfer fails or an initially conceived pregnancy is interrupted (by miscarriage or abortion), the agency hires her out up to two more times to either the same or different client parents. Surrogacy workers are not regarded as employees, but only their reproductive service is contracted. That allows agencies to classify the money paid to the surrogacy worker as a reward for the surrogacy worker's time and commitment as well as compensation for possible adverse effects to her health (see also Farrugia, Penrod, & Bult, 2010). As such, the money is not taxed and part of an unofficial economy. No governmental guidance exists regarding the contents of a surrogacy contract, which puts surrogacy workers at risk of exploitation.

place'. In addition to preferring no or mediated contact with the surrogacy worker, according to Ala, client parents choose commercial agencies because of their long-standing experience, professional guidance and good judgement of who makes a good surrogacy worker. Occasionally, however, Ala found herself in the situation where she needed to remind the client parents of the quality of their service:

> We choose one successful candidate who fits our needs as well as the needs of the Ministry of Health. That's it. *One.* [Emphasis hers]. Such a fuss about the choice, {mimics the voice of a client parent:} 'and I like this one more, and this one less'. No! We remind the parents of the circumstance that we really understand our work and once you have turned to us, listen to our opinion! (…) You can choose the most amazing, beautiful, smart and educated and whatever [woman] but if she doesn't get pregnant, then what have you got?!
>
> (Ala, surrogacy agency coordinator, September 2014)

Framing the option to not meet the surrogacy worker, but communicate, if desired, via the agency, is presented as an advantage and, as such, undergirds the economic framing of Russian surrogacy. Following a neoliberal orthodoxy (McGregor, 2001, p. 83), surrogacy workers are disposable (Rudrappa, 2015) and consumable for client parents.

However, not all client parents liked this calculated approach. Nadezhda and her husband Arkady, for instance, were appalled by the attitude of Ala's agency when they first considered the agency route and booked in for a consultation. 'We found so much coldness there, as if we came to buy carrots', Nadezhda recalled. After they had left, they knew they would rather take up the challenge to find a direct arrangement.

Direct Arrangements

In direct arrangements, surrogacy workers and client parents meet in person and conclude a contract directly between one another. They commonly find each other on websites such as meddesk.ru, where intending client parents and surrogacy workers upload requests and advertisements (Fig. 3.1).

The two examples of Figs. 3.2 and 3.3 (see pp. 62 and 63) show how the advertisements may vary in detail. Such online advertisements commonly include the financial expectations or offers, such as detailed in Fig. 3.2. Like the woman offering her surrogacy service in Fig. 3.2, some (intending) surrogacy workers, especially those who are experienced, advise intermediaries and agencies to refrain from contacting them to recruit them into their database. Once first contact is established between a surrogacy worker and client parents, they negotiate the details of the arrangement, such as the monthly allowance and final compensation. If both sides are interested, they meet in person. Often the first meeting occurs with an appointment with the client parents' doctor to gain medical approval, and once details are worked out and agreed upon, a contract will be negotiated and signed. Client parents take the initiative in providing this contract,

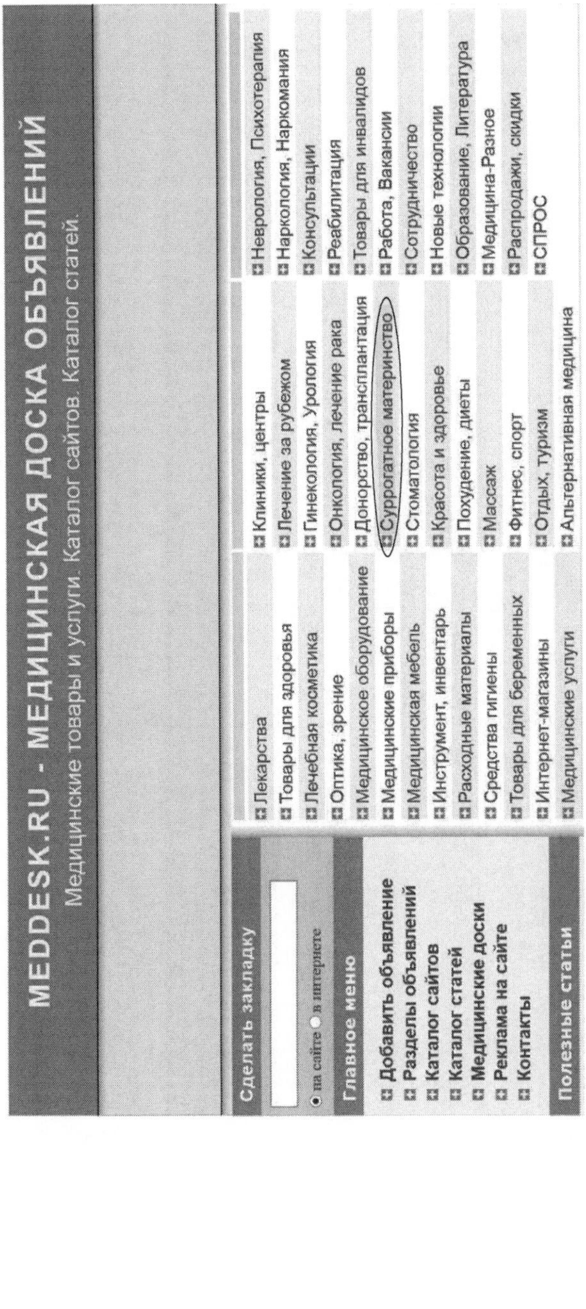

Fig. 3.1.   Meddesk – Medical Adverts. Highlighted: The Portal for Advertisements for Surrogacy.

Раздел: Суррогатное материнство

СТАНУ СМ.

Ищу порядочных био. Есть свои дети. Рожденые в срок. Также есть опыт рождения двойни по программе. Всё роды естественные. Ищу программу только в Барнауле. Посредников прошу не беспокоить. Есть частично анализы. Врачом одобрена. 900/200/150/20.25 если двойня.

КОНТАКТЫ:

Автор:	См С Опытом. Ищу Био
Город:	Барнаул
Телефон:	
E-mail:	Написать Автору Объявления
Сайт:	Скрыт

Fig. 3.2.   'I will be a s[urrogate] m[other]'.
Translation: 'I am searching for decent bio[-parents]. I have my own children. Births were full term. I also have experience in birthing twins in a [surrogacy] programme. All births were natural. I am looking for a [surrogacy] programme only in Barnaul. Intermediaries, please don't bother. I have recent test results. I am approved by a doctor.
900.000₽ [final compensation] (£14,940)
200.000₽ [in addition in the case of twins] (£3,320)
150.000₽ [in addition in the case of Caesarean section] (£2,490)
20.000₽ [monthly allowance during the pregnancy] (£332)
25.000₽ [monthly allowance during the pregnancy in case of twin pregnancy] (£415)'

but experienced surrogacy workers in my sample reported playing an active role in amending contracts. For client parents, opting for a direct arrangement means they make significant savings on agency service charges, and for surrogacy workers, entering a direct arrangement could entail the advantage of greater transparency and more rights. At the same time, direct arrangements also mean the absence of a mediator. They are commonly sought by individuals who prefer interpersonal contact with their counterparts. In direct arrangements, client parents and surrogacy workers carry more risks and responsibilities in managing the interpersonal relationships and the risks of surrogacy arrangements than when mediated through agencies.

Раздел: Суррогатное материнство   🖨 версия для печати

Срок объявления истек

Рекомендуем воспользоваться **другими объявлениями** или поиском на сайте.

СЕМЬЯ ИЩЕТ СУРМАМУ

В поиске сурмамы из г. Улан-Удэ. Нужна здоровая, с + резусом сурмама до 35 лет, ответственная, адекватная, без кесарево, без замерших беременностей. Вознаграждение достойное

КОНТАКТЫ:

Автор:	Био
Город:	УЛАН-УДЭ
Телефон:	Срок Публикации Истек
E-mail:	Написать Автору Объявления
Сайт:	Скрыт

Fig. 3.3. 'Family is searching for a surmama'.
Translation: 'On the search for a surmama from the city of Ulan-Ude. Must be healthy, with a positive rhesus factor, up to 35 years old, responsible, adequate, without Caesarean section, without "frozen pregnancies".[6]
Exemplary reward'.

How Surrogacy Workers Make Their Decision.

Most surrogacy workers reported that they had an idea of what they wanted from the arrangements in terms of contact with their client parents and what to expect depending on the type of arrangement. They commonly obtained this information from talking to other surrogacy workers online or simply from reading forum posts, and chose either a direct or an agency arrangement accordingly.

However, not all surrogacy workers had the liberty of choice. For some first-time surrogacy workers, and in particular those who relied on accommodation being provided, agencies appeared to be a safer option than muddling through online offers and contracting with strangers. In addition, larger, established agencies reassured first-time surrogacy workers that agencies were the best option. Agencies also attracted women who intended to avoid their clients and welcomed the agency's minimum-to-no-interaction policy. Surrogacy worker Ilya reported

---

[6]In the advertisement, the intending parents rule out considering a woman with previous experience of 'a frozen pregnancy'. The term 'frozen pregnancy' refers to an unexpected and abnormal termination of foetal development in the early stages of the pregnancy. The pregnancy ends with foetal death and premature termination. A 'frozen pregnancy' may also include a blighted ovum, whereby a fertilised egg implants in the uterus but fails to develop into an embryo.

the approach of her acquaintance Alisa, who had worked through an agency twice:

> Working with an agency motivated her, she said: {Imitates Alisa's voice} 'Because I also don't want to know [the client parents]'. 'I gestate, give birth, and receive my money – my relationship with the agency was excellent. They didn't oblige me to travel [*unlike Ilya who travelled on her client parents' request*] and they gave me my money, all as it should be'.
> (Ilya, surrogacy worker, November 2014)

Ilya herself only considered direct arrangements. She wanted contact and a supportive relationship with the client parents throughout the arrangement. Reflecting and comparing her own experiences with Alisa's, she concluded 'I would hardly have been able to do that'. Likewise, surrogacy worker Asenka stated that 'the emotional support is more important' than choosing the highest-paying arrangement under unrewarding conditions. The experienced surrogacy worker Yuliana shared Alisa's approach of not wanting contact. Making apple crumble in her agency-provided accommodation where she lived with three pregnant women and two others preparing for embryo transfer, she reflected that had she been in her client mother's situation, she likewise would have avoided contact with her sur-rogate. In her first surrogacy pregnancy, she had not met her client parents once, not even after giving birth, and, pleased with the experience, she returned to the same agency. Two months pregnant with twins, she emphasised that once again, she had no desire to meet and engage with her client parents. However, she was willing to negotiate some level of contact if that was their client parents' desire.

> If the *bio[logical] parents* want to get in touch with me, if that is *their desire*, I won't resist them. But, as far as I am concerned, I have not the slightest motivation to talk to them. The request to get in touch would certainly not come from me. [emphasis hers]
> (Yuliana, surrogacy worker, September 2014)

Finally, surrogacy workers also reported what they called 'VIP arrangements' that were mediated not by an agency, but the client parents' own mediators, and which offered extraordinarily high compensation for particularly stringent conditions during the pregnancy. Alexandra recalled her disappointment when she saw an offer advertised for 2,000,000₽ (£33,200), nearly triple the pay she received for her previous surrogacy arrangement, but for which she couldn't apply as she only just had given birth. The conditions included not leaving the provided accommodation and being under constant surveillance. 'It's like a golden cage. But for that money, I could pull myself together and be a good girl and do it'.

These accounts by agency representatives and surrogacy workers demonstrate how agency arrangements provide a setting where interactions between surrogacy workers and client parents rarely happen and are less desired. Surrogacy workers who are aware of this prefer the prospect working through agencies. However, agencies were also the place to go to for women without alternatives, regardless of their awareness concerning the relationship with the client parents. Surrogacy workers who, on the contrary, want to meet their client parents personally, and whose circumstances allow to arrange for that, chose to enter direct arrangements with the intention of laying the groundwork for a relationship with their client parents. However, as I will discuss further on in this chapter, their aspiration is that such a relationship will last only for the duration of the surrogacy arrangement. The expectation of a transient relationship is embedded in the cultural understanding of surrogacy as a 'business arrangement'. Surrogacy workers in Russia perceive their client parents to be their employers. Their intention to seek out client parents with whom they feel comfortable neither diminishes the arrangement's contractual character nor challenges the hierarchical relationship.

The Relationship (Is) Work

After having described the different settings for the serious game of surrogacy, I now turn my focus to how surrogacy workers develop their agency as players and how they relate to their client parents during the pregnancy. To guide my analysis, I complement my conceptual framework of 'serious games' with Viviana Zelizer's (2012, p. 149) concept of relational work. Zelizer describes relational work as a process during which:

> ...for each distinct category of social relations, people erect a boundary, mark the boundary by means of names and practices, establish a set of distinctive understandings that operate within that boundary, designate certain sorts of economic transactions as appropriate for the relation, bar other transactions as inappropriate, and adopt certain media for reckoning and facilitating economic transactions within the relation.
>
> (Zelizer, 2012, p. 146)

First, I address relationships that developed because surrogacy workers considered it their duty to be receptive to their client parents' wish to be in contact and establish a relationship. Next, I explore relationships between surrogacy workers and client parents that worked out to each party's satisfaction, and finally, I show how surrogacy workers coped when relationships failed.

Relationship (Work) as a Duty

Anyuta, a 27-year-old married woman from a small town in north-eastern Ukraine, had just signed her contract with her client parents and was waiting for the embryo transfer. She had chosen a direct arrangement not because she wanted to establish a relationship with the client parents but because she did not want to be separated from her child and husband. All of the agencies she contacted made it mandatory to relocate and live in accommodation provided by the agency. Anyuta unequivocally regarded both the physical efforts of pregnancy and birth and the management of the personal relationship between herself and client parents as work. She explained how she attuned herself from the onset to comply with her client parents' demands:

> During the pregnancy, I am sort of their hired worker, therefore I need to carry out their requests… if the bio-mama wants to watch over my pregnancy at every step and turn, I consider that her right. And I won't oppose her. (…) [The relationship during the pregnancy] will be whatever way they want it to be. We can keep a pregnancy diary, and *they* can be in touch and talk to me so I can share with them the feeling of being pregnant with *their child*. [Emphasis added]
>
> (Anyuta, surrogacy worker, February 2015)

Anyuta's statement clearly shows how she considers relational work as part of her surrogacy tasks. Casting herself as the client parents' hired worker, Anyuta considers it her job to establish and maintain a relationship that satisfies her employers and guarantees a smooth arrangement. To achieve this, Anyuta intends to commodify not only her embodied reproductive labour of pregnancy and birth (Cooper & Waldby, 2014) but also her emotions. Attuning herself to 'sustain the outward countenance that produces the proper state of mind in others [the client parents]' (Hochschild, 2003, p. 7) demands both emotion work (Hochschild, 1979) and emotional labour (Hochschild, 2003) of her. Anyuta maneuvered her 'serious game' within the cultural and contextual framing of surrogacy as an economic exchange that she is familiar with, and by coding the client parents as her employers, she is reproducing it. The social stratification between her and her client parents reinforces their hierarchical relationship. Contractual partners in surrogacy arrangements are hardly on egalitarian terms, and as Block (2012, p. 138) points out, 'relational work (…) comes in more or less egalitarian varieties (…) [and] in their relational work, individuals routinely take advantage of existing social hierarchies'. The client parents in my sample both consciously and unconsciously took advantage of the superior position granted to them by a higher economic status and reinforced by their contracts. Surrogacy workers in return consciously granted client parents these advantages and thus co-created the structural inequalities (Ortner, 1997).

The finding that Anyuta engaged in relational work in order to fulfil all her duties as a 'hired worker' contradict Haylett (2015), who studied the relationships between surrogate mothers and intending parents in the United States. Haylett (2015, p. 117) argues that

> …relational work within the surrogate-[intended parents] relationship is a failure if the surrogate comes to think of herself as a subordinate who has just rented out her body to people of higher-class status.

In Russia, maintaining that the surrogacy worker is the subordinate, is part of what makes the relationship work. Surrogacy workers see managing the relationship with their client parents as their duty.

Another example that illustrates this cultural notion equally well is the account of surrogacy worker Olesya. Olesya became a surrogacy worker through a St. Petersburg agency, and Evgenya, Olesya's client mother, had chosen the 'bargain package' including the provision of a surrogacy worker and coordination of embryo transfer. In other words, once pregnant the agency handed the management of the pregnancy and consequent communication other to Evgenya. Olesya invited me to her home for a first interview only a few days after the embryo transfer, and before she even new whether she was pregnant. Despite the kind of arrangement she had with Evgenya, she had met the client mother online twice so far, and each time only briefly. Their first encounter was in the office of their agency, when Olesya was presented to Evgenya as a possible candidate,[7] and the second time on the day of the embryo transfer, in the waiting room of the clinic, 15 min before Olesya was called in for the procedure; that day was also when I was introduced to both women and could sense their nervousness and insecurity in how to relate to each other. Sitting in her kitchen for our first interview, with her youngest child present and playing next to us, Olesya explained to me that she perceived her role and consequently her tasks towards Evgenya as attuning to *her* preferences. As a surrogacy worker, she saw this attunement as her duty. She felt that she owed her client mother a relationship that would allow her to draw closer to the child in utero. She said:

> I understand that [the biological parents] want to spend a lot of time with me, and check what I eat (...). To run from them, to avoid them, I do not regard as correct. As a surrogate mother, I need to attune to the idea that they are more worried than I am. I am helping, but they are giving their own, and their one and only [hope], [into the care of] another person.
>
> (Olesya, surrogacy worker, September 2014)

Olesya expressed that in letting Evgenya intrude her life as she wished, she was hoping for a working relationship to be established and to become familiar with her client parents. She did not regard it as contradictory to desire as well as to feel a duty to establish a relationship with her client mother. When I prompted Olesya to tell me more about her client mother and their relationship so far, she replied

> We have talked very little; I don't know [much about her]. (...) If this pregnancy will be confirmed with God's grace, then I think I will bring her here [to my home] for her to see the type of home where her baby will grow.

---

[7]This type of encounter in the office is not common, but was the agency's procedure in a 'bargain package' such as Evgenya's. As Evgenya was expected to arrange all further steps after a successful embryo transfer with Olesya, the two women were presented to each other for Evgenya to accept or decline her as a potential surrogacy worker.

Olesya's plan to reach out to Evgenya and welcome her into her was an alternative solution should Evgenya not take initiative to reach out to Olesya for a closer relationship. Olesya was made aware by her agency that initiatives that came from the surrogacy workers were not welcomed and inappropriate. Yet by making a 'plan B', Olesya was prepared to introduce modifications or even her own rules into the game, and having been matched to a client mother who paid the agency for a bargain arrangement rather than a fully supervised arrangement gave her more leeway to act. Her strategy went beyond the dichotomy of either obeying or resisting (MacLeod, 1992). Instead, Olesya strategized. She had assessed and understood the complexity of the game and played with the given rules and with her own agenda in mind.

Working under a regular agency contract, Anna and Mila had different experiences. During Mila's first, fully agency-mediated surrogacy pregnancy, her client parents infrequently enquired about her well-being, alternating personal calls with sending regards via the agency. On the day of delivery, Mila's client mother was present at the birth with Mila's permission. The client parents' attention gave Mila a sense of support and being valued. Two years later, and eight weeks pregnant in her second arrangement, her client parents had neither introduced themselves personally nor sent a message through the agency. 'And maybe I won't [ever meet them]' explained Mila, 'It all depends on the parents' preference'. Intrigued how matter-of-factly Mila gave this explanation, yet noticing the soft worry lines on her forehead and a note of submissiveness in her voice, I reinforced my question: 'And *your* wish? Do *you* want to meet them?' Mila responded: 'Well, if the parents have the desire to meet me, why should I be against it? I won't refuse them'. I risked insisting one more time: 'And *your* wish?', whereupon she replied:

> Of course, I would like to see them, meet them, and have a relationship. (...) For me personally, I find it easier. I don't know how it is for others, but for me it makes it easier. To see them at least once and talk – and understand their attitude.
>
> (Mila, surrogacy worker, September 2014)

Mila emphasised and insisted that the intention and initiative of seeking contact should come from the client parents' side, and like Olesya, ranked her own expectations and needs second by attuning herself to the accommodating of her client parents' wishes (Siegl, 2018a). Surrogacy worker Anna, five months pregnant with her second surrogacy child through an agency arrangement, also did not know these second client parents and shared Mila's approach. Even though she wanted to meet them and satisfy her curiosity about whose child she was carrying she explained that she didn't feel entitled to request her agency to contact her client parents. Instead, she pointed out that the client parents had her number, so 'if they want to, then they will call me, and I will be there'. Both Mila and Anna considered it their duty to be receptive to the client parents' expectations. It was their expression of agency to adapt to the given circumstances. As Näre (2014, p. 225) points out, 'to be an agent does not necessarily mean resisting or acting against someone or something, but being receptive and adapting to one's circumstances'. Furthermore, Mila and Anna knew, based on their repeated arrangements with the same agency and experience with their agency's approach, that requesting contact from their client parents would not only be a venture in vain but could even cause them trouble with the agency. Therefore, in order to reach their goal of successfully completing the arrangement and receiving full financial compensation, they chose to content themselves with their circumstances and, accept their client parents' choice of having a completely detached arrangement. Furthermore, taking the path of least resistance engendered less emotional turmoil for them.

Relationships That Work

Not all relationships centred around the client parents or where the surrogacy workers were expected to perform a larger share of the relational work. In some cases, more likely in direct arrangements, in which both sides were able to carefully choose their arrangement partners, relationships worked out in a mutually satisfactory and beneficial way. In such cases, both sides made efforts to address, reassess and shape their boundaries and during this process established, maintained and repeatedly negotiated their interpersonal relations (Zelizer, Bandelj, & Wherry, 2012).

One such case was the relationship of the surrogacy worker Asenka and client mother Katarina.[8] When Asenka, a single mother from nearby Kronstadt, first decided to be a surrogacy worker, she had registered with a St. Petersburg-based agency and by chance was matched with client parents who, though living several thousand kilometres away in Ulan-Ude, visited her twice during the pregnancy and stayed in frequent contact. For her second arrangement the following year, and richer in experience, Asenka decided to actively seek a local matching and the potential for a pleasant relationship. She undertook an avid search until she found client mother Katarina who shared her approach of wanting a mutual beneficial relationship; Katarina could not have imagined an arrangement without personally relating to her surrogacy worker and did not want to get involved with an agency. Nevertheless, for Katarina, surrogacy remained a form of work with an inherent 'employer–employee relationship', as does any transactional relationship. As the manager of her own company, the comparison came easily, and she emphasised that she always tried to treat Asenka 'as I would want to be treated'. For her, the commercial core of surrogacy was inevitable, yet indisputably she acknowledged and deeply appreciated Asenka's care work for her unborn child. She accompanied Asenka to all the pregnancy appointments,

---

[8]In my sample, the majority of surrogacy workers would speak at length about their relationships with client mothers, yet had little to say about the client fathers. When recruiting client parents, client fathers expressed little or no interest in being involved in this research. The absence of client fathers' voices is a limitation of this study that I have addressed elsewhere – see Weis and Norton (2020).

assisted with shopping and was on call in case Asenka needed any help. Asenka appreciated Katarina's efforts and moral support, and for her it

> ...was an additional plus that the child could recurrently hear the mother's voice and in such moments, I pointed it out to the child 'Listen! Listen! That is your mother talking!' because I believe that this [awareness] needs to be there early.
>
> (Asenka, surrogacy worker, August 2014)

Like Asenka, also Ilya chose all three of her client parents carefully. She explained:

> There are people who care only about the business [side], who don't seek, who don't need a personal tone. They want you to perform your duties conscientiously, like in an employer-employee relationship. (...) I see [surrogate motherhood] as a service, a paid [service], quite delicate and fine in every aspect and where emotions predominate.
>
> (Ilya, surrogacy worker, August 2014)

Ilya's choice to spend more time searching for a good match worked out for her. Despite the inevitability of a commuting arrangement, Ilya and her client mother Nadezhda established a close and mutually supportive relationship.[9] Every time Ilya came to St. Petersburg, she lodged with Nadezhda and her husband, and on two occasions, Nadezhda travelled to Ilya's hometown to participate in the ultrasound appointments and spare Ilya the journey to St. Petersburg in the midst of winter.

In both examples, Asenka and Katarina, and Ilya and Nadezhda, the women 'played their game' with the intention of accomplishing both the economic exchange and the personal relationship with their own and each other's benefit in mind. In order to achieve their multiple goals, they recognised each other's needs and were aware that surrogacy sits at the cusp of trust and work. For Ilya, the layer of the personal, cordial relationship with her client parents softened the edges of surrogacy's foundation, the 'employee–employer' arrangement. While for client mother Katarina, the social relationship did not have the same effect, the economic framing of surrogacy as a business arrangement was on a par with the gratitude and affection she felt for Asenka. The business of surrogacy and the fondness towards the person she hired for the work were both separate, yet simultaneous. In both cases, besides understanding the arrangements as essentially commercial and work, both parties attached great importance to having good rapport and a supportive relationship with each other. Their cases show that when surrogacy workers and client parents (client mothers in most cases) engage with each other, the resulting cordial relationships can be supportive and

---

[9]Ilya continued to live her hometown Yartsevo, close to Smolensk by the Belarusian border, and commuted on demand via the 16 hours train ride to St. Petersburg.

affirmative. However, these relationships do not shake the very foundations of surrogacy and its cultural framing in Russia. Surrogacy remains coded as an economic exchange and a commercial service.

Relationships That Don't Work

Personal relationships can fail, yet the nature of the surrogacy arrangement demands that relational and physical work is required to continue until the child is born – or in rare cases, a surrogacy worker decides to have an abortion.[10] In such cases, surrogacy workers have to be strategic and make creative efforts in their relational work to resolve unexpected situations or terminations of personal relationships (Zelizer, 2012). As outlined at the beginning of the chapter, surrogacy workers seek to lay strategic groundwork when choosing either direct or agency-mediated arrangements to prevent unpleasant surprises. Surrogacy relationships lie at the intersection of the intimate and economic sphere, which can add extra friction to the unpredictability of the dynamics of human relationships.

Surrogacy worker Diana, bitterly disappointed by the lack of contact with her client parents, had been unaware of the agency policy to keep both parties separated. This embitterment was intensified by her roommates contact with their client parents. Diana never received a call or a card, while her cohabitants received gifts and met their client parents personally. This is how her story unfolded:

> In the beginning, I felt uncomfortable about the absence of communication, because... if I carry a baby for someone, I want to know what awaits [the child], and that I am not just an incubator, but helping someone to achieve a wonder (...). But then, as time went by, on the contrary, I began enjoying this arrangement, because nobody was trying to get into my mind, nobody was trying to wring answers from me about how I feel, what I ate, how often I took walks, how I spent my free time – I felt entirely free. I slept when I wanted, ate chips when I wanted, and salted sunflower seeds as well, that I shouldn't have been eating but that I craved... I used to pick up my child, and carry her around, which is forbidden because it puts pressure on my uterus – all in all, it was great.[11] I was doing fine.
> (Diana, surrogacy worker, May 2015)

When Diana said she wanted to be seen as being more than just an incubator, but as someone helping to achieve a wonder, she did not imply that she had an

---

[10]I have not encountered a case in my sample. In all cases, abortions of a surrogacy pregnancy were performed on medical indication.
[11]Her one-year-old child lived with her. That was a rare exception, as she could not find anybody in whose care she could leave the child. However, it meant that she received a lower final compensation for bringing her child.

altruistic motivation. She was frank about her financial motivation. Instead, she sought confirmation that the client parents were decent people who would treat the child accordingly and not like a commodity. She feared that the client parents' attitude towards her as a commodity could reflect their attitude towards the child as a commodity which they bought through her service. Yet, witnessing how her fellow surrogacy workers' initial delight transformed into annoyance and even distress over obtrusive control, Diana reconsidered her situation. She became aware of the amount of relational work and emotional strain she was spared. Re-evaluating her situation, she no longer felt that she was missing out, but that she had the advantage of maintaining her peace, privacy and dignity. She was deprived of a relationship, but she was able to change her own emotions from disappointment and frustration into appreciation (Hochschild, 1979), which compensated for her initial concerns over the client parents' attitude. Diana not only learned the rules of the game but also began to make up and enact her own rules. In fact, flouting the rules of her agency became a game for her. The triumph of now feeling more privileged than her housemates empowered her to rely more on her intuitive knowledge. As the doctors were satisfied at the bi-weekly appointments, her 'mischief' of caring for her own young child by picking her up carrying her, and of eating what she wanted to eat, went unnoticed, and her pregnancy ended successful.

Finally, the example of surrogacy worker Marcella, who initially was in direct contact with her client parents and terminated the contact on her own account against her agency's advice. From the onset, Marcella's client parents called her on a regular basis and attended to her medical appointments to make sure not to miss a nuance of the pregnancy. Presented as a token of gratitude they regularly brought Marcella food, which was equally intended to ensure that Marcella ate what *they* thought was beneficial. Initially, Marcella felt privileged to have such solicitous client parents. Over time, however, the tension grew as Marcella increasingly felt her boundaries intruded upon. At the end of her second trimester, Marcella felt the client parents had overstepped every mark, prying into her privacy and questioning her personal integrity. When the client parents were unreceptive to Marcella's requests to grant her some privacy, she turned to the agency. First, she asked her coordinator to speak to her client parents on her behalf, but when the more subtle attempts failed, Marcella decisively broke with the rules of the game. She pressed the agency director to prohibit the client parents from contacting her. From initially accommodating the role of a recipient obedient worker, she resisted and toughened up her game. Her determined move to disrupt the structure despite what was at stake proves her resourcefulness and courage despite her structural disadvantage (MacLeod, 1992).

Applying the extended serious games approach to the women's moves enables us to analyse how the women assessed and adapted to the conditions they faced according to their personalities and capabilities (Näre, 2014). Diana and Marcella acted with their own agenda in mind while gauging what was appropriate and what was required of them. Diana chose to be an adaptive 'player' in the 'serious game' (Ortner, 1996, 2006; Näre, 2014). She expected to establish a relationship with her client parents, but the client parents scotched her efforts from the beginning. Enmeshed in the power dynamics of being seen and seeing themselves as the employee obliged to act according to the agency's and client parents' demands, Diana developed strategies of coping with the circumstances that reinforced and co-created the hierarchical structures in which she found herself. She shifted her attention to the positive aspects that the absence of the client parents yielded for her, and through her creative efforts achieved satisfaction. Marcella, by contrast, took the daring step of breaking with the given structure by demanding the client parents changed their behaviour. She enacted her agency and relational work by 'marking the boundaries of the relation' (Toledano & Zeiler, 2016, p. 171). Her actions showed determination and resilience. She dutifully had performed her relational work by investing into the relationships; however, her boundaries being broken, she contested and attempted to renegotiate terms before requiring a termination (Zelizer et al., 2012).[12]

After Childbirth

The literature on surrogacy arrangements and relationships between surrogacy workers and client parents in Northern America has shown how surrogacy workers value a good personal relationship with their client parents during the pregnancy and expect a lasting bond thereafter as a confirmation of the appreciation of their priceless gift and selfless deed. This has impressed itself firmly on the public understanding of surrogacy in northern America and western Europe. In this final section, I show how the expectations and experiences of surrogacy workers in Russia diverge from this narrative as all parties expect the relationship to end with childbirth. This doesn't preclude that some may welcome a light, non-committal continuation. Conversations with surrogacy workers over their expectations for what may come after handing over the child or children and receiving their final compensation revealed that they had no expectations for future contact and were of the general opinion that it was client parents' right and privilege to make the decision regarding the course of an eventual future relationship.

When I asked surrogacy worker Ilya at the time of preparing for her third surrogacy arrangement how she remained with her previous client parents and whether she had ever taken the initiative to stay in contact, Ilya was taken aback by my presumption that she had or would ever try to do so. To her, the idea of a surrogacy worker taking the lead in continuing a relationship with the client parents was preposterous. She replied vehemently:

> I have never taken the initiative! That would be disreputable, or, at least, not nice. Different people have different approaches to it. Maybe [the client parents] really want to forget *how* their child was born and that [the client mother] wasn't able to give birth herself. As far as I know, [infertility] is very painful for many. Therefore, they want to reach that phase [parenthood] and move on. They will express their gratitude in words and in material gifts... and

---

[12]Despite her rebellious act, the agency hired her a second time, when she became pregnant with triplets.

then they will return to their lives, where a new stage is awaiting
them now. In essence: what place do I have in it?

(Ilya, surrogacy worker, November 2014)

Ilya's rhetorical question at the end expressed an imperative shared by many
surrogacy workers: 'unless *the client parents* want you in their lives, *you* do not
have a place there and you should not impose yourself'.

Like Ilya, many surrogacy workers had chosen to carry the commissioned
pregnancies primarily with the intention of earning money. Philanthropic motives
came second. Consequently, they entered into arrangements with clear financial
expectations and had no expectations of bonding with their client parents or even
becoming fictive kin (Haylett, 2015, p. 149). These intentions are formed within a
cultural framing of surrogacy as an economic exchange, not a 'labour of love' or
'gift' as it is in the United States, United Kingdom and Israel (Berend, 2012,
2016b; Jacobson, 2016; Teman, 2010; van den Akker, 2003). Once the contract
was concluded and the child and money were exchanged, the game ended.

As indicated earlier, surrogacy is expensive and client parents and surrogacy
workers commonly find themselves coming from different socio-economic strata.
Surrogacy worker Inga poignantly articulated this divide, along with her indif-
ference about a relationship during the commissioned pregnancy, and her
contentment with parting for good at the end of the arrangement:

> We have hardly anything in common. We are from different social
> classes. That is always the case. The *biomamas* and the *surmamas*
> are different: different age, different upbringing, different
> residential areas. It is like a friendship that does not go beyond
> the level of an incidental, friendly acquaintance with a next-door
> neighbour. For the time that we live next to each other, we act
> friendly, we interact with each other. Then one moves away and
> the memories fade. We are not kin. Kin would keep in touch even
> over thousands of miles. [Bio parents] are like fellow travellers, like
> someone who accompanies you for a certain distance on a long
> journey. (…) We accompany each other for these nine months.
> And then we part and do not meet again.
>
> (Inga, surrogacy worker, October 2012)

In addition to the differences between herself and her client mother Anastasia,
Inga points at the temporality of the arrangement and the transient nature of their
relationship. Consanguineous kinship is important in Russian culture, and Inga's
account shows that she draws an unambiguous line between herself and the client
parents. Such accounts from surrogacy workers in Russia are in stark contrast to
the accounts of US-American surrogates where both sides emphasise their
closeness by referring to each other in fictive kinship terms (Berend, 2016b;
Haylett, 2015). Speaking to me in the waiting room of a St. Petersburg fertility
clinic, Inga ranked her client parents as nodding acquaintances.

Ilya accentuated the social and economic stratifications between client parents and women who offer gestational service. Thinking of her first two sets of client parents, she said: 'Besides the pregnancy and the birth, which we planned together, we had nothing in common. We had nothing else to talk about'. Acknowledging on the one hand that her task was completed once the couples who hired her became parents, and that they wanted to move on, she also emphasised her own desire to move on:

> And to be fair, I wasn't interested in talking about baby stuff with them either – [14 years after having had my own child] I don't even remember what little children need...
>
> (Ilya, surrogacy worker, November 2014)

Speaking with Ilya's third client mother Nadezhda separately about their relationship, Nadezhda, who kept describing the close relationship she had to Ilya, struggled to find the words to describe the nature of their relationship. My question 'Who is she to you?' prompted a pensive silence. After stirring her coffee a few times, Nadezhda cautiously began formulating her thoughts, while pausing between each sentence.

> I don't know. But I regard her very highly. I regard her with love. Sometimes I even want to hug her, hug her tightly – but to define who she is for me, I cannot. Your sister is your sister, your aunt is your aunt, that is clear. A friend? I don't know. A good friend. Yes... I don't know. More like... closer to family than to a friend, because we feel each other closely. For real, I feel it when she feels poorly. She says, 'you really do feel it' and she feels it, and the little one does. The distance does not matter, the feelings travel. Somehow, like that... But there is no definition, there is no term for it.
>
> (Nadezhda, client mother, April 2015)

First-time surrogacy worker Anyuta shared Inga's and Ilya's approach of not having expectations of a relationship beyond the arrangement. Early on in the pregnancy, she already expressed her expectations particularly strongly. Anyuta regarded it as her client parents' right to be in contact with her during the pregnancy and her duty as a 'hired worker' to comply with their demands. However, and on this point she was adamant, once she had given birth, she would terminate all contact. In response to my question about whether she could imagine any form of future contact, she replied 'Categorically no! Categorically no further communication. We will part forever'. For her, the birth marked the turning point of the relationship, and the point where Anyuta could fully (re)claim her agency. In her role as a 'hired worker', she considered it her duty to accommodate the client parents' wishes, possibly even beyond her comfort zone, yet by radically cutting ties after birth she intended to recover full integrity over her life.

After these accounts of how surrogacy workers expected arrangements to end, I want to close this chapter with how surrogacy workers experienced the end of their surrogacy arrangements. In Anna's first surrogacy pregnancy, her client mother Svetlana, from Krasnoyarsk in the southern Central Siberian Plateau, lived about 4000 km from St. Petersburg. Svetlana travelled to St. Petersburg five times to attend appointments and spend time with Anna. With satisfaction, Anna recalled how they were in regular contact during the pregnancy. Then, to my surprise, she narrated how contact ended immediately after Svetlana left St. Petersburg with her newborn. Probing about whether occasional contact would not have been an option, or maybe something she would have appreciated, Anna vigorously replied 'Of course not!' and pointed to their contract that stipulated that 'I was not to disturb [the client mother] after the child's birth'. Anna even destroyed her contract copy with the client mother's contact details and deleted her number from her phone 'to prevent the temptation [of calling]'. By taking this step of self-discipline, Anna forestalled not only a temptation to contact Svetlana but also being put in her place by her. Within the limits of her power, she took as much control as she could in her situation. In the weeks immediately postpartum, she occasionally felt an urge to call Svetlana and enquire about the child's well-being, as she had never seen the child, but only heard him cry as nurses carried him out of the theatre to hand him to the client mother waiting outside. In the moments when the urge to know welled up, she was glad she had been wise enough to forestall acting upon this temptation. Looking back at the two past surrogacy arrangements, she didn't miss being in touch with the client parents.

Surrogacy worker Lyubov searched for her client parents by reading through women's infertility stories until she offered her gestation service to a woman who she felt was most deserving. Looking back at the pregnancy, she described the relationship with her client parents as neutral and business-like throughout, and her client mother as 'not of a chatty nature'. Her client mother accompanied her to the pregnancy screenings and made it no secret that her main interest was Lyubov's state of health, her weight gain and the baby's growth. She was also interested to know about her emotional state or family matters as it could directly affect the pregnancy. Lyubov commented on the sparse communication with:

> I have enough friends [for support when I need it]. Surrogacy –
> that is work. (…) Communication that is limited to business
> matters has its advantages: it won't be so difficult to part later.
> (Lyubov, surrogacy worker, March 2015)

As Lyubov did not expect any postpartum interaction, she didn't mind the silence after handing over the child.

These examples show how surrogacy workers in Russia intrinsically understand surrogacy as a temporary, contractual arrangement and not as an opportunity to create life-long bonds. The understanding of the relationship as transient goes hand in hand with the economic approach. However, not all relationships ended definitively with childbirth. One surrogacy worker became a nanny and two women stayed in contact with their client parents as they had the prospect of carrying a sibling. In two further cases, surrogacy workers and client parents simply continued to stay in touch but expressed no intention to reveal to the children the nature of their acquaintance.

Analysing the relationships between surrogacy workers and client parents shows that within Russia's cultural framing of surrogacy as a business arrangement, relationships between surrogacy workers and client parents are expected to be transient and relational work is seen as one of the surrogacy workers' duties. Before entering into surrogacy arrangements, surrogacy workers seek information about the options and then decide on their preferred form of arrangement, which is either agency-mediated or direct with the client parents, and thus, they choose the setting and a given set of rules for their 'serious games' (Ortner, 1997, 2001, 2006). The more the women knew about the micro-politics of the arrangement options, the more likely they were able to make their choices strategically; surrogacy workers who wanted contact with their client parents chose direct arrangements, whereas surrogacy workers to whom personal contact with their client parents was irrelevant or undesirable, chose agencies. Once surrogacy workers entered into surrogacy arrangements and began to engage with the client parents' expectations, they began to execute their moves with skill and intention (Ortner, 1997, 2001, 2006), strategically alternating between resistance, adaption, reception (Näre, 2014) and temporal accommodation. Most surrogacy workers I talked to regarded adapting to the expectations of their client parents with respect to the quality and frequency of contact to be their duty as 'hired workers'.

Similarly to the way surrogacy workers maintained that they should attune their expectations and actions to the wishes of the client parents during the pregnancy, they also considered it the client parents' privilege to choose how to relate postpartum and that they would act accordingly. Often this meant that surrogacy workers and client parents parted ways, and in many cases, surrogacy workers themselves had little intention of staying in contact. Instead, they felt inclined to let the relationships fade, as they were aware of the social and economic stratification between themselves and their client parents and saw little common ground upon which to base their relationship, other than having provided their gestational services. In a few cases, surrogacy workers ended the relationship with their client parents to reclaim power over their private lives and personal integrity.

Surrogacy workers anticipated and negotiated their surrogacy relationship with their client parents to be transient, an expectation which has been embedded in the cultural framing of surrogacy as an economic arrangement. They gained satisfaction from having completed an arrangement and having given birth to a child or children, instead of from ongoing affirmation of their service by the client parents.

Gabriela's Story Continued

Fieldnotes, 5 March 2015

Miscarriage diagnosis. Walking with Gabriela.

Gabriela miscarried. Today the doctors confirmed what she had already known. She wasn't surprised but resigned.

I wasn't present at the ultrasound appointment when she was told, as her agency didn't approve of my presence. Instead, I waited for her outside the building, and walked with her to the metro station afterwards. She had no time to spare between the appointment and getting back to work in time, else she would get in trouble with her supervisor.

'I had an inkling about it, that this had happened, because a few days ago I had this dream. I dreamt about a hen without feathers. Dead'. She paused. 'Dead, plucked and cleaned, ready to be thrown into a pot and be made into soup. At home in Moldova, when you dream of a hen, the dream tells you that you are pregnant with a girl. When I was pregnant with my daughter, I also dreamt of a hen. That hen was fat, and happy. She fluttered. She was alive. And then I gave birth to a big, healthy baby girl. I knew from the beginning that I carried a female foetus for those biological parents. So when I had that dream, I knew'.

She fell silent until we reached the metro station, and as we parted, she said she would be in touch.

Gabriela grieved. She grieved the loss of the pregnancy, the loss of time and the loss of the money. Most of all, she grieved the consequences, which were additional months of separation from her own children, who she had left in her mother's care in Moldova, if she wanted to try for surrogacy again.

All that grief left little space to grieve for the loss of the foetus, or for the client parents' loss. She struggled to sympathise with them as to them she was only a gestational carrier, a hired worker, and as a foreign citizen, a low-paid worker with diminished rights. At today's appointment, like at all previous pregnancy-related appointments, the client parents were absent, and an agency employee only attended to take care of administrative tasks, but not to provide Gabriela with emotional support. Gabriela had seen the client parents once, prior to signing their contract, because the couple had requested to 'view' Gabriela in person to ascertain she met their expectations.

This morning, after confirming to her that she had lost the pregnancy, the doctor had already informed her that she could try again – after all, she had signed a contract for three attempts – but that she would have to wait a minimum of three months.

After having spent a year already in Russia, the reunion with her children had yet again, been postponed to an unpredictable date in the future.

Fieldnotes, 4 April 2015

Café Petrushka, St. Petersburg. Notes after recording the second and final interview with Gabriela.

As we were getting ready to leave, Gabriela pulled out her phone and asked me whether I wanted to see her children. Of course. The picture was taken in a supermarket, probably by her mother, who currently cares for them. It shows a lanky boy, tall for his age, standing beside his younger sister in her preschool dress, blonde curls framing her face. The girl is standing on her tiptoes to be able to reach the bars of the shopping cart. Gabriela's eyes remained fixed on the screen as she turned the phone around for me to see the image. Caressing the image on the screen with her index finger she said, 'Look at my little girl, who I left behind for this'.

For this – the endeavour of surrogacy in Russia, far from home, far from her children

For this – the twice-shattered hope that she could quickly make the needed money and ease her family's financial burden

For this – the worries, the stress, the emotional and physical pain, and the grief over the additional and unpredictably long separation from her children.

A month after I last met Gabriela in the café, I left Russia. As agreed with her, I did not follow up on her. Neither did she, and so I don't know whether she was successful in her third attempt, how long she waited and when she was able to return home to her family. Her story illustrates the precarity and uncertainties of surrogacy work and the additional challenges faced by women who migrate for surrogacy work – as I will explore further in the following chapter on reproductive migrations.

Chapter 4

Reproductive Migrations

Conversation with commuting surrogacy worker Ilya, when she was pregnant for client parents in St Petersburg.

Ilya: '[To travel] to Moscow, that is nothing for me, that's 400 km. And there are plenty of clinics [in Moscow]. And I don't travel every day, or every week. St. Petersburg, that is twice as far. There were two trains a day to Moscow, that is do-able. But here [to St. Petersburg], to come and to return home, that is a bit more problematic'.
Christina: 'How many hours does it take?'
Ilya: '17'.

In this chapter I take a closer look at the geographic and geopolitical aspects of the social organisation of Russian surrogacy. I trace surrogacy workers' (temporary) migration and commuting patterns to and within Russia and how this differentiates the practise of surrogacy in Russia from the social and geographical organisation of surrogacy elsewhere. I begin this chapter by showing why the market in surrogacy is concentrated in Moscow and St. Petersburg and how that impels surrogacy workers to travel to these reproductive hubs from other parts of Russia, as well as from its neighbouring countries. I then explore differences in how surrogacy workers experience the resulting geographic and geopolitical stratifications of their migration and commuting realities for their commissioned pregnancies.

   In order to emphasise the exceptional mobility of many surrogacy workers in Russia and to explore how their experiences differ amongst themselves and from locally living surrogacy workers, I introduce the terms *migrant surrogacy worker* and *commuting surrogacy worker*. I define a *migrant surrogacy worker* as a woman who relocates from her hometown to the place where her surrogacy arrangement is implemented, living there for the entire duration of the surrogacy process, from the preparatory hormone treatment for the embryo transfer and until the delivery of the child.[1] I refer to surrogacy workers as *commuting* when

---

[1]In local St. Petersburg parlance, these women were referred to as '*prieshzhiye*' ['those who have come here'] or '*inogorodniye*', which translates to 'non-residents' or 'foreigners', contrary to local Piterskiye [long-standing residents of St. Petersburg], derived from the term Piter for St. Petersburg, as locals affectionately refer to the city in everyday speech.

Surrogacy in Russia, 81–109
Copyright © 2021 Christina Weis
Published under exclusive licence by Emerald Publishing Limited
doi:10.1108/978-1-83982-896-620211012

they regularly travel for appointments for the pregnancy, but continue to reside at home (with their family) until a few weeks before their delivery date. The frequency of such travel, and the destinations, depend on the client parents' requests, and at a minimum include a medical examination prior to the embryo transfer, for the embryo transfer, for medically required ultrasound appointments and for the delivery.

It is not possible to give precise numbers or a percentage of how many women migrate or commute in order to be surrogacy workers in Russia as there are no official records available for surrogacy in Russia in general. However, my ethnographic data suggest that the numbers of 'mobile surrogacy workers' are significant and mobility amongst surrogacy workers is a core part of the social organisation of surrogacy in Russia. In this chapter I also introduce the terms *geographic* and *geopolitical stratification* and in doing so, expand upon Colen's (1995) conceptual framework of stratified reproduction. These terms will aid to capture and conceptualise migrant and commuting surrogacy workers' specific experiences and to call attention to these kinds of reproductive stratifications on the rise for the providers of reproductive labour within the increasing fragmentation of the global reproductive supply chains. 'Stratified reproduction' describes 'the power relations by which some categories of people are empowered to nurture and reproduce, while others are disempowered' (Davis-Floyd, 1997, p. 399). Building on this foundation, I conceptualize '*geographic* and *geopolitical stratifications*' as the process that separates commuting and migrant surrogacy workers from locally living surrogacy workers. Geographic and geopolitical stratifications impact commuting and migrant surrogacy workers firstly when they are being chosen, evaluated and categorized by client parents and commercial agencies based on judgments and imaginaries about the significance of their geographic origin, place of residence during the pregnancy and citizenship, and secondly how they are treated and experience the pregnancy while commuting or having (temporarily) relocated for the pregnancy.

I further draw on Bourdieu's (1986) concept of the convertibility of different forms of capital to argue that for many women intending to be surrogacy workers, mobility, which I conceptualise as the ability to travel and the readiness to do so on demand, is a necessary complementary capital to reproductive capital for migrant and commuting surrogacy workers. Mobility is essential to enable them to convert their reproductive capital into economic capital.

I have organised this chapter as follows. First, I outline the development of Moscow and St. Petersburg as Russia's surrogacy hubs, which triggered the recent 'inflows' by migrant and commuting surrogacy workers. Next, I analyse the migrant and commuting surrogacy workers' patterns of mobility and different kinds of geographic and geopolitical stratification that they experienced.

Russia's Repro-hubs: St. Petersburg and Moscow

Reproflows describe the flows of reproductive actors, technology and substances across distinct reproscapes (Inhorn, 2011, 2015). In Russia, migrant and commuting surrogacy workers have joined these reproflows as 'bio-medically technologically savvy [actors]' (Roberts & Scheper-Hughes, 2011, p. 2) who seek to maximise their earnings, minimise the search or waiting time for a match, and disguise their surrogacy work as general labour migration if they prefer to not tell at home. In Russia, women travel from all over and even from the neighbouring former Soviet Union countries to Russia's repro-hubs Moscow and St. Petersburg, and to a lesser degree to other larger cities to find client parents.

In 1995, doctors implemented the first surrogacy arrangement in Russia in St. Petersburg. Since then, St. Petersburg and Moscow have developed into Russia's main sites for assisted reproduction. These cities host the majority of Russia's private and state-run fertility clinics, as well as commercial surrogacy agencies and gamete banks (see also Kirpichenko, 2020). Today fertility clinics can be found in almost every city across Russia. Yet, higher salaries, better career opportunities, a vibrant cultural life and the proximity to Europe motivate highly qualified specialists to migrate to work in Moscow and St. Petersburg. The resulting density expands choice of competing clinics, along with their qualified specialists, prestige and websites presenting highly competitive success rates, and it attracts patients from all over Russia and abroad (see also Weis, 2021). Furthermore, fertility clinics elsewhere in Russia, especially east of the Ural Mountains where the population density rapidly decreases, are widely dispersed.[2] As a consequence, fertility patients still need to travel a considerable distance for a consultation and those who can afford it therefore often opt for Moscow or St. Petersburg straightaway.[3]

In the context of surrogacy, such reproductive flows of patients to Moscow and St. Petersburg result in a high demand for donor gametes and surrogacy workers, which in turn had led to a surge of commercial agencies providing these services. To meet the demand in surrogacy workers, agencies in turn have started recruiting women from all over the country as well as from Ukraine and Belarus.

---

[2]The Siberian and Far Eastern federal districts occupy 66% of the country's territory, yet only 18% of the Russian population lives there (Gorshkova & Klochkov, 2011, p. 611).
[3]Dr Nikolai, who himself moved from a regional capital east of the Ural Mountains to St. Petersburg, reflected: 'The doctors leave and search for better places (...) and the local clinics have to employ young doctors... so 5–7 years ago, when I was the senior doctor in [Siberian clinic] — they wanted to open an IVF lab there. And they told me that this profession demands a proper and long education and loads of experience – and now this young lad is working there, he just finished university, and he has no experience. (...) Nevertheless, he is already working in reproduction. And there are many such clinics. And I don't know what I would do [as a patient] ... go there, or not go there? (...) It is always better to look for a clinic that is already working [well]. [Patients] are coming from the periphery to the centre, because here, in clinics like ours, we do 1,500 [IVF] cycles in a year compared to a clinic that does 100 a year. In the beginning, when [patients] think the situation is not so dire, they go to a nearby clinic, but then they don't get the desired outcome, and have wasted their money, then they are ready to do anything, and they approach those clinics where it is better'.

Likewise, women from all over Russia and the neighbouring countries have become aware of opportunities for reproductive labour in Russia's metropolises and so come to St. Petersburg and Moscow for higher compensation or quicker matches with client parents.

Here, two kinds of reproflows have emerged, one of migration and one of commuting. The trajectories of *migrant surrogacy workers* are predominantly one-dimensional: they 'flow in' to where surrogacy arrangements are taking place, remain there from embryo transfer until birth and 'flow back' after delivery. Migrant surrogacy workers are most commonly hired by surrogacy agencies who provide them with accommodation for the duration of the arrangement. *Commuting surrogacy workers* in turn criss-cross Russia, sometimes travelling to multiple destinations over the course of the pregnancy. Commuting arrangements demand a predisposition for constant mobility and are more common in direct arrangements. Depending on the client parents' place of residence and preferences, commuting surrogacy workers travel for the initial medical examinations, to meet potential client parents, to sign the contract, for the embryo transfer, ultrasound appointments and finally for the birth.[4] Intending surrogacy workers who used the online platform 'Meddesk' to post their advertisements to find client parents indicated their inclinations and conditions regarding relocating or commuting for the pregnancy in the advert. The frequency of offers indicating inclination to travel or temporarily move was high and illustrates that migration and long-distance commuting were not exceptional, but necessary and common practices in Russia. Below are three examples of surrogacy workers' advertisements containing offers of their willingness to travel and relocate to accommodate the surrogacy arrangements. All the advertisements are from Meddesk, and were posted in spring 2015 (Figs. 4.1–4.3).

I see this mobility as a form of capital that surrogacy workers need to possess in order to use their reproductive capital to transform it into economic capital. Finding a surrogacy arrangement on the 'periphery' of Russia was rare and even then, client parents might prefer to travel with their surrogacy worker to seek the treatment of experts in St. Petersburg and Moscow. Consequently, the more

---

[4]A close reading of the multiple offers on the Russian medical service website Meddesk by surrogacy workers, who indicated their readiness to travel in their advertisement, showed four distinct trends. (1) A clear predisposition to relocate to wherever client parents want their surrogacy worker to live (without bringing their own children). (2) The offer to relocate under the condition of bringing their own child/ren or entire family. (3) Offers that implied they would live at home during the pregnancy, but commute to all required appointments and relocate to where the client parents requested the birth to take place. (4) Offers for arrangements with client parents only within close proximity of their home.

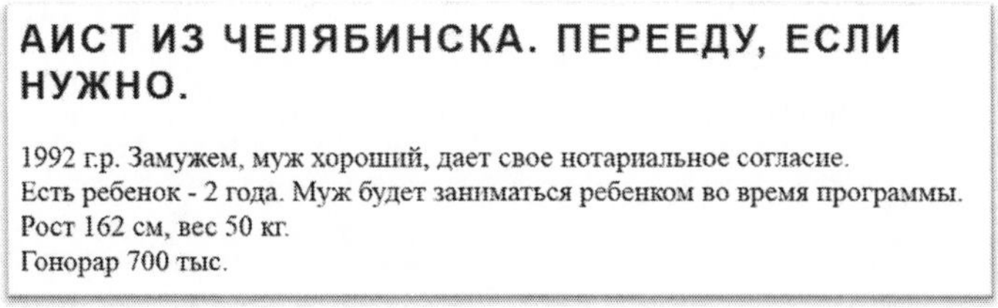

> **АИСТ ИЗ ЧЕЛЯБИНСКА. ПЕРЕЕДУ, ЕСЛИ НУЖНО.**
>
> 1992 г.р. Замужем, муж хороший, дает свое нотариальное согласие.
> Есть ребенок - 2 года. Муж будет заниматься ребенком во время программы.
> Рост 162 см, вес 50 кг.
> Гонорар 700 тыс.

Fig. 4.1. 'Stork from Chelyabinsk. I will move, if required'.
Translation: 'Born 1992. Married, good husband, who will give his notarial consent. I have a child of 2 years. My husband will take care of the child during the programme.
Height 162cm, weight 50kg
Compensation 700,000₽ (£11,620)'.

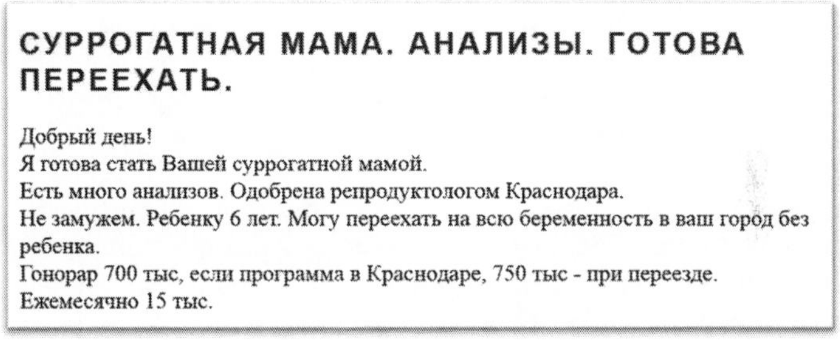

> **СУРРОГАТНАЯ МАМА. АНАЛИЗЫ. ГОТОВА ПЕРЕЕХАТЬ.**
>
> Добрый день!
> Я готова стать Вашей суррогатной мамой.
> Есть много анализов. Одобрена репродуктологом Краснодара.
> Не замужем. Ребенку 6 лет. Могу переехать на всю беременность в ваш город без ребенка.
> Гонорар 700 тыс, если программа в Краснодаре, 750 тыс - при переезде.
> Ежемесячно 15 тыс.

Fig. 4.2. 'Surrogate mother. Test results [available].
Ready to change residence'.
Translation: 'Good day!
I am ready to be Your surrogate mother.
I have many test results. I was approved by a fertility doctor in Krasnodar.
I am not married. [My] son is 6 years old. I can change residence to [live in] your city for the entire' pregnancy without [my] child.
Compensation 700,000₽ (£11,620), if the programme is in Krasnodar, 750,000₽ (£12,450) when moving.
Monthly 15,000₽ (£249)'.

ВЫНОШУ ВАМ МАЛЫША

Выношу вашего малыша со всей заботой и ответственностью. Перееду на весь срок в любой город вместе с сыном. Мне 26лет. Сыну 1,5. Рожала сама. Кровь +. Инфекций нет. На руках есть УЗИ на 12-13 день цикла. Все подробности в личной переписке

Fig. 4.3.   'I will carry your baby'.
Translation: 'I will carry your baby with care and responsibility. I will relocate for the entire period to any city together with my son. I am 26 years old. [My] son is 1 1/2. I gave birth myself [vaginal delivery]. Blood [rhesus factor] +. No infections. I have ultrasound images ready of my 12-13th day of the cycle. All further details in private exchange'.

flexibility and mobility that surrogacy workers offered, the better their chances of finding a (quick) match.[5]

Geographic and Geopolitical Stratifications in Selecting and Paying Surrogacy Workers

One matrix of geographic and geopolitical stratifications of surrogacy workers' reproductive bodies and labour is based on their geographic origin or residence before and during their surrogacy pregnancy. Geographic and geopolitical stratifications play out in the imaginations and preferences of agencies and client parents and impact on surrogacy workers' reimbursement.

Selecting a 'Provincial' Surrogacy Worker

As St. Petersburg and Moscow have evolved into Russia's 'repro-hubs' for surrogacy, women seeking to become surrogacy workers travel to these cities from all over Russia as well as neighbouring countries. Some women come on their own

---

[5]It is important to note that all but one of the commuting surrogacy workers I met and interviewed travelled by train; the surrogacy worker from Yakutsk flew to St. Petersburg together with her client parents. Russia covers nine time zones. The well-known 'Trans-Siberian Express' leaves Moscow daily to travel 144 hours (about six days) to Vladivostok in the Far East, covering 9289 km on the way. Many Russians are familiar with long-distance train travel as well as long-distance commuting for employment (see, for instance, Saxinger, 2015; Saxinger et al., 2014). By the time I had spent several months in St. Petersburg, taking 12–14 hours overnight trains to cities north and south of St. Petersburg as well as to the Belarusian capital Minsk to meet research participants, I had adopted a similar attitude. Towards the end of my fieldwork I too referred to a 40-hour-long train journey from Moscow to Omsk as 'it's just two nights and a day'.

initiative to find a match, or once they have found a match with client parents online. Others are hired by commercial surrogacy agencies who provide them with accommodation (which is deducted from their final compensation) for the duration of the surrogacy programme.

Agencies in St. Petersburg and Moscow, who recruited surrogacy workers from beyond their municipality, do so for two reasons: Increasing demand needed to be met for surrogacy workers, and secondly, because recruiting and being able to offer client parents surrogacy workers from a 'rural origin' – as they referred to almost anyone outside Moscow and St. Petersburg – brought additional advantages. Sveta, a representative from the Moscow-based agency 'Mobile Surrogacy', listed the following reasons for her agency's targeted recruitment of 'rural girls'.

> Central Russia – that means rural poverty [*bednoe naselenie*] and an excellent environment. And that means that [the women] are healthy, yet with a minimum of needs and demands. [Women] in Moscow want a lot of money [for their surrogacy services] and their health is poor. Therefore, the majority of the girls who we offer [to our clients] come from Central Russia – fresh air, mountains, forests... they grow up on their own fresh and nutritious diet. They are healthy. (...) We invite them to live [in Moscow or St. Petersburg during their pregnancies] because here the medical supervision is better. But, in general, when they come from such environments, their health is good.
>
> (Sveta, surrogacy agency representative, January 2015)

Mobile Surrogacy's recruitment approach is representative of that of other agencies in my sample. Sveta's statement shows agencies' intention of economising on costs while maximising success rates: hiring surrogacy workers from the provinces was a strategy to provide the healthiest bodies to undergo the best treatment to achieve the best results at lower costs. During our conversation in a fashionable gallery café in a Moscow high street, Sveta further elaborated that *Muscovites* and *Piterskiye devotchki* [girls] demand a higher compensation because of high living costs; but in her opinion, metropolitan women's reproductive capacity is poor value for money as they live stressful lives, often manage several jobs, are exposed to noise and exhaust pollution and often only afford a poor quality diet or highly processed food that was low in nutrition. She therefore preferred 'the village girls', whom she credited with outstanding health and sturdiness, and whose diet she romanticised as fresh and healthy because of its home-grown character. Such subsistence farming, which is common in Russia, is not limited to the rural population, but has become a necessity for many residents of provincial towns and cities, who 'lack sufficient purchasing power to afford a minimally healthy diet' (Liefert, 2004, p. 35; see also; Humphrey, 2002). When economic sanctions were introduced in the winter of 2014, and the Russian government in response boycotted US and European food products, rural as well as town dwellers have been hit hard by rising food prices and the decreasing availability of products (Ivolga, 2016). Drawing on this, agency staff went on to describe 'village girls', as they commonly differentiated and belittled their migrant surrogacy workers, as less pampered and spoiled. Advertising them as ideal candidates to intending father Pawel, agency owner Eliza first described the migrant surrogacy workers as more compliant with their guidance because of their lack of education and their dependence of the agency, given they were non-locals. She then asserted that, having grown up in harsher conditions, they were 'made of a substance' that enabled them to 'give birth in the field or in the forest'; in other words, they were simply 'created to give birth'.

Another bonus of recruiting migrant surrogacy workers and accommodating them in groups of three to eight in agency-owned or rented apartments was that it gace agencies the opportunity to offer their clients the option of close supervision. Migrant surrogacy workers in provided were exposed to scheduled and unannounced surprise visits and video surveillance. Client parents were further guaranteed that visits from husbands and partners are prohibited.

Analysing the practice of commercial surrogacy in India, sociologist Amrita Pande (2014b, p. 82) argued that the 'naturalisation of skills effectively *cheapens* women's labour'. In Russia, migrant surrogacy workers are particularly often dismissed as 'village girls' and as such deemed healthier, more resilient and less pretentious. This, along with the assumption that the previous births of their own children had taken place without access to cutting-edge technology, dismissed as births 'in the fields and forests', made them more valuable to the agency. At the same time, agency staff described their experiences as unspoiled, and their knowledge as innate, and thus beneath notice. Furthermore, agency staff maintained that all surrogacy workers do is 'being pregnant', hence 'they are not doing any work', whereas all the work and 'skilled labour', such as the fertilisation, the (medical) supervision and the medical assisted delivery, is performed by professionals (see also Weis, 2013). Such devaluing of surrogacy workers' efforts and skills, and thus cheapening of surrogacy workers' labour, is applied particularly to women from a rural or provincial background.

Graded Payment Schemes

Once they had been devalued in this way, migrant and commuting surrogacy workers faced discounted offers for their reproductive labour. Agencies as well as client parents made no effort to conceal the fact that they expected migrant and commuting surrogacy workers to work for a lower fee. In 2014, an agency listed the following payment offer on their website (Fig. 4.4).

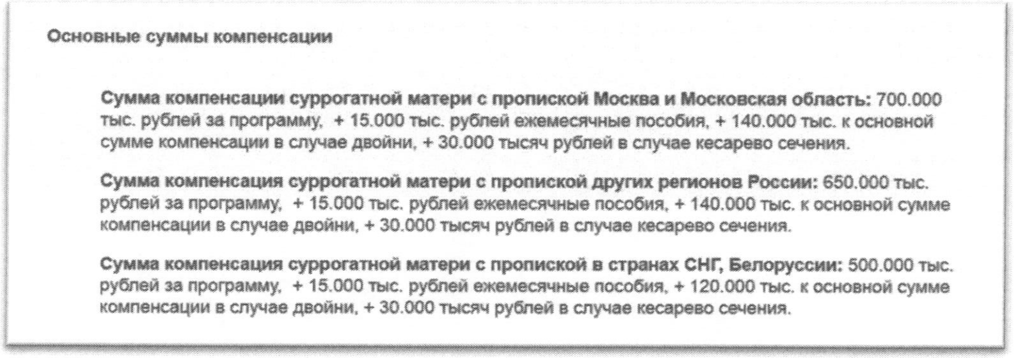

Основные суммы компенсации

Сумма компенсации суррогатной матери с пропиской Москва и Московская область: 700.000 тыс. рублей за программу, + 15.000 тыс. рублей ежемесячные пособия, + 140.000 тыс. к основной сумме компенсации в случае двойни, + 30.000 тысяч рублей в случае кесарево сечения.

Сумма компенсации суррогатной матери с пропиской других регионов России: 650.000 тыс. рублей за программу, + 15.000 тыс. рублей ежемесячные пособия, + 140.000 тыс. к основной сумме компенсации в случае двойни, + 30.000 тысяч рублей в случае кесарево сечения.

Сумма компенсации суррогатной матери с пропиской в странах СНГ, Белоруссии: 500.000 тыс. рублей за программу, + 15.000 тыс. рублей ежемесячные пособия, + 120.000 тыс. к основной сумме компенсации в случае двойни, + 30.000 тысяч рублей в случае кесарево сечения.

Fig. 4.4.   Screenshot of Agency Website: Compensation Based on Women's Origin.
Translation:

Principal amounts of compensation

'**Compensation for surrogate mothers with residence permit in Moscow and Moscow region:** *700,000 Roubles (£11,620) for the programme + 15,000 Roubles (£249) monthly allowance + 140,000 Roubles (£2,324) basic compensation in the case of twins + 30,000 Roubles (£498) in the case of Caesarean section.*

Compensation for surrogate mothers with residence permit in other regions of Russia: *650,000 Roubles (£10,790) for the programme + 15,000 Roubles (£249) monthly allowance + 140,000 Roubles (£2,324) Roubles basic compensation in the case of twins + 30,000 Roubles (£498) in the case of Caesarean section.*

Compensation for surrogate mothers with residence Permit in CIS countries and Belarus: *500,000 (£8,300) Roubles for the programme + 15,000 Roubles (£249) monthly allowance + 120,000 (£1,992) Roubles basic compensation in the case of twins + 30,000 Roubles (£498) in the case of Caesarean section'.*

These prices are quite low in comparison to the 800,000–1,000,000₽ (£13,280–16,600) that local women in Moscow and St. Petersburg were already receiving at the time I took this screenshot in 2015, and prices have gone up since. However, the differentiation by origin or residence, and thus the reduction applied to the fees of migrant and commuting surrogacy workers to Moscow, has remained the same and is consistent across agencies.

Alexander, the manager of 'Promise' in St. Petersburg, commented, for instance, that

> …naturally, the payment for *Piterskiye* is the full payment. If they come from other cities, the payment decreases, and if they are living with their children, they 'step down further'.
>
> (Alexander, agency manager, September 2014)

By living with their children, Alexander meant surrogacy workers bringing their young children to live with them. It is important to note that women's reduced payment is not reflected in the charge for client parents.

Agencies' standard approach of applying lower payments to migrant surrogacy workers has also been adopted by surrogacy workers and client parents seeking direct arrangements. Compared to the above-described 800,000–1,000,000₽ for surrogacy workers living in Moscow and St. Petersburg, the women whose advertisements I listed earlier (Figs. 4.1 and 4.2) asked 700,000₽ around the same time in 2015. These women were discounting their reproductive labour in order to compete with agencies prices and to offset the travel costs incurred for their client parents, as client parents are expected to cover their surrogacy workers' travel. The figures, however, show that in the end, the ones really bearing the costs of mobility were the surrogacy workers.

Surrogacy worker Gabriela, from the Republic of Moldova, felt the effects of these reproductive stratifications based on geographic and geopolitical factors in a most humiliating way. As described already in the opening of the book, Gabriela moved to St. Petersburg with the intention of becoming a surrogacy worker. She first found herself a job in a factory and arranged accommodation and the necessary residence and work permit as a foreigner. She impressed her agency and because she spoke Russian fluently and informed them that she was currently living and working in St. Petersburg, they did not enquire further into her nationality and citizenship. Gabriela liked the agency's offer of 800,000₽ and so she agreed to the conditions – however, when prompted to produce her passport to be copied, handing it over revealed her Moldovan citizenship, upon which she was told 'for your kind we offer 600,000₽'.

In 2014/2015, when I collected most of my data on surrogacy workers from CIS countries, surrogacy agencies and client parents were cautious and hesitant about employing two groups of potential surrogacy workers, Ukrainian and Central Asian women, albeit for two different reasons.[6]

When the armed conflicts flared up in southern and eastern Ukraine (Katchanovski, 2016), travelling to Russia to become a surrogacy worker became a (temporary) migration strategy allowing some women and their families to leave the conflict zone. Conversations with agency staff, surrogacy workers, client parents and doctors corroborated my observations that the number of online advertisements posted by Ukrainian women increased. Yet, with the increase in political tensions between the Ukrainian and Russian government, client parents and agencies in Russia grew more and more reluctant to work with Ukrainian surrogacy workers. Alexander, the manager of the agency 'Promise' explained, for instance, that

> We are avoiding the Ukraine. I discussed [the matter] with our lawyer, what to do with [the applications from Ukrainian women] (…) and he said 'you have surrogate mothers from Russia? Work with them right now, and (…) when the border conflict settles, we will work with them as usual'.
>
> (Alexander, agency manager, September 2014)

Client parents likewise agreed that employing surrogacy workers from a war zone was too risky and worried that a surrogacy worker's emotional turmoil could have negative effects on the pregnancy. Client parents neither wanted them to stay in the conflict zone, nor did they want to insist that they stay in Russia when bad news, such as casualties or a home having been bombed or burnt down, might drive them to rush home – whilst pregnant with their baby. Client mother Nadezhda named her worst-case scenario as a sudden border closure on the part of Russia with her non-Russian surrogacy worker and (in utero) baby on the other side. Ukrainian surrogacy workers, in response, lowered their financial expectations to compensate for their drop in popularity.

---

[6]CIS stands for the Commonwealth of Independent States and includes Armenia, Azerbaijan, Belarus, Georgia, Kazakhstan, Kyrgyzstan, Moldova, Tajikistan, Turkmenistan, Ukraine and Uzbekistan – besides Russia. CIS citizens can enter Russia visa-free and can legally stay for three months. After three months, they either need to leave the country, and return and repeat the immigration procedure, or if they want to extend their stay, and reside and work legally in Russia for more than three months, they need to obtain a work permit [*patent na rabotu*]. Those who fail to comply with these regulations, or whose paperwork is delayed, are automatically criminalised (Pachenkov, 2010), and can be deported and banned from re-entry. These bureaucratic obligations were necessary for surrogacy workers with Moldovan, Ukrainian, Uzbek, Kyrgyz and Tajik citizenship. Surrogacy agencies who hired surrogacy workers from the CIS could obtain these permits for them, even though surrogacy is not recognised as official labour. The money that surrogacy workers received from their agencies is classified as compensation, not a salary. According to one agency in my sample, surrogacy workers who receive their work permit through an agency are not permitted to take up additional employment. If they did obtain it, the sponsoring agency would be fined. Although I have been given this information by agencies, I have not been able to find out under what category or job title they obtain the work permit for their surrogacy workers.

Women of Central Asian origin, as detailed in chapter two, 'Becoming a surrogacy worker', are less likely to be chosen by surrogacy agencies and client parents based on racist prejudice: despite passing the medical requirements and generally being regarded as fertile, many agencies and client parents felt uncomfortable working with a woman of Central Asian origin as they attributed them with sexual promiscuity or risk of contracting sexual disease and not adhering to their hygienic standards.

To summarise, migrant and commuting surrogacy workers in Russia are stratified in their selection process and with regards to their compensation as their reproductive bodies and labour are evaluated and discounted according to their residence or origin: women from a rural background were preferred, yet paid less. This stratification has become normalised and routinised in the social organisation of surrogacy in Russia. As a consequence, surrogacy workers from outside the reproductive hubs lowered their financial expectations on their own initiative to compete in the market for reproductive labour. Furthermore, intending surrogacy workers with citizenship from Russian's neighbouring CIS countries experienced additional geopolitical stratifications and a discount was applied to their reproductive labour purely based on their citizenship.

During the Pregnancy: The Lived Realities of Mobilised and Immobilised 'Carriers'

The second matrix of geographic and geopolitical stratifications of commuting and migrant surrogacy workers' reproductive bodies and reproductive labour becomes evident in the way they experience their pregnancies either as peripatetic or as confined to a location far from home. Comparing the experiences of migrant surrogacy workers and local surrogacy workers and following commuting surrogacy workers' journeys shows how the treatment and experiences of migrant and commuting surrogacy workers are marked by geographic and geopolitical stratification. In the following sections I analyse these stratifications along the course of the arrangement: the embryo transfer, the pregnancy and the birth and what comes afterwards.

On Call: The Embryo Transfer(s)

For many, the Internet is the first point of contact for surrogacy opportunities and their willingness to travel is a necessary precondition. When contacting an agency, women are first instructed to fill in an application form. Women who made it into the next round were requested to undergo a medical examination, consisting of all the tests listed in Medical Order No. 107. At the time of my fieldwork, St. Petersburg-based agencies either requested women to travel to St. Petersburg (at the expense of the agency) or to undertake the medical examination in their home town and inform them of the results. If the results were satisfactory, the women signed a contract and were entered into the database. Whether a surrogacy worker was requested to travel to St. Petersburg for the medical examination, or requested to test at home, depended on which option was cheaper for the agency. Similarly, what migrant surrogacy workers who came for the initial test and qualified were either advised to stay in town, or to return home and be prepared to travel on call. In either case, once matched with client parents, the surrogacy worker would then undergo hormone treatment through self-medication or under the supervision of an embryologist. In the case of home self-medication, the women only relocate for the embryo transfer.

Migrant surrogacy worker Alexandra's experience illustrates this process. After filling out the online form and being selected to proceed to testing, she was asked to travel approximately 40 hours by train from her small town close to the Kazakh border to Moscow. She left her two young children with her 16-year-old sister as her husband worked away from home several days at a stretch, and set off. In Moscow, a doctor associated with the agency approved her candidature, and Alexandra was given a contract to sign there and then. Returning home, she presented the contract to her husband and announced 'See what that piece of paper means? When they call, I have to go!' That meant, having been entered onto the agency's database, the agency instructed her to be on call, and once client parents were matched and the date for the embryo transfer was set, she would have to act by taking the hormones as instructed and travel to Moscow for the transfer; failure to respond unconditionally would mean a breach of contract with the penalty of having to reimburse all the incurred costs. The weeks following her return from Moscow were marked by waiting and tentative preparedness, without receiving any indication of when it would be time to go. This approach was common amongst agencies as it reduced their travel expenses and accommodation costs at the expense of migrant surrogacy workers, who had no say in the timing. Instead, they were on call without the ability to plan ahead and were expected to respond once instructions came, with no possibility of a compromise. However, this procedure also meant that agencies had no control over whether medication was taken appropriately or the individual right amount of dosage was given and the surrogacy worker was optimally prepared for the transfer: local surrogacy workers from the same agencies attended regular appointments to measure the growth of the uterine lining.

In direct and commuting arrangements, surrogacy workers and intending parents always met in person before signing a contract; if client parents paid for their commuting surrogacy workers' travel, they often combined this first meeting with a medical appointment to get medical approval to proceed, and surrogacy workers were expected to have all the results of their medical examinations at hand. Once approved, contracts were signed and the embryo transfer was scheduled; until then, commuting surrogacy workers returned home. As with migrant surrogacy workers in agency arrangements, commuting surrogacy workers' medical appointments in direct arrangements were scheduled by the client parents. Yet, while direct arrangements were more personal and could give surrogacy workers more leeway to negotiate compromises, the client parents' more favourable position of being able to choose from several available candidates meant there was a higher risk that they could potentially take advantage of commuting surrogacy workers. Ilya's experience illustrates how her client parents' higher socio-economic status, along with the cultural notion that they were her employers who had hired her to do a job, led to her being exploited when they took advantage of her inexperience.

> There were these people – I came to Moscow for them. I came with all the analyses done, I had paid for them out of my own pocket, and came at my own expense, and they, as it turned out, only wanted to sit in a café with me, to meet me. They didn't even introduce me to their doctor. (...) I had no previous experience then. They told me to come, and I dropped everything. I took unpaid leave from work, and came!
>
> (Ilya, surrogacy worker, November 2014)

At that time, Ilya lived about 400 km from Moscow. Unlike Ilya, these client parents were in no hurry to find a surrogacy worker, and hadn't regarded it as necessary to notify Ilya that they were merely viewing and comparing candidates. Following this experience, Ilya only agreed to meet clients if a doctor's appointment was scheduled. It is common practice for client parents to reimburse their potential surrogacy workers' travel expenses, however, not to provide them in advance, in order to avoid 'freeloaders' who wanted a free trip to St. Petersburg or Moscow. By not advancing tickets, travelling to meet client parents was often a financial strain for the intending surrogacy workers and there was a risk that their reimbursement would be withheld. Both client parents and surrogacy workers manoeuvred in a state of uncertainty and financial insecurity. However, the situation was more distressing and aggravating for the surrogacy workers, who in every case were financially worse off and more precarious than client parents. Thus, commuting surrogacy workers' (expected) readiness to travel put them in more precarious economic situations than their local peers.

Returning to migrant surrogacy worker Alexandra: a few weeks after returning from Moscow with the signed contract, she received the call to prepare for her scheduled embryo transfer. Her agency sent her instructions on how to take the oestrogen and a train ticket to Moscow. Alexandra quit her job in a casino, placed her two young children in the care of her teenage sister the next ten months, notified her mother that she had found a better paid job in Moscow, packed her suitcase, said goodbye to her husband and boarded her train. Arriving at Moscow's *Paveletskaya* station after a two-and-a-half-day journey, she was met by an agency representative. This representative, however, did not take her to her accommodation to rest and to prepare for her embryo transfer, as she had been led to expect. Instead, the representative took her to Moscow's *Oktyabrskaya* train station to depart for St. Petersburg on the next overnight train. She was tersely briefed that 'plans have changed' and the client parents now expected her in St. Petersburg. When she arrived in St. Petersburg the next morning, having by this point travelled for over three days, a second agency representative met Alexandra and took her directly to a clinic for her embryo transfer. Alexandra felt disoriented and confused about the sudden change in plans, the sparse information and the unexpected relocation. Yet what distressed her more than being treated like a commodity was the humiliation of having to undergo the embryo transfer without being given the opportunity to shower after three days on the train. While Alexandra's agency avoided giving direct answers about whether it was common to (re)allocate surrogacy workers between St. Petersburg and Moscow, as they had branches in both cities, I collected several stories by surrogacy workers that confirm the practice: to suit the demands of their client parents, agencies relocated migrant surrogacy workers around the time of the embryo transfer, as well as for delivery.[7] In another example, Kira from southern Ukraine signed a contract with the same agency as Alexandra for an arrangement in Moscow. However, when her pregnancy test was positive, she was sent to live in agency-owned accommodation in the outskirts of St. Petersburg. Over time she found out that her client parents were Muscovites who didn't want to run any risks that she would meet them; in addition, accommodating her in St. Petersburg rather than in Moscow was cheaper for the agency. She was not privy to any of this information, but she paid close attention to what was being said, and often prompted the driver or other service staff for any information she could get.

The success of an embryo transfer depends on many factors, and Diana's story below demonstrates what may happen when embryo transfers fail.

> When I arrived [in St. Petersburg], I thought [the embryo transfer] would succeed at the first attempt. But it didn't... [even though] my body was in the best of health. I was sent back. The agency didn't want me anymore (...). They said 'we won't vex the [client] parents a second time'.
>
> (Diana, surrogacy worker, May 2015)

Diana was sent back to Vologda after the pregnancy test result was negative. But like all surrogacy workers in her agency, her contract stipulated that she would undergo three embryo transfers. Sending her home after the first failed attempt was not about her failure to conceive, but it was simply cheaper to send her back than to provide her with accommodation and subsistence until the next embryo transfer.[8] While some women welcomed being sent home to be with their families, for others it meant considerable stress: What would they tell their employer in St. Petersburg, if they had managed to find a job on the side? What would they tell friends and family about their sudden return if they were unaware of the surrogacy arrangements? Yet most of all, how would they deal with and explain to friends and family the impending, unpredictable next departure? Such questions were not part of agencies' considerations. When Diana returned to St. Petersburg for her second attempt a few weeks later, the embryo transfer was successful.

---

[7] In cases where migrant surrogacy workers were relocated for the birth, the reason was to produce birth certificates with the desired birth city so that client parents could more easily conceal the surrogacy pregnancy and construct their own birth story.

[8] During the two-week wait between undergoing the embryo transfer and receiving the results, surrogacy workers who worked with and were accommodated by the agency 'Happy Baby' shared a room with another woman. Once the pregnancy was confirmed, and a room became available, they were upgraded to a private room.

These experiences of migrant and commuting surrogacy workers at the onset of their arrangements show that mobility is an essential capital for surrogacy workers in Russia. Yet it is more than just the quality or state of being mobile but also the readiness to be prepared for the required mobility, and in that respect, mobility is a form of convertible capital (Bourdieu, 1986) that not only comes with financial costs but also additional tolls on the mobile surrogacy workers. Once contracts are signed, their movements and mobility are at the discretion and under the scrutiny of the employing party. Mobility is a form of capital that is necessary for women from less desirable locations: unless they are willing to undertake commuting or temporary migration, they are not able to convert their reproductive capital into economic capital. Compared to locally living surrogacy workers, migrant and and commuting surrogacy workers experienced additional uncertainties about their residence and the degree of mobility and flexibility demanded of them.

The Pregnancy: Nine Months of (Im)Mobility

The previous section has highlighted the precarious states of mobility that migrant and commuting surrogacy workers are left in. The necessary availability to travel upon request is yet another stressor on top of managing the unpredictability of a successful embryo transfer. In the following sections, I explore first migrant surrogacy workers' and then commuting surrogacy workers' experiences of pregnancy: once pregnant, migrant surrogacy workers enter a phase of imposed immobility and inertia, whereas commuting surrogacy workers, by contrast continued to travel, often over large distances.

Migrant Surrogacy Workers: Nine Months of Inertia

The agencies' code of conduct regarding pregnant surrogacy workers is simple: once pregnant, surrogacy workers stay put.[9] This mandate of inertia and imposed immobility is clearly outlined in surrogacy contracts and affects migrant and local surrogacy workers equally. At a minimum, a compromise is met that surrogacy workers can travel around the city. In some cases, they may be prohibited from driving. This rule mainly serves to guarantee their close supervision and to exclude any risks associated with travelling, such as accidents or missing appointments.

While restricted mobility affects all agency surrogacy workers alike, local surrogacy workers continue to live with their families in their familiar social surroundings and may continue to work. However, the imposed restrictions isolate migrant surrogacy workers from their families, even in cases of emergency. When I asked agency manager Veronica whether migrant surrogacy workers are able to see their children during the pregnancy, she replied 'Of course, of course. They talk on the phone, over Skype. Every day'. 'But not *in person*' I assured myself that I understood her correctly. 'No, not in person. Of course not. [Our surrogate

---

[9]In an interview in April 2020, the manager of a smaller agency based in St. Petersburg reported that they had changed their approach and as of 2019, they are allowing non-local surrogacy workers to commute based on individually agreed conditions.

mothers] don't travel'. Agencies go further than that by restricting migrant surrogacy workers in provided accommodation from receiving family visits. The agency 'Happy Baby', for instance, only permits visits from surrogacy workers' children if a female relative accompanies them. These visits are restricted to one or maximum of two per pregnancy, are not to last longer than a week, and the visitors may not stay in the surrogacy workers' accommodation. Visits by husbands are not permitted at all, as staff member Ala explained:

> The husband mustn't visit. There are five [women] living together! Bringing in a man cannot be considered correct. (...) – and beside that, we prohibit sexual intercourse in general. If a man comes, I suppose it would be hard to keep oneself away from him.
> (Ala, surrogacy agency coordinator, September 2014)

In addition to the travel and visiting restrictions, a number of women, especially those from provincial towns, were overwhelmed and even intimidated by the size and pace of the metropolis, and during the entire pregnancy did not go out to visit cultural sites or even go for a walk. Their experience of St. Petersburg consisted of the clinics and the nearby supermarket. A conversation with Vitali, the driver for 'Happy Baby', in which he derided the surrogacy workers, confirmed my impressions. He said:

> They rest and they sleep all day long (...) and when their pregnancy is over and I take them to the airport and ask them what they have seen and what they will be able to tell their folks back home about St. Petersburg... there is nothing. Most of them don't even know *what* there is to see. I have told them many times to not sit and wait until the pregnancy is over and done with, but to go out – but it is useless.
> (Vitali, driver for surrogacy agency, September 2014)

In his opinion, which was shared by his agency staff colleagues and expressed without hesitation, the majority of (migrant) surrogacy workers were poorly educated, lacked interest in culture, and spent their days in idleness watching TV. Or they engaged in unnecessary quarrels, as Ala commented. 'They have nothing better to do all day long but to fight and reconcile. And sometimes they don't reconcile. That is their amusement, their pastime'. What went unnoticed, fortunately for the women concerned, was the crucial and cruel fact that many migrant surrogacy workers' financial precarity compelled them to save shares of their monthly food and transport allowance by cutting unnecessary spending such as entry to cultural sites or a café visit on Nevsky Boulevard in order to send money home to provide for their children.

Migrant surrogacy worker Mila described her days living in provided accommodation at the edge of St. Petersburg with a hint of irony as 'we suffer [*stradaem*]'. The meaning of her answer is threefold. Firstly, she referred to physical experience of being pregnant and coping with morning sickness, back pains, swollen feet and other related discomforts. Secondly, she emphasized an implicit gendered meaning of '*stradat*", which is often used to discredit women's reproductive labour (Glenn, 1992).

Confined to idleness because agency surrogacy workers are prohibited from pursuing an additional paid job, are far from their families and without their usual household and childminding chores, their surrogacy pregnancies appear undemanding in comparison to their own previous pregnancies. By mockingly calling their surrogacy pregnancies 'suffering [*stradanie*]', Mila was discrediting the reproductive labour of surrogacy workers. However, the third nuance attached to *stradanie* acknowledged these very plights of idleness, confinement and loneliness. Instructed to 'do nothing but be pregnant', surrogacy workers had little to no distraction to take their minds off their pregnancies, which aggravated the physical discomforts and mood swings. Mila packed all of this into her one-word answer '*stradaem*'. Listening to the conversation, Mila's housemate Yuliana added 'Well, what *can* we do? We prepare food, we clean, browse the internet, walk to the shop... and once, we collected apples'. (For a description of the surroundings of two agency residences, including where Yuliana and Mila lived, see Appendix 4.)

Migrant surrogacy workers' confinement to idleness came in useful for the agencies, as it eased their monitoring. Furthermore, agencies commonly installed surveillance cameras in communal areas. While surrogacy workers were told that these cameras only recorded images and no sound, the women often mistrusted the accuracy of the information. Alexandra cynically called the accommodation a reality show for the agency. Yet at the same time, the living conditions in the agency-provided apartments often exceeded the women's living conditions at home and for the duration of the arrangement offered comfort and amenities that they could never afford. 'I felt like an empress [*tsaritsa*] here!' exclaimed 24-year-old Kira cheerfully when she showed me around the house and led me to her private room where she pointed out the double bed and flat-screen TV. Never in her life had she had a room of her own – at home in the Ukraine she shared first with her younger brother, and after the birth of her daughter, with her child. Experiencing such a contrast led many migrant surrogacy workers to overlook the agencies' interference in their lives and compliantly exchange privacy for comfort.

While the agency-imposed travel restrictions for all pregnant surrogacy workers was the general rule, I witnessed incidents during my extended stay in St. Petersburg when migrant surrogacy workers were compelled to travel and thereby subjected to heightened precarity and risks. In the following, I illustrate two cases.

The first case concerned the Uzbek citizen Afareen, who had come to St. Petersburg for work together with her husband, leaving their children with their extended family. Both had found employment with an affluent family as a maid and gardener and were accommodated by their employer. To quickly increase the amount of their savings, Afareen opted for surrogacy and was matched with client parents from Nizhny Novgorod, 1220 km east of St. Petersburg. A few weeks into the pregnancy, the client parents, aware of Afareen's working and living circumstances, insisted on her quitting her job. The agency likewise insisted on her compliance and without her employment, Afareen had to find new accommodation, which proved difficult, as landlord after landlord turned her application down. At that point, her client parents offered, via the agency manager, to accommodate Afareen in their spare apartment in Nizhny Novgorod. Without involving Afareen in the decision, the agency manager agreed with the client parents to assume the supervision of their surrogacy worker, and pregnant Afareen was put on a train to Nizhny Novgorod. Once there, Afareen was not allowed to talk to me, and the agency manager considered her role and responsibilities completed. Even though in earlier meetings and interviews the agency manager firmly insisted that pregnant surrogacy workers may not travel under any circumstances, she was prepared to make exceptions when it eased her workload and suited the client parents.

A second case concerned Alexandra, the young mother from Orenburg, who had come to St. Petersburg via Moscow and who had left her two young children in her 16-year-old sister's care. One afternoon, at two months pregnant, she received a distressing phone call from her frantic sister. The nursery had discovered the children's care situation and threatened the sister that they would remove them into state care unless the mother made an immediate appearance. Alexandra feared the agency would not let her make the journey of over 1000 km and devised a plan: she would collect her children, bring them to St. Petersburg and present the agency with a *fait accompli*. By coincidence, the agency manager paid a surprise visit to Alexandra's apartment the same day and noticed Alexandra's state of despair. She was urged to explain herself and subsequently permitted to travel the following day to collect her children under the following conditions: by plane, at her own expense, taking the risks and responsibility upon herself if she had a miscarriage. She was instructed to return within one day and handed a set of syringes to administer hormone injections in case she started bleeding. She was told that if she miscarried, she would be held responsible and would have to reimburse the client parents and the agency all the expenses that had been incurred. Later, an agency employee commented on Alexandra's case that they knew her to be a headstrong woman and feared that she would choose to terminate her surrogate pregnancy rather than risking losing her children, and therefore proposed the trip.[10]

Afareen's and Alexandra's experiences illustrate that when a migrant surrogacy worker's mobility during the pregnancy became more valuable to their agencies than her staying in one place, the required mobility was enforced, whereas travel that was essential for surrogacy workers but which did not directly benefit the agency was granted at the sole responsibility of the surrogacy worker. Local surrogacy workers were much less likely to encounter such situations, which again highlights the more precarious position and the inherent geographic stratifications of migrant surrogacy workers. The exceptional character of these two cases also highlights that agencies have no guidelines in place of what to do in unexpected, yet possible events, such as the serious illness or death of a family member, that might require a migrant surrogacy worker to travel or return home.

Commuting Arrangements: Continuous Motion

Contrary to the (self-)imposed immobility of migrant surrogacy workers, commuting surrogacy workers, who were commonly in direct arrangements, experienced

---

[10]It is legal for a surrogacy worker to terminate her pregnancy under the same abortion rules that apply to all pregnant women in Russia. However, influential figures in the surrogacy business have been proposing law changes for years that would deny surrogacy workers the autonomy to make decisions over their bodies and pregnancies.

continuous mobility on demand as they commuted on a regular basis for screening and appointments to the locations requested by their client parents. The frequency of travel depended on the client parents themselves: how often they wanted to see their surrogacy workers, or them to be seen by a doctor of their choosing, as well as how much travel they could afford; the latter also affected the level of comfort at which the surrogacy workers travelled. As noted earlier, client parents who chose direct arrangements, as well as women from locations which required a commute if not a relocation, often did so for financial reasons: the realities of the inherent geographic stratifications in the Russian markets in surrogacy disregard commuting and migrant surrogacy workers' reproductive bodies and reproductive labour. Rada's experience illustrates this point. Rada, from Medvezhyegorsk, a small town on the shores of Onega Lake in the Republic of Karelia to the north of St. Petersburg, commuted for all three surrogacy pregnancies. For the first and the third, she commuted to St. Petersburg, and for the second one to Moscow. She always travelled by train, and her client parents usually paid her tickets in the *platskartniy* compartment in advance (Figs. 4.5 and 4.6).

Fig. 4.5.   Platzkartniy Category Train Compartment.
Source: Author, 24/08/2014.

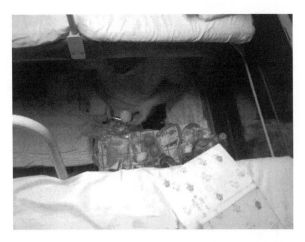

Fig. 4.6.   View from My Platzkartniy Upper Bunk Bed onto My
Travel Companion Preparing His Supper. *Source:* Author, 13/05/2015.

Looking back, she described her first client parents as particularly anxious after experiencing several failed IVF attempts, both on their own and with previous surrogacy workers.

> Sveta, the bio-mama, she was so fastidious, she worried about everything. She tried [to conceive] herself many times, and then had many girls and when it finally worked out, she wanted to control the entire process.
>
> (Rada, surrogacy worker, November 2012)

Trying to compensate for her onlooker role in Rada's pregnancy, she requested that Rada to travel to St. Petersburg at least once a month, and at each visit, booked two appointments for the same screening at two different private institutions to ensure no potential pathology would be missed and ensure the best care. Yet despite the investment, or because of it, the same client parents were rather frugal when it came to providing for Rada and compensating her for the expenses sue incurred, as Rada recalled, still aggrieved:

> Sveta saved every *kopeyka* [penny] (…). For everything I had to buy, I needed to provide the receipts and she would give me precisely the amount, down to the last *kopeyka*. (…) [Once] she told me 'Rada, there are no *platskartniy* tickets left. I will buy you a sleeper ticket, but pay only for the price for *platskartniy*' – so like 'the ticket costs 3000₽, but I will only give you 1000₽'. Is it my fault that there is no *platskartniy* ticket? If you decide to go for this, then be genuine until the very end!
>
> (Rada, surrogacy worker, November 2012)

Rada had no choice but to pay the difference for this ticket because her contract stipulated that she had to attend the appointment. As the pregnancy progressed, she would have had the right to get a set of maternity clothes paid for by the client parents, but as Rada continued, 'But I pitied these people, so I only went to get myself a cheap pair of trousers – I didn't want to spend more of their money'. When I asked Rada how she felt about the regular long commutes, she replied, laughing. 'Long? That!? That is not far! To the Urals, that is a long way! But not this!! It's a night. [Moscow] is just a bit further than St. Petersburg. (...) You get on [the train] in the evening, and in the morning, when you wake up, you are in Moscow'. After the first surrogacy experience in St. Petersburg, it was Rada's second arrangement that took her to Moscow, where 'I also have a lot of relatives (...), so when I went there, it was nice. I met up and spent time with them, I was there for 2–3 days', which made the commute more worthwhile than going for the appointment only.

Karina, an acquaintance of Rada, also commuted regularly to St. Petersburg for both commissioned pregnancies. As both she and her client parents continued to work, they agreed to schedule the appointments on Saturdays, which allowed Karina to take a night train after her Friday shift, attend the appointment on Saturday morning, spend time with the client parents and return home either Sunday night or Monday morning, ready to go to work. Though Karina prided herself on being resilient and insisted that the arrangement suited her, as she basically worked two full-time jobs and therefore made a decent income, the busy schedule took a toll on her family life:

> My children told me that I am neglecting them. I was physically unable to give them more attention, because I had to travel regularly, or I was in such a state that I simply had to sleep... but my children wanted attention. That is my story, the unpleasant nuances in my experience.
>
> (Karina, surrogacy worker, December 2012)

In contrast to the mobility restrictions that commercial surrogacy agencies imposed on pregnant surrogacy workers, many women in direct arrangements worked based on this commuting model that turned the 'gestational carriers' into 'gestational couriers'.[11]

There were three main reasons for the popularity of these types of commuting arrangements despite the burden it placed on the pregnant women, the risks it posed to the pregnancy and the limitations of monitoring it placed on the client parents. First, was the difficulty of finding a suitable local surrogacy worker. Second, was the preference for a non-local surrogacy worker to avoid or minimise the risk of meeting the surrogacy worker in the future and of the surrogacy worker exposing the surrogacy arrangement if the parents kept it secret. Third, cost-effectiveness:

---

[11]During my research visit in 2014/2015, 12 of the 18 direct arrangements I observed in my research were commuting arrangements.

commuting surrogacy workers, particularly if they came from abroad, were more likely to agree to work for less money in order to offset their travel costs. Nevertheless, as Karina highlighted, although commuting while pregnant was physically tiring and took a toll on them and their families, it provided them with an agency that migrant surrogacy workers did not have, as well as with the opportunity of earning a dual income. For many commuting surrogacy workers, the commuting is a strategy enabling them to combine nurturing and spending time with their own families for as long as possible, sometimes maintaining their regular employment, and earning the surrogacy income at the same time. Furthermore, it gave them the opportunity to partake in the surrogacy markets by drawing on their capital of mobility to convert their reproductive capital into economic capital.

Delivery and Departure

After the divergent experiences during the pregnancy, commuting and migrant surrogacy workers' experiences converged again at childbirth; what is most notable is that, regardless the form of arrangement, the forms of (im-)mobility and measures imposed during and after childbirth continued to serve first and foremost the requirements of client parents and agencies.

Surrogacy workers, like any women in Russia, are entitled to a three-day stay in the maternity clinic for post-partum care. After that, agencies usually accommodated their migrant surrogacy workers for up to one further week to recover, rest during the retraction of the uterus and if necessary, access medical care, and to make preparations to return home. In most cases, agencies bought their surrogacy workers a plane ticket for the return journey, to minimise the physical strain as well as make the journey safer, as many women travelled with their final compensation in cash.

However, not all deliveries and departures went smoothly, and in several cases timing and mobility was once again oriented towards the needs of the agency or the client parents, regardless of the adverse impact on the surrogacy workers. The following two examples illustrate how the geographic stratification continue to demarcate differences and extend from the pregnancy into the post-partum period to affect migrant surrogacy workers' mobility even after delivery.

Once more, I return to migrant surrogacy worker Alexandra, who was first sent on from Moscow to St. Petersburg and then travelled back home to Orenburg to fetch her children. On the day she went into labour, the intended maternity clinic, which was used to handling surrogacy arrangements, was closed for its bi-annual disinfection day. The ambulance therefore took Alexandra to the nearest available clinic, where the general staff were not briefed on surrogacy deliveries. Despite notifying her agency that she was on her way to hospital, Alexandra had to undergo the delivery on her own without assistance from her agency. She recalls seeing the child – 'so white, such big eyes' – as he was handed to the client mother who had arrived just as Alexandra was delivering the child. Even though the client parents had not intended for Alexandra to ever see them, she managed to see at least the client mother. 'After I gave birth, I opened my eyes when she came in – literally for two, maybe three minutes we talked. She showed me the child, said thank you'. Alexandra was then put under anaesthesia to surgically remove the placenta and when she woke up, she recalled that a nurse asked her 'You won't mind if we put you in with a woman and her child, will you?' Still dazed from the anaesthesia, exhausted, overwhelmed by just having delivered a child and given it to the client parents, and without support from the agency or knowing her rights to a single room as a surrogacy worker, Alexandra agreed.[12]

> I hadn't fully come to all my senses yet when they asked me. I wasn't against it *then*, but once I had fully woken up and found myself in a room with a new-born, I regretted it. It was difficult, psychologically difficult. (...) They don't have the right to put me with a woman and her new-born! Can you imagine?! I don't have a child after giving birth, and then here I am, with a mother and her new-born. And she begins to ask: Where is your little one? And I tell her that the boy is sick, and that he is somewhere – I was not going to tell her that I was a surrogate, because of the gossip that would go around in the hospital.
>
> (Alexandra, surrogacy worker, August 2014)

Alexandra's anger grew as she found out that the agency representative Malvina had arrived at the hospital in the meantime to take care of the paperwork for the child and support the client parents, and thus knew of Alexandra's unacceptable situation, but regarded it as unnecessary to intervene.

On the following day, the information that she was a surrogacy worker leaked from a nurse to the general staff, including the cleaners, which led to a cleaner verbally abusing her. Alexandra could no longer take it. Upset and humiliated she left the clinic to return to her shared apartment where she had left her two little children in the care of her fellow surrogacy workers. As she told me her story, her voice was often quivering with upset.

> I cried. I was so upset and humiliated. A cleaner bullied me out! I carried a child and the bio[logical] parents didn't even come to thank me! (...) [The bio-papa], he rushed to church, to pray! They didn't come to see me any further – even though they simply could have come to see me there [in the clinic], to ask how I feel and so on. I think to act so indifferent, that is not correct!
>
> (Alexandra, surrogacy worker, August 2014)

---

[12]Alexandra and other surrogacy workers reported that it is a routine procedure of giving birth in Russia to have the placenta removed instead of waiting for the women to deliver the placenta.

On the evening of the same day that she returned to her accommodation, barely 36h after the delivery, she received a phone call from the agency. 'They said: "Alexandra, can you move out within a day or two? We need your place for a new girl'". She fumed as she recalled the conversation:

> They needed to put another surrogate, another girl, in my place. I should leave as soon as I could. I was no longer of use, so I was supposed to leave as soon as I could. And I told them 'I am not going anywhere!'
>
> (Alexandra, surrogacy worker, August 2014)

On top of intending to deprive Alexandra of the usual week to rest and recover, Malvina, the manager, further broke the news that since Alexandra had brought her children, she was responsible for buying her own return tickets. Alexandra's voice vibrated with anger as she tried to keep her countenance while narrating:

> [Tickets] are expensive when you buy them 24 hours in advance, especially for the plane. But what was most insulting was that they wanted to kick me out – again. And I told them: 'I am not going anywhere, not until my belly has shrunk!' I told them that first they kick me out from the hospital, and now from the apartment.' I am not going anywhere!' That's what I told them!
>
> (Alexandra, surrogacy worker, August 2014)

Alexandra did stay for the full week before she returned to her hometown with her two children. The unexpected expenses of travelling to fetch her children, higher rent charges by the agency for accommodating her children (which were subtracted from her final compensation), paying the occasional childminder and general living expenses in St. Petersburg, and the short-notice plane tickets to return home diminished her earnings substantially. A year and half later, when we met in Moscow after she had left her husband (who had cheated on her during the surrogacy stay in St. Petersburg) and was preparing for another surrogacy pregnancy, she reflected on her first surrogacy experience. Looking back, she knew that not having been local, but a *priezzhaya,* had weakened her position with the clinic and the agency substantially.[13] 'I should have sued them' she concluded, but acknowledged that at that time she had neither the mental and physical strength nor the means to pay a lawyer and remain in St. Petersburg to fight for her rights. She was convinced that agencies are aware of migrant surrogacy workers' particular vulnerability and precarity, and take advantage by treating them accordingly, with impunity.

---

[13]'*Priezzhaya*' [приезжая], short for '*priezzhiy rabotchiy*' [приезжий рабочий] – the gastarbeiter/labour migrant – is a common way for agencies to refer to their migrant surrogacy workers. In the everyday speech, the term refers to temporary and seasonal migrant workers.

While in Alexandra's case, the delivery of the baby marked the end of her utility and thus the agency's 'hospitality' to the extent that her agency even wanted her accommodation vacated a week ahead of time to accommodate the next surrogacy worker for the next pregnancy, migrant surrogacy worker Irina was not permitted to leave after the delivery as planned, in order to return to her family, but her agency insisted on an extended stay for the sake of the client parents' peace of mind.

Irina had carried a child for a male same-sex couple with German citizenship. After Irina had delivered the child and signed the required document in which she relinquished her parental rights, her agency 'Surrogacy Exclusive', responding to their clients' apprehension that there could be difficulties at the passport control, insisted that Irina remain available in St. Petersburg until the fathers had successfully left the country. In a note of gratitude to the agency upon arrival in Germany without any interruptions, the two fathers posted a praise on the agency's professionalism, especially their foresight to 'keep our surrogate mother at our disposal until our day of departure'. Once they had left, the agency and Irina's presence were no longer needed, and the agency provided her the return ticket. Both cases illustrate how migrant workers' departure was not at their own, but at their agencies' discretion.

In the case of commuting surrogacy workers, contracts stipulated their relocation to wherever the client parents wanted them to give birth, between three to six weeks prior to the expected delivery date, depending on circumstances such as medical recommendations and whether the surrogacy workers were carrying a singleton or twin pregnancy. Client parents picked the birth places for various reasons of their own, such as having a preferred clinic, proximity to their home, or proximity to the location they wanted to be entered on the birth certificate.

While awaiting the delivery, commuting surrogacy workers are either accommodated in rented apartments or aparthotels, or less frequently, are hosted by their client parents. The commuting surrogacy workers I met gave mixed accounts about these final weeks of their surrogacy journeys. While some jokingly described the weeks awaiting delivery as a pleasant break from household chores and full-time mothering, for others the memories of loneliness and long and boring days predominated. Nastya, who carried twins and was accommodated in her client parents' home, described her experience.

> I had to go there one and half, or two months before the birth. Of course I didn't want to go there any earlier than necessary, because, you understand, it is one thing to have a good relationship – but to live, in the family – in a stranger's family, that is not comfortable, because you want to feel like you are at home. And... well, but it was fine. There was no bad attitude, it was all fine. Though morally it was difficult, and I wanted to return home as fast as possible.
>
> (Nastya, surrogacy worker, November 2012)

Daria, who also gestated twins and was accommodated in the home of her client parents, had a more positive experience:

> They never rented something extra, because when I came to visit earlier, for a day or two, for the screenings – I felt very comfortable there, we felt each other *[my drug druga tchustvovaly]* – (...) we agreed that it would be better for them and for me if we lived together. Because at such an advanced stage of the pregnancy it is more difficult to do even the simplest things, such as daily shopping – and even to tie shoelaces, because I had this big belly.
> (Daria, surrogacy worker, November 2014)

For Lyubov, who spent the time leading up to the birth in a rented apartment in a foreign city on her own, it was a lonely experience. Unlike some surrogacy workers who received regular visits from their client mothers to distract them and assist them with shopping, Lyubov only received regular text messages checking whether she was all right or needed anything. She described how she felt lucky that it was summer and she could undertake daily walks to distract herself whereas a birth during winter, with temperatures below zero and snow and ice on the streets, would have ruled out such a distraction.

Such wholly positive experiences leading up to the birth as Daria reported were rare. Instead, both migrating and commuting surrogacy workers frequently described the pregnancy, and especially the final weeks before delivery, as a period of endurance – or as Mila (quoted earlier) described it, as a 'suffering' *[stradanie]*. By then they had spent nearly a year separated from their children and partners, and were often hiding their surrogacy pregnancies from friends and wider family, unable to reach out for support.

Unlike pregnant women who are fulfilling their wish for their own child, and may spend the weeks leading up to birth nesting and preparing themselves for motherhood and the beginning of something new and joyfully anticipated, surrogacy workers were anticipating the delivery because it would bring an end to the arrangement and enable them to return to their family lives and privacy. The feelings of discomfort and the geographic relocation even assisted some in their ongoing emotion work of staying detached from the surrogacy child and remaining morally prepared to give the child to the client parents – as described in chapter two, 'Becoming a surrogacy worker'.

In short, for surrogacy workers, and migrant and commuting surrogacy workers in particular, the birth did not mark a beginning, but an ending and the return to their own lives with privacy and bodily integrity. It was these prospects that sparked joy and chatter on the evening of Marcella's departure from St. Petersburg in September 2014 after delivering triplets. Given these exceptional circumstances of a triplet birth, Marcella's agency had granted her mother permission to visit to assist her daughter in the days before and after birth, and to help her with packing and the return journey to the Republic of Moldova – by train. Visiting Marcella's accommodation on the evening of her departure, I witnessed the lugging and lifting of bags, the checking that Marcella did not leave anything behind, and the avoidance of interaction with the other surrogacy workers who sat with me in the kitchen. Only when the taxi driver called and Marcella returned to the kitchen to say her goodbyes, the glum kitchen suddenly erupted in chit-chat, laughter and well-wishing. Marcella's mother, standing by the door, let out an emphasised groan and commented. 'For a week! For a week nobody here says a word to each other, and now, now that they are separating, now they can't keep their traps shut!' As described earlier, migrant surrogacy workers in their agency-provided accommodation, in most cases, were not friends, but women from different parts of the country and Russia's neighbouring countries, tolerating each other's presence while they were sharing accommodation for the period of their surrogacy pregnancy. They preferred to keep to themselves, not to reveal too much about themselves, and were encouraged by their agencies to report each other for trespassing rules. Yet when the moment of departure came for Marcella, she couldn't hold back her joy over the departure and successfully completing yet another surrogacy arrangement. 'That is normal! That is normal!' shouted Yuliana, the two-months pregnant surrogacy worker from the Ukraine, in response to Marcella's mother's annoyance. 'No. It is perversion', replied Marcella's mother as she left the kitchen to get in the taxi.

Conclusion

Mobility, in the form of reproductive commuting and migration, and the concomitant geographic and geopolitical stratifications, characterises the social organisation of commercial surrogacy in Russia. As Moscow and St. Petersburg have become Russia's major 'repro-hubs', the preeminent destinations for the majority of the 'repro-flows' for assisted reproductive treatment, women across Russia and from the neighbouring former Soviet Union states have responded by drawing on their capital of mobility so they can capitalise on their reproductive capacities. In order to distinguish the two different forms of mobility, I have coined the terms *migrant surrogacy worker* and *commuting surrogacy worker.* I have extended Shelee Colen's (1995) theoretical framework of stratified reproduction to *geographic and geopolitical stratifications* to analyse the meaning and experiences of Russia's reproductive migrants. Surrogacy workers in Russia are geographically and geopolitically stratified when their bodies and reproductive labour are desired, valued and compensated based on their geographic origin, place of residence and citizenship – and the imaginaries relating to these characteristics. These stratifications impact on migrant and commuting surrogacy workers' experiences during the commissioned pregnancy.

My analysis of the social of organisation of surrogacy in Russia, with its intrinsic geographic reproductive stratifications, shows that reproductive flows and practices depend not only on transnational inequalities (Ginsburg & Rapp, 1995, p. 1) but increasingly also on regional disparities: as St. Petersburg and Moscow have emerged as Russia's 'repro hubs', and as the demand for surrogacy workers increases, local agencies rely on hiring surrogacy workers from all over Russia and the surrounding countries to meet it. However, as these women (temporarily) migrate or commute to the hubs, their reproductive labour is disregarded despite the fact that agencies often prefer to recruit women from outside the metropolises, as they attribute them with having better health and greater resilience – in the words of the agency managers – 'village girls' that were simply 'created to give birth'. While presenting this framing as a compliment to women's fertility and reproductive capacities, the choice of words shows how agencies systematically reduce surrogacy workers from individuals to reproductive vessels.

Agencies also preferred women from outside the metropolises for the reason that they expected them to be satisfied with a lower salary, and in response to the competition to be selected by an agency, many migrant surrogacy workers complied. The price regime set by commercial agencies automatically applied a discount to the fee for migrant surrogacy workers based on their location and has rippled through the markets in surrogacy in Russia. Effectively, it has led to women from outside Russia's surrogacy hubs lowering their compensation expectations in order to compete on the neoliberal market in assisted reproduction.

The experiences of commuting and migrant surrogacy workers contrast starkly. While the frequency with which commuting surrogacy workers were expected to commute for appointments varied according to their client parents' preferences, they nevertheless had to comply with the demands, and often, commuting took a toll on surrogacy workers' family life. Migrant surrogacy workers, by contrast, experienced externally imposed as well as self-imposed immobility and inertia. Commercial agencies restricted their travel which meant that they were separated from their partners and children. In addition, many migrant surrogacy workers from rural places felt overwhelmed by the pace of life in the metropolis which deterred them from going out. Equally, many could not afford to treat their surrogacy as an extended holiday and take the opportunity to visit cultural sites, as they were saving every penny to support their families back home.

Yet while these forms of mobility impacted and took their toll on the surrogacy workers' private lives, for many women they also presented the opportunity to become surrogacy workers in the first place, as they enabled women to hide the surrogacy pregnancy from their social circle by pretending to temporarily migrate for a fictional job. It also offered an opportunity to partake in the reproductive marketplace to women who would otherwise be unable to find client parents in their own cities and districts. The sheer size of Russia, the concentration of assisted reproductive treatment facilities in St. Petersburg and Moscow, and to a lesser extent in other larger cities, the familiarity with commuting work based on the Soviet past, and the cultural notion of seeing surrogacy as a form of work with a temporary relationship to the client parents, all provide the conditions for such reproductive migrations, which today are intrinsic to the market in surrogacy in Russia.

Chapter 5

Disruptions and Reconfigurations

> In my opinion, they are not going to stop [surrogacy] any time soon.
> Surrogacy is a very beneficial [method] of advanced reproductive
> technologies. Surrogacy in Russia is a paid programme, it is legal,
> and it is clearly legislated. It is a kind of work. I don't think they will
> be shutting it down. No, definitely no.
>
> (Dr Lydia, embryologist, April 2020)

This chapter concerns itself with the emergence of SARS-CoV-2 and the impact the resulting illness COVID-19 has on the practice of surrogacy in Russia. Further, it addresses how the disruptions to surrogacy and related events during the lockdown in 2020 were instrumentalised by conservative and homophobic politicians to incite against queer individuals and those seeking to build non-heteronormative families, and to restrict their access to surrogacy. In this chapter, I draw on legal documents and media coverage, and with regards to empirical data, exclusively on interviews and cyberethnographic observations that I have collected from January 2020 until March 2021.

Disruptions: The Impact of COVID-19

In December 2019, the outbreak of the novel coronavirus SARS-CoV-2 was recorded in China and followed by a local travel ban on 23 January 2020 (Chen, Yang, Yang, Wang, & Bärnighausen, 2020). Shortly after, Russian Far East regions bordering China closed their borders with China to stop the virus from spreading into Russia (Reuters, 2020a). In March 2020, Russia went into a national lockdown and closed all its borders for international travel. For Russia's surrogacy industry, that meant that international client parents were unable to enter Russia to pick up their newborn babies. Depending where foreign client parents were from, some were able to enter Russia in the summer of 2020.

As global reproductive flows were jerked into an uncomfortable standstill (König, Jacobson, & Majumdar, 2020), worldwide thousands of children were born to surrogates, with parents unable to enter the countries where they were born in order to pick up their children (Denton, 2020; Roth, 2020; Vlasenko, 2020; Widdicombe, 2020). Images of hotel rooms turned into makeshift nurseries filled with cradles, in some cases over 50 in a room, and nurses busying themselves feeding and swaddling crying infants, caused an outcry.

Surrogacy in Russia, 111–118
Copyright © 2021 Christina Weis
Published under exclusive licence by Emerald Publishing Limited
doi:10.1108/978-1-83982-896-620211014

In Russia, it remains impossible to establish how many children born via surrogacy were not able to be taken home by their non-resident parents due to local and global lockdown and travel restrictions; even before the COVID-19 pandemic, there were no official statistics in Russia of how many children were born through surrogacy. On July 29th, 2020, The Guardian's Russia correspondent Andrew Roth estimated that 1,000 children born to surrogates were awaiting their parents (Roth, 2020), and an unknown number of children were yet to be born to pregnant surrogacy workers. Left in limbo, some newborns were being cared for by nannies, hired privately by commercial surrogacy agencies or the overseas client parents themselves, some were placed in state institutions (SPBdeti, 2020) and some were temporarily taken home and looked after by the surrogacy workers who gave birth to them. In such cases, the surrogacy workers received additional pay Some agency representatives approved of this solution, considering it the best solution for the babies – yet when feeding, nurturing and caring for these babies at home, these women inevitably developed a bond, as did their own children, which made parting from the baby much harder. In addition, caring for these babies entailed a severe disruption of their private lives, as anxious client parents demanded several videos calls a day to be able to check on their children. In many cases, communication between surrogacy workers and foreign client parents had to take place via Google Translate or WeChat inbuilt automated translation apps, and in some instances, agencies ceded these makeshift arrangements entirely to the surrogacy workers and the foreign parents. This excerpt of a conversation with an agency manager in April 2020 illustrates:

Christina: So just to be clear – so that I understand it right: In this arrangement the surrogate was working for you and you paid her after the delivery, the usual money she gets, but after the birth it is the parents who have to take care of the child.

Alexander: Yes. Right.

Christina: And how do they communicate? Do they have a translator?

Alexander: I think yes. I think they communicate through WeChat and they have internal translators from Russian to Chinese, sorry no, Chinese to English, because they speak English.*

Christina: Ok, so they are just communicating with each other by text messages. They are not calling each other.

Alexander: I think so, yes.

To clarify, by 'internal translators', Alexander is referring to the inbuilt automated app translation.

For a number of client parents, the long-desired moment of holding and bringing their babies home arrived by the end of the summer 2020, as Russia started to reopen its borders to some countries. One agency owner confirmed a successful diplomatic arrangement with the Chinese government that allowed the parents of 15 surrogacy-born children to collect their children in St. Petersburg in autumn 2020. At the same time, another agency owner estimated that there were still between 150 and 200 babies, aged between one and nine months and born to Chinese nationals, 'stuck in Russia' (see also Dandan & Shiyu, 2020).[1] Yet with fluctuating infection numbers, restrictions and permissions as to who could travel to Russia continuously changed throughout 2020, making it difficult for client parents to travel.

Further to unreliable numbers on how many children were born through surrogacy and had later been collected by their genetic parents – and how many remained in limbo in Russia – there remains a dearth in knowledge on many children were never collected, but ultimately placed in orphanages or taken in by the surrogacy workers who then also did not receive their final compensation for their work.[2]

While we continue to know little about how these children are doing, what impact these first months of placement in different emergency care arrangements is having on the children's development and despite cases of children never being collected by their intended parents, some fertility clinics in Russia returned to implementing new surrogacy arrangements, in November 2020, for locals and foreigners alike. Agencies were simply factoring the possibilities of new travel restrictions and lockdowns into their service packages for client parents, such as the agency that provided the following details via email:

> If the parents are unable to promptly come to pick up the born child, we discharge the child from the hospital under the guardianship of an infant professional nanny. She lives with her child (children in case of twins) in a separate apartment. At the same time, we draw up documents for the child (birth certificate, medical insurance policy). To do this, at the stage of concluding an agreement with the parents, we draw up all the necessary powers of attorney. We also have the opportunity, even in a pandemic, to issue invitations for the entry of parents for their children, on the basis of which a Russian visa is issued to parents. (We got accreditation from the Ministry of the Interior).
>
> (Agency correspondent, November 2020)

---

[1] It is important to note that foreign client parents come to Russia from all over the world. However, in 2015, Russia saw a rapid increase in Chinese nationals seeking assisted reproductive treatment, and soon, Chinese client parents represented the largest share among international client having surrogacy arrangements in Russia (Weis, 2021).

[2] On 29 October 2020, Konstantin Svitnev published an open letter on his law company's website reporting that three babies born to parents from the Philippines have spent the first year of their life placed in 'a state-owned orphanage for mentally ill children' and demanding from the Russian state their return to their parents. These children were born prior to the COVID-19-related lockdown, but their parents' arrival was further delayed due to the lockdown and travel ban disruptions, and criminal investigations (Svitnev, 2020; see also; The Economist, 2021).

Reconfigurations: Challenges and Potential Changes to the Current Liberal Policy Context

By the end of the summer of 2020, at the same time as international client parents were still struggling to come to Russia and retrieve their babies, and agencies and private fertility clinic were reorganising their provision of surrogacy, for locals and foreigners alike, members of the Russian State Duma were already debating changes to the current surrogacy laws. Then, in January 2021, the Russian State Duma declared the existence of a draft bill to amend the current regulation of surrogacy in Russia. If accepted, the new bill would prohibit foreigners and unmarried couples from seeking surrogacy in Russia (Takie Dela, 2021). To recap, under the current law, commercial, gestational surrogacy is legal for married and unmarried heterosexual couples and single women, Russian citizens, residents and foreigners alike. While single men are not explicitly mentioned in the law, successful law cases in favour of paternity for single fathers through surrogacy and egg donation have also helped create a precedent establishing the practice of offering surrogacy to single men and same-sex couples. To date, the liberal regulation of surrogacy makes it one of the most permissive places to seek surrogacy, 'a reproductive paradise, a country where almost everybody willing to have a child through ART may fulfill [*sic*] their dream' (Svitnev, 2012a).

However, the newly drafted bill would restrict surrogacy to married heterosexual couples with residence permits in Russia. Further, intending parents seeking surrogacy would need to have been married for at least one year, be at least 25 years old but not older than 55, and couples would need a valid medical reason for the use of surrogacy. Though the latter is already required by the current law (but occasionally overlooked by favorable doctors), the climate around surrogacy has been changing since 2020. And here, one incident stands out in particular: In January 2020, the police entered a Moscow apartment to find a dead infant, and three further newborns, all born to surrogacy workers for client parents from abroad who couldn't come to Russia in time to be there for the birth and who were being cared for by a hired nurse.[3] Doctors declared the reason for the infant's death to be SIDS (sudden infant death syndrome) (Vasilyeva, 2020); yet in July 2020, the fertility doctors involved in this case were arrested and charged with child trafficking (RapsiNews, 2020).[4] Investigations into child trafficking and inflicting death by negligence were also initiated against Konstantin Svitnev, lawyer and director of the surrogacy agency Rosjurconsulting that implemented and oversaw the surrogacy arrangement (Dzhafarov, 2020; Vasilyeva, 2020); in November 2020, an international arrest warrant had been

---

[3]The client parents of the deceased infant came from the Philippines. In January 2020, when these client parents were unable to arrive in Russia in time for the birth of their child, borders were still open and the circumstances leading to them missing the birth of their child unrelated to COVID-19. (My gratitude to my colleague Maria Kirpichenko who commented on a draft of this chapter and alerted me to the detail.)

[4]The Economist (21 March 2021) reports the said infant '[dying] while recovering from an operation on his brain'.

issued for Svitnev, who had left Russia and was staying in the Czech Republic at the time of the arrests (RapsiNews, 2020). On 01 January 2021, Konstantin Svitnev, in an interview given to surrogacy.ru, rejected charges and referred to himself as 'the first reprodissident in Russia and the world' (Svitnev, 2021).

Over the the past decade, Svitnev has played a crucial role in making surrogacy available to single men and gay couples, as it was he and his law firm that won the precedent cases that helped subsequent cases of single men win paternity over their surrogacy-conceived children.[5] However, an increasing number of politicians, emboldened by the hostile anti-LGBTQI+ (lesbian, gay, bisexual, transgender, queer and intersex) rhetoric of the government, have been campaigning for legislation to 'prioritise heterosexual marriage' and discriminate against 'non-traditional lifestyles and choices'. Within this current climate, the investigations against the lawyer who set the precedent by winning parental rights court cases for single men (including homosexual men) were driven by explicit anti-gay sentiments (Carroll, 2020.) The allegations of child trafficking have no legal grounds, yet nevertheless, 'investigators [were] planning to arrest more suspects including single Russian men who used surrogate mothers to have babies via IVF treatment (...) because of their non-traditional sexual orientation' (Vasilyeva, 2020). The online news portal EU-OCS (European Observatory of Crimes and Security) (2020) is quoting the arrestees' lawyer Igor Trunov stating that

> They want to connect baby trafficking to the idea of sexual orientation, knowing how that resonates with the wider public. (...) They understand no one is going to stand up for gays.

As a consequence, several homosexual men who are fathers through surrogacy in Russia have fled the country to escape the threat of interrogation, arrest and separation from their children (Bocharova, 2020).

Once the draft bill was announced in January 2021, commercial agencies and fertility doctors began to act with more caution and to alter their practise. For instance, a Russian embryologist commented in personal correspondence that since the surrogacy bill had been announced, 'we have stopped working with non-traditional patients (I mean single fathers), including Chinese patients. And we do the surrogate programme only when there are strict medical indications'. The Australian non-profit organisation 'Growing Families' that provides information about surrogacy options worldwide announced on their website's section for Russia that 'NOTE THAT as of January 2021 RUSSIA is no longer accepting Single men/gay couples for surrogacy' (capitals in original; website visited 8 March 2021). A representative added in personal correspondence that 'no

---

[5]To recap – in the case of gay couple seeking parenthood through surrogacy in Russia, only one man of the two can legally be recognised as the father in Russia. In the case of foreign client fathers, the second father can seek legal recognition of his role in his country of origin (or residence), if possible, there. Konstantin Svitnev won paternity for the first single man to become father through surrogacy in 2010 (Surrogacy.ru, 2021).

reputable Russian agency has been able to accept single men since this time'. In Russia, one agency manager described their agency '[being] in waiting', meaning they are not facilitating new arrangements while closely monitoring the political landscape, while another private clinic with an in-house agency dismissed the potential restrictions as 'rumours'. Avoiding addressing sexual orientation directly, the international correspondent stated boldly that, with regards to serving international client parents, even if a ban on foreigners came into force, all contracts signed prior to that date would guarantee that 'everything will be smooth'; a potential new travel ban would be circumvented by issuing medical invitations for foreign patients.

According to the Vice Speaker of the State Duma, Pyotr Tolstoy, co-author of the bill, it is a direct response to the children left (temporarily) stranded in Russia due to the COVID-19 lockdown and travel ban (Kuznetsova & Gubernatorov, 2021). According to *The Moscow Times* however, the bill's explanatory note, in fact, reveals its underlying homophobia by noting that the use of surrogacy by single men and women does not align with traditional Russian family values (Avilov, 2021). Further, according to Kuznetsova and Gubernatorov (2021) the explanatory note also states that the practise of surrogacy 'creates direct and indirect possibilities of harming the national interest' by posing 'a threat to public and economic security, personal security, and biological security', which neces-sitates a ban on foreigners accessing surrogacy in Russia, which in turn would prevent any further export of children born to surrogate mothers in Russia (Litvinova, Manuyilova, Veretennikova, & Makutina, 2021).

This is not the first time that a bill has been proposed which would ban some or all aspects of the current practise of commercial surrogacy in Russia. In 2013, State Duma Deputy, Yelena Mizulina, called for a ban on surrogacy for fear that it 'threatens mankind with extinction' (Krainova, 2013). In February 2014, Vitaly Milonov, Deputy of the Legislative Assembly of St. Petersburg, announced his intention to put forward a bill that would ban the use of surrogacy services by single men, and as a result, by men in same-sex relationships. That bill would have permitted only heterosexual couples, regardless of their marital status, to be allowed to use the service of 'surrogate mothers'. However, his intention was never realised. In March 2017, Senator Anton Belyakov proposed a bill that would ban all surrogacy in Russia (RapsiNews, 2017); however, in October 2018, the State Duma Committee on Family, Women and Children firmly rejected the bill (Zen, 2018).

In light of international developments, in particular the clampdown on sur-rogacy in various countries that rapidly gained popularity for transnational sur-rogacy because of their scarce or liberal regulation such as Nepal, Thailand and Cambodia, the Russian case raises the question of which direction the Russian state will take. Rather than completely banning surrogacy, will Russia take a similar route to India? The Indian government first banned same-sex couples from accessing surrogacy in 2013, not through law, but through new visa rules for client parents (Chauduri, 2013), and followed this with a ban on commercial surrogacy for all foreigners, restricting access to altruistic surrogacy to heterosexual, married, Indian couples only (Rudrappa, 2017). Yet while the Indian state reasoned that the ban of commercial and transnational surrogacy would protect Indian surrogates (Rudrappa, 2018), in Russia, concerns about the commercialisation of surrogacy were never part of the discussion. Among the authors of the Russian bills, and its commentators, there is a striking absence of focus on the well-being of surrogates in Russia and the impact the bills would have on them. Instead, what is foregrounded in the debate in Russia is firstly the concern to protect the national interest by ceasing the export of children, and secondly, the protection of traditional Russian family values.

As such, the developments in surrogacy legislation are in accord with the wider demographic and reproductive politics in Russia: the increasing hostility towards and criminalisation of homosexuality and non-heteronormative identities and living arrangements (Belyakov, 2018; Davydova, 2019), the (re) orientation towards conservative, regressive family values (Reuters, 2020b; Shadrina, 2015) and the resulting pressure placed on Russian women and young families to have more children and contribute to demographic growth (Rotkirch, Temkina, & Zdravomyslova, 2007). In 2013, Sergei Kalashnikov, then head of the Duma's Public Health Committee, even responded to Mizulina's proposal to ban surrogacy by saying that surrogacy could be part of a national strategy to tackle infertility and stop fertility decline (Krainova, 2013), a stance widely taken by fertility doctors (see introduction, page 6). Both the proposed bill and the current media coverage of it disregard the surrogacy workers and their labour, as well as the often-essential egg providers; instead, they highlight Russia's national interests and hint at the fear that Russia is losing reproductive capacity, as Russian women's reproductive labour is exported elsewhere. Furthermore, the proposed bill and the discussion around it fails to consider – or deliberately ignores – those surrogacy workers who come to Russia from its neighbouring former Soviet Union countries for surrogacy work and, thus, contribute their reproductive labour to the demographic growth of the Russian population.[6]

Thus, Dr Lydia, who predicted during the height of Russia's first COVID-19-related lockdown in April 2020 that 'they are not going to stop [surrogacy] any time soon', might be right. In the light of recent developments and with regards to how surrogacy practices have been established in Russia since the first surrogacy

---

[6]Few surrogacy workers actually addressed the notion of their partners' or wider families' unease over their sovereign use of their reproductive capacities for financial gain. Anna explained how she concealed her two surrogacy pregnancies from her in-laws to spare her husband their mockery over not keeping her reproduction under his control and letting others take advantage of her fertility, and Karina summarised the taunting her partner had to endure as 'What were you thinking of, to allow your woman to give birth for someone else?'. Migrant surrogacy worker Yuliana, who is from the Ukraine and was carrying her second surrogacy pregnancy as we talked in St. Petersburg, even poignantly addressed the very notion of a woman's reproductive capacity belonging to her husband and, therefore, to his fatherland, when she explained that her husband only very reluctantly let her go abroad to carry children for someone in Russia. 'Well, why?!! I am his wife! I am his property!'.

worker gave birth in St. Petersburg in 1995, it is impossible to escape the impression that the potential restriction of surrogacy in Russia is less about moving towards a ban of surrogacy, and more about reserving surrogacy for childbirth that is in the national interest, where only the right kind of people are allowed to become parents.

Conclusion: At Crossroads

At present, commercial gestational surrogacy remains legal in Russia, but it finds itself at crossroads. Since the first case of gestational surrogacy in Russia (in St. Petersburg in 1995), commercial gestational surrogacy has been established into a normalised and routinised practice in the privatised fertility sector, and since the mid-2010s, Russia's reproductive hubs St. Petersburg and Moscow have been attracting client parents no longer only from all over Russia, but the world. Furthermore, and this makes the practice of surrogacy Russia stand out on the global scale, Russia's reproductive hubs have even attracted surrogacy workers from beyond Russia's borders; these women come to Russia hired and guided by agencies, as well as on their own initiative and with the intention of becoming surrogacy workers. Despite, and also because of Russia's liberal laws that allow locals and foreigners alike to hire a surrogacy worker, the last decade has also seen repeated attempts from conservative politicians and campaigners to ban some or all aspects of surrogacy (Cook, 2017; Krainova, 2013; RapsiNews, 2020). The most recent example is the attempt to curb surrogacy in Russia and restrict its access to heterosexual, married residents in Russia, citing the disruptions caused by the COVID-19 pandemic.

Alongside these internal developments of surrogacy in Russia, the past years have also witnessed constant and rapid reorientations of global reproductive flows for transnational surrogacy, as governments in popular transnational surrogacy destination countries increasingly restrict or prohibit commercial surrogacy in some or all of its forms. As India and Mexico, to name two examples, no longer receive foreign nationals to enter commercial surrogacy arrangements, countries in South-East Asia and the former Soviet Union, such as Russia, gain in popularity (Vertommen et al., 2021; Weis, 2021; Whittaker, 2018). Inevitably, these global reproductive flows have also been affected by the travel restrictions, border closures and quarantine mandates as a result of the COVID-19 pandemic (König, Jacobson, & Majumdar, 2020). Nevertheless, intending parents continue to seek routes to parenthood, and for many, time is critical (Keaney & Moll, 2020) – and so clinics, agencies and entrepreneurs likewise seek legal loopholes and ways to revive (transnational) surrogacy amidst constantly changing guidance, rules and (travel) restrictions.

Zooming back into Russia: It is possible that the current draft bill to restrict surrogacy services to married heterosexual couples will be passed. It is likewise possible that the bill will be dismissed alike previous attempts, and further, that the current setback of global reproductive travel is temporary and that once

Surrogacy in Russia, 119–124
Copyright © 2021 Christina Weis
Published under exclusive licence by Emerald Publishing Limited
doi:10.1108/978-1-83982-896-620211016

restrictions are eased, local as well as international demand for surrogacy in Russia will surge again. Regardless of the outcome of the bill and the reconfigurations of the global reproductive flows, commercial surrogacy will remain possible in Russia. Therefore, against the backdrop of the recent local and global developments, we need more empirically grounded analysis of the Russian surrogacy market and its actors to gain a better understanding of how it functions. This feminist ethnography, based on 15 months of on-site, face-to-face data collection and additional digital ethnography, is a pioneering contribution. With this work, I contribute in particular to the understanding of surrogacy from the perspectives and experiences of the women who offer their reproductive labour and make a living by making life. In this ethnography, I have shown how the reproductive labour of surrogacy is culturally framed and socially practiced as an economic exchange, and that it is permeated by intersecting reproductive stratifications, of which a surrogacy worker's ethnicity, citizenship, place of residence, and inclination and ability to travel or relocate for surrogacy play a major role. Furthermore, I have shown how distinctively different practises and understandings of surrogacy in Russia are from surrogacy practices and arrangements in other parts of the world.

Surrogacy workers in Russia do not question the morality of commercial surrogacy. Instead, they consider surrogacy a commendable act and opportunity to earn an income. They regard surrogacy as work, and as workers, entitled to adequate pay. This conception of themselves and their work distinguishes women in Russia from surrogates who enter commercial surrogacy arrangements in the United States and Israel and go a great length to downplay the importance of financial motivation and instead describe surrogacy as the ultimate gift and a labour of love (Berend, 2016b; Jacobson, 2016; Ragoné, 1994; Smietana, 2017; Teman, 2010). Furthermore, unlike in Gujarat, India, where Pande (2014b) describes surrogacy agents advising surrogates that business-mindedness is unwelcome – likewise in the United States where psychologists screen out women with overtly economic motivation (Smietana, 2017) – Russian agencies approved of surrogacy candidates' financial incentives. They maintained that financial motivation makes a better worker. I showed how clearly surrogacy workers in Russia elaborated that to them the children they are gestating as surrogates are not '*theirs*', but belonging to the client parents, and that therefore, they don't feel kinship bonds. This understanding stands in stark contrast to the kinship experience of women in South Asia, as demonstrated in ethnographic studies in India conducted by Rudrappa (2015), Majumdar (2017) and Pande (2014b), and by Whittaker (2016) in the context of Thailand. Analysing the relationships between surrogacy workers and their client parents during and after their arrangements, I show that in Russia, both the surrogacy workers and the client parents expect the relationship to be transient. The economic framing gives both parties defined responsibilities within their roles as 'employer' and 'employee', which they appreciate. Surrogacy workers in particular emphasised that they did not need or expect ongoing contact and a continued confirmation of their client parents' gratitude for their own satisfaction. Research in the United States and Israel in contrast found that surrogates regarded a cordial, lasting relationship as a marker of success as it affirmed them in having undertaken a labour of love and given a priceless gift: that of a child as well as that of parenthood (Teman, 2010). Client parents failing to recognise the dimension of the gift by letting the relationship fade or even terminating contact are, therefore, a cause for dissatisfaction and grief (Berend, 2014; Jacobson, 2016; Teman, 2010).

With regards to surrogacy workers' ethnic identity and how it shaped their experience of surrogacy, I have shown that in Russia, agencies and client parents shared the preference for ethnic Russian or Slavic women, and rejected and discounted the work ethos and integrity of women of Central Asian origin, due to racist preconceptions of their cleanliness and cultural suitability. In other words, the predominantly 'white' client parents preferred to reproduce their whiteness with the reproductive labour of 'white' surrogates. In the United States, and in most transnational surrogacy arrangements whereby client parents from the Global North travel to surrogacy destinations in the Global South, previous research has seen the opposite preference. As Harrison (2014, p.150) summarises the phenomenon: 'the raced body of the surrogate can be read as a text that marks her liminality both socially and legally; when a surrogate's skin color reflects the lack of genetic tie between herself and the child, this serves as "evidence" of the authentic connection between the child and its biological parent(s)'. Therefore, it serves to establish the client parents' parenthood and to dismiss the same from the surrogacy worker. Finally, another distinct feature of the social organisation of surrogacy in Russia is that it rests on and propels surrogacy workers to migrate or commute. To highlight these experiences and intrinsic differences, I have coined the terms 'migrant surrogacy workers' and 'commuting surrogacy workers' and analysed how their mobility exposes them to greater stratifications and risks, while at the same time giving them a financial disadvantage compared to women living and working as surrogates locally. As the global reproductive landscape is changing and increasingly becoming more fragmented (Weis, 2021; Whittaker, 2018; Whittaker, Inhorn, & Shenfield, 2019), we will continue to witness an increasing number of women migrating, commuting and crossing borders to perform reproductive labour, including becoming surrogacy workers – such as the Indian women going to Nepal to bear children for gay Israeli men, and the Kenyan women who were sent to India for embryo transfers and back to Kenya to give birth (Rudrappa, 2018). Turning our analysis to understanding the experiences of the travelling surrogacy workers is paramount. By extending Colen's (1995) conceptual framework of reproductive stratifications to include geographic and geo-political stratifications, I am offering two more lenses with which to further examine and analyse the reproductive stratification of surrogacy in Russia, and globally.

One of the core arguments of this book has been that surrogacy is stratified in multiple, intersecting ways. Surrogacy workers and client parents are from different socio-economic backgrounds. In every arrangement in my sample, client parents were financially well off, in secure, permanent employment, and able to afford spacious accommodation in often prosperous neighbourhoods, whereas surrogacy workers were often financially struggling and eager to improve their precarious situation and housing conditions. In other words, there was not a single arrangement whereby a woman of high(er) socio-economic standing offered her reproductive and emotional labour and her time to a person of a lower socio-economic strata. Ethnic stereotyping by commercial agencies and client parents led to ethnic stratifications among surrogacy workers that created a hierarchy of preference; the most favoured choices at the top of the hierarchy were Slavic Russian women, followed by other Slavic women, followed by Russian women from an ethnic minority and finally women of Central Asian origin. These ethnic stratifications make it harder for ethnic minority and Central Asian women to find surrogacy arrangements, or often compelled them to lower their financial compensation in order to compete with Russian and other Slavic surrogacy workers. Likewise, geographic stratifications impacted on surrogacy workers' earnings, as women who commuted or needed accommodation provision were paid less to offset costs while performing the same reproductive labour. Geopolitical stratifications added to these discount schemes. The ways in which the different forms of stratification intersect in women's experiences of carrying a commissioned surrogacy pregnancy in Russia vary, as do women's individual responses to the conditions that mark their experience. It is misleading to focus on which group experiences the most intensive stratifications when becoming a surrogacy worker. For some women, exactly the same the conditions that led to other women's experiences of stratification were enabling for them; mobility, in the form of commuting or re-locating, could be an opportunity to conceal the surrogacy arrangement or to use the surrogacy money as start-up capital in a new city. Some Central Asian women 'filled' a certain demand for Muslim women for the increasing numbers of client parents from countries with a Muslim population. These examples do not mitigate the intrinsic risk of exploitation when women in precarious living and working conditions offer their reproductive labour to commercial agencies or client parents who are at a material advantage, and therefore, when push comes to shove, legal advantage. Furthermore, racialised imaginaries permeate surrogacy as they do across the spectrum of assisted reproduction (Cromer, 2019; Moll, 2019; Nahman, 2013). It is, therefore, important to reiterate that surrogacy workers are not victims of an unjust system, but active players with courage, wit and skill (Ortner, 2006) in locally and globally stratified markets in reproductions. Global surrogacy remains one of the prime examples of stratified reproduction (Colen, 1995). As there are many ways of 'doing surrogacy', as emphasised in the very beginning of the book, every analysis needs to be situated within the local circumstances.

Another core argument of this book has been that surrogacy in Russia is culturally framed and socially organised as an economic exchange. And here I want to reiterate what I demonstrated throughout the book: that a simplified equation of 'surrogacy as a business transaction = a cold-hearted endeavour' would do gross injustice to surrogacy workers – and to client parents alike. The notion of surrogacy as an economic exchange is just one set of rules to guide the 'serious game' of surrogacy. The framings of surrogacy as a gift exchange or a labour of love (Berend, 2016b; Ragoné, 1999; Teman, 2010) are alternative framings – yet while they immediately trigger positive associations, the unvarnished commodification narrative causes discomfort. Yet in Russia, it is this framing of surrogacy as an economic exchange that provides surrogacy workers with a reference to make sense of their experience and that guides them through their arrangements; it teaches them to regard surrogacy work as transient and as much an economic opportunity as a morally appropriate act. The economic framing makes surrogacy arrangements no less emotional or intense. Regardless of the cultural framing, surrogacy remains women's immense embodied and emotional labour. Surrogacy workers conceive, carry and give birth – at the risk of their own life.

Where Do We Go from Here?

It is no longer enough to just list Russia as one of the countries where surrogacy arrangements are possible. Over the last decade, Russian surrogacy has established itself as an important player in the rapidly changing global reproductive landscapes. Regardless whether Russia will stay the 'reproductive paradise' or whether the government will curb the international market and restrict access, it is high time to take a closer look at the assisted reproductive service industry in Russia.

In Russia, the acceptance of surrogacy by doctors and politicians (as I have shown in chapter 1) is rooted in the notion that Russia's future lies in more children and in the cultural understanding that a woman's ideal self-realisation is that of a mother. The expansion of the services is therefore driven not only by local and international client parents seeking to achieve parenthood but also by proponents who regard surrogacy as the modern solution to both issues: overcoming involuntary childlessness and contributing to the growth of the Russian nation. As analysed in chapter 5, the concerns driving the proposed restrictions align with this understanding, as they are intending to keep surrogacy accessible for the people who the current government regards as 'the right kind of parents': heterosexual, married couples with residency.

Yet what about the surrogacy workers? Throughout the book, I have shown how many actors in surrogacy arrangements are only concerned about the rights and well-being of surrogacy workers when it contributes to a healthy pregnancy and successful birth of children: from the doctor who lamented the stress levels among precariously working and living mothers who turn to surrogacy and intermittent egg provision to make ends meet, to agencies accommodating migrant surrogacy workers in video-surveilled apartments, where their families have no or limited visitation permission and their welcome is over as soon as the next surrogacy worker's embryo transfer is scheduled, even if that means within a day or two of delivery. The calls for restrictions continue to disregard how conditions could be improved for surrogacy workers and what changes to the current practice would better protect their rights.

At a time when calls for international regulations of (transnational) surrogacy are getting louder, and while savvy, profit-oriented agents continue scoping out legal loopholes and permissive legislations to keep transnational surrogacy going, it is futile to keep arguing whether surrogacy is good or bad, empowering or exploitative. Instead, we need to centre those who do the work; any reform of surrogacy has to start with understanding and centring the needs of the surrogacy workers, and with improving their physical, mental and emotional health and well-being during and after the arrangement. To do so, we need to listen to their stories and acknowledge that their accounts hold the truth of their lived experience. Further, policymakers need to acknowledge that there is no one way of practising surrogacy, but that surrogacy practises are embedded in the local moral framework and local political governance (Smietana, Rudrappa, & Weis, 2021). Therefore, any reform also has to take local social practises and cultural framings into account. With this book, I am contributing to this effort that I demand by foregrounding the voices of Russia's surrogacy workers.

Appendix 1

Overview of Participants

Surrogacy Workers

	Name	Age at Beginning of Participation in Research	Form of Arrangement	Local/ Migrant/ Commuter	Number of Surrogacy Pregnancies and Other Information	Place of Origin[1]	Place of Surrogacy Arrangement and Birth	Date(s) of Recorded Interview(s)
1	Alexandra	28	Agency	Migrant	1	Orenburg	St. Petersburg (SPB)	December 2012 January 2013 August 2014 (Skype) August 2014 (Moscow)
2	Oksana	34	Agency	Local	5 embryo transfers (ET), 1 pregnancy	SPB	SPB	October 2012 January 2013 September 2014
3	Asenka	27	1st Agency 2nd Direct	Commuter	2	Kronstadt	SPB	August 2014
4	Rada	36	Direct	Commuter	3	Medvezhyegorsk, Republic of Karelia	SPB (1, 3) Moscow (2)	November 2012
5	Mila	29	Agency	Migrant	2	Brest, Belarus	SPB	September 2014

6	Svetlana	25	Direct	Commuter	1, preparing for 2nd	Belgorod	SPB	September 2014
7	Yuliana	28	Agency	Migrant	2 (twins in the first arrangement)	Kherson, Ukraine	SPB	September 2014
8	Marcella	32	Agency	Migrant	2 (triplets in the second arrangement)	Chisinau, Moldova	SPB	September 2012 September 2014
9	Kira	26	Agency	Migrant	1	Odessa, Ukraine	SPB	Ethnographic notes
10	Olesya	29	Agency	Local	1 miscarriage, preparing for next attempt	SPB	SPB	September 2014
11	Olya	34	Agency	Local	1	SPB	SPB	n/a
12	Galina	25	Agency	Migrant	1	Ukraine	SPB	Ethnographic notes
13	Inma	x	Agency	Local	1	SPB	SPB	Ethnographic notes
14	Anna	31	Agency	Local		SPB		December 2014 March 2015
15	Elisaveta	30	Direct	Local	2	SPB	SPB	November 2014

(Continued)

Name	Age at Beginning of Participation in Research	Form of Arrangement	Local/ Migrant/ Commuter	Number of Surrogacy Pregnancies and Other Information	Place of Origin[1]	Place of Surrogacy Arrangement and Birth	Date(s) of Recorded Interview(s)
16 Gabriela	31	Direct intended; Agency	Migrant	1 failed embryo transfer, 1 miscarriage	Hincesti, Moldova	SPB	April 2015 April 2015
17 Ilya	33	Direct	Commuter	3 (twins in first arrangement)	Yartsevo	SPB (1,3) Moscow (2)	November 2014
18 Zemfira	x	x	n/a	Preparing for surrogacy	Saratov	n/a	Ethnographic notes
19 Daria	32	Direct	Commuter	1, preparing for 2nd surrogacy	Kursk	SPB	November 2014
20 Gul'nur	x	Direct	Commuter	Preparing for surrogacy	Belorestk	Ufa	January 2015
21 Nadya	30	Direct	Commuter	1 (twins)	Medvezhyegorsk	SPB	November 2012
22 Katya	19	Direct	Commuter	Preparing for surrogacy	Moscow Oblast	Moscow	February 2015

#	Name	Age			Preparing for surrogacy			
23	Anyuta	27	Direct	n/a	Preparing for surrogacy	Odessa	n/a	February 2015
24	Alsu	20	Agency	Migrant	1	Ufa	SPB	n/a
25	Diana	25	Agency	Migrant	1	Vologda	SPB	May 2015
26	Ira	28	Direct	n/a	Preparing for surrogacy	Eastern Ukraine	Intended: Kiev	February 2015
27	Lyubov	28	Direct	Commuter	1	Leningrad Oblast	Luga	March 2015
28	Kristina	x	Agency	x	ET	x	SPB	Ethnographic notes
29	Tara	x	Direct	Commuter	1	Perm	Moscow	n/a
30	Inga	26	Direct	Local	Unsuccessful ET	SPB	SPB	October 2012
31	Karina	36	Direct	Commuter	2	Medvezhyegorsk	Moscow, SPB	December 2012 December 2012
32	Nyurguyaanax		Direct	Commuter	Preparing for surrogacy	Yakutsk	SPB	December 2012
33	Irina	x	Agency	Migrant	1	x	SPB	Ethnographic notes
34	Dasha	29	Direct	Commuter	1	Krasnodar	SPB	December 2012

(Continued)

Name	Age at Beginning of Participation in Research	Form of Arrangement	Local/ Migrant/ Commuter	Number of Surrogacy Pregnancies and Other Information	Place of Origin[1]	Place of Surrogacy Arrangement and Birth	Date(s) of Recorded Interview(s)
35 Ksenya	x	Agency	Local	1, preparing for 2nd surrogacy	SPB	SPB	December 2012
36 Lenya	x	Agency	Local	1, preparing for 2nd surrogacy	SPB	SPB	December 2012
37 Yuliya	24	Agency	Commuter	2 unsuccessful ET, stops trying	Tikhvin	SPB	October 2012
38 Vera	35	Agency	Local	1 pregnancy, miscarriage in the 2nd	SPB	SPB	October 2012
39 Ksyusha	x	Direct	x	1 pregnancy	x	x	n/a
40 Anina	x	x	x	ET	x	SPB	n/a

[1]To assure anonymity and confidentiality, I have changed the origin of some surrogacy workers to nearby towns.

Client Parents

Name	Age at Beginning of Participation in Research	Agency/ Direct	Rounds of Surrogacy Pregnancy/ Miscarriage	Children through Surrogacy	Place of Pregnancy/Birth	Date of Recorded Interview(s)
1 Katarina	36	D	2	2	SPB	October 2011 August 2014
2 Anastasia	34	D	4 attempts (1 miscarriage, 1 abortion)	2	Pregnancy at surrogacy worker's home, birth in Chelyabinsk	October 2011 November 2011 (via email)
3 Aleksey (husband of Anastasia)	x	D	4 attempts (1 miscarriage, 1 abortion)	2	Pregnancy at surrogacy worker's home, birth in Chelyabinsk	n/a
4 Lyuba	40s	D	1	Surrogacy worker pregnant at time of interview	SPB	October 2011
5 Pawel	28	A	Preparing for surrogacy	none	SPB	January 2012
6 Evgenya	54	D	Miscarriage	No children through surrogacy, but a child from previous IVF cycle	SPB	October 2014

(Continued)

Name	Age at Beginning of Participation in Research	Agency/ Direct	Rounds of Surrogacy Pregnancy/ Miscarriage	Children through Surrogacy	Place of Pregnancy/Birth	Date of Recorded Interview(s)
7 Nadezhda	32	D	1	1	SPB	November 2014 November 2014 April 2015 May 2015
8 Arkady (husband of Nadezhda)	33	D	1	1	SPB	n/a
9 Yana	40s	D	3 failed attempts with 3 surrogacy workers	0	SPB	February 2015
10 Matvey	60s	A	1	1	SPB	February 2015
11 Gulya	x	x	x	x	SPB	n/a

Agency Staff

	Name	Role	Agency	Location	Date of Recorded Interview(s)
1	Malvina	Owner/ manager	Happy Baby	SPB	December 2012
2	Eliza	Owner/ manager	Happy Baby	SPB	January 2012
3	Ala	Secretary	Happy Baby	SPB	September 2014
4	Vitali	Legal advisor	Happy Baby	SPB	September 2014
5	Veronica	Owner/ manager	Growing Generations	SPB	August 2012 September 2012 November 2012 September 2014
6	Taisiya	Owner/ manager	Precious Gift	SPB	Ethnographic notes
7	Alyona	Secretary	Precious Gift	SPB	Ethnographic notes
8	Ira	Representative	Precious Gift	Moscow	Ethnographic notes
9	Vladimir	Press spokesman	Precious Gift	Moscow	Ethnographic notes
10	Mirela	Owner/ manager	Wonderchild	SPB	Ethnographic notes
11	Anya	Secretary	Wonderchild	SPB	Ethnographic notes
12	Alexander	Owner/ manager	Promise	SPB	September 2014 March 2014 January 2019 June 2019 November 2019 April 2020
13	Elena	Secretary	Promise	SPB	September 2014
14	Sveta	Representative	Mobile Surrogacy	Moscow	January 2015
15	Igor	Country representative	Sensible Surrogacy	SPB	November 2014

(Continued)

Name	Role	Agency	Location	Date of Recorded Interview(s)
16 Grigory	Lawyer/owner	Surrogacy Exclusive	SPB/ Moscow	August 2014
17 Dr Boris	IVF specialist	Surrogacy Exclusive	SPB	October 2012
18 Nikita	Lawyer	Surrogacy Exclusive	SPB	October 2012
19 Natalia	Secretary	Surrogacy Exclusive	SPB	November 2012

Medical Staff

Name	Role	Medical Unit	Location	Date of Recorded Interview(s)
1 Dr Vladislav	Head of clinic	SPB Fertility Unit	SPB	September 2012
2 Dr Natalia	IVF specialist	SPB Fertility Unit	SPB	September 2012
3 Dr Irina	IVF specialist	SPB Fertility Unit	SPB	Ethnographic notes
4 Dr Andrey	Head embryologist, IVF specialist	NewLife Fertility	SPB	September 2012 November 2012 August 2014
5 Dr Dimitri	Owner of clinic, IVF specialist	Radiant Creation	SPB	October 2012
6 Dr Victoria	IVF specialist	Radiant Creation	SPB	October 2019
7 Dr Pawel	IVF specialist	Fertility Centre	SPB	September 2012
8 Dr Nikolai	IVF specialist	Our Children Fertility Clinic	SPB	October 2014

(Continued)

Name	Role	Medical Unit	Location	Date of Recorded Interview(s)
9 Dr Feotistov	IVF specialist	Our Children Fertility Clinic	SPB	December 2012
10 Dr Natali	IVF specialist	Human Reproduction Centre	SPB	Ethnographic notes
11 Dr Danila	IVF specialist	Urban Fertility Clinic	SPB	October 2014
12 Dr Alexey	IVF specialist	Urban Fertility Clinic	SPB	October 2014
13 Dr Igor	IVF specialist	Ocean Fertility Centre	SPB	October 2012
14 Dr Vladislav	IVF specialist	Family Centre	SPB	November 2014
15 Dr Nicola	IVF specialist	Global Fertility Clinic	SPB	September 2012
16 Rita	Former IVF nurse	European Fertility Centre	SPB	September 2014
17 Dr Ivan	Psychologist	Maternity Ward D	SPB	November 2014
18 Dr Elvina	Senior Obstetrician	Maternity Ward D	SPB	November 2014
19 Dr Vasili	Obstetrician	Maternity Ward D	SPB	November 2014

Appendix 2

Notes on Research Relationships

In this appendix, I share my fieldnotes and personal reflections on meeting surrogacy workers for the first time and establishing research relationships in order to give a more detailed insight into my recruitment experiences and challenges. When conducting an ethnography, scoping for participants and learning how to best approach and recruit potential participants is, in fact, part of the ethnography, as the researcher is learning about their respective research site, the dynamics of existing relationships between people who might become participants and put quite simply, the 'do's and don'ts'. Furthermore, these account provide a further insight into the demographics of surrogacy workers in Russia.

In the following, I give seven examples of meeting surrogacy workers in St. Petersburg. These examples include recruitment via agencies, medical gatekeepers and posting online advertisement, and are taken from both research visits in 2012/2013 and 2014/2015.

Galina

Fieldnotes, October 2014

Galina, 25 years old, is from the Ukraine and a first-time surrogacy worker. Today is the appointment for the embryo transfer. Agreeing to meet me, we were introduced by her embryologist prior to her embryo transfer at the clinic. After introducing myself, I told her that I have been to Ukraine a few times, to the capital Kiev, and in the south west to L'viv and Chernovtsy. She replied that she would have liked to travel, but never had the chance. Aged 25 when we met, Galina is married and already has two children. She asked about my husband and children, and I told her that I am neither married nor have children. She replied: 'You Western girls marry late and get lots of education. Not like us girls from the Ukraine'. And I answered: 'Yes, indeed, I am one of those Western girls that go for education instead of children'.

Today wasn't a good day for an interview, as she could have been called in for her embryo transfer anytime, and I did not want to simply use the minutes spent with her in the waiting room to get as much out of her as possible either. I offered to meet at any time later this week or the coming week. She agreed to meet but hesitated to suggest where. Though she has moved to St Petersburg four months ago, together with her family, she isn't familiar with the city and still feels lost taking the metro on her own. After the appointment today she was picked up by the agency's driver, who brought her to the clinic earlier, to be taken home. Before she was called in for her appointment, she told me she is from the Donbass and that 'I am here because of the war' – the armed conflict that flared up in the eastern part of the Ukraine in 2014 between pro-Russian separatists and pro-government forces, which displaced thousands of civilians. She moved to Russia with her family to escape the war. Becoming a surrogacy worker is motivated by the need to quickly make money to support her family in St Petersburg, where rent and living costs are much higher than in the Donbass.

My notes of my short encounter and the few minutes of the hushed conversation between me and Galina in a corner of the clinic's waiting room quickly show that, besides being of similar age and both women, we had little else in common. Unlike her and the other surrogacy workers, I have never been pregnant and have no children. Holding a German passport, I was able to travel easily and freely without having to take many visa restrictions into consideration, and because I was supported by government funding and scholarships, I was able to pursue higher education. By bringing up my travels to the Ukraine, I looked for a shared experience with Galina, but it only highlighted our differences further.

Realising that such varying degrees of social separation may pose a risk of distrust between the researcher and participants (see also Emmel, Hughes, Greenhalgh, & Sales, 2007), going forward I adopted a more careful strategy of often downplaying stark differences, such as education, and instead emphasising on my true interest in their experience and knowledge on pregnancy and surrogacy, and my desire to learn through their accounts and from their expertise – while striking a balance between being honest about my background and answering any questions they had.

Kira

I met Kira, a 26-year-old single mother from the south of Ukraine, by chance in an agency car in September 2014. Following the unexpected and spontaneous offer of an agency to catch a lift and be shown around the surrogacy apartments at the edge of St. Petersburg by the agency's driver, Kira was already sitting in the front seat as I got in. She had just been picked up from the hospital where she had given birth three days earlier and had been waiting in the car when the driver dropped in at the agency and was given the task to take me with him.

Confronted with my presence and taken by surprise that the driver had started to tell me about her without asking for her consent or even involving in her conversation, she sat silent, staring out of the window. Uncomfortable with his disregard over Kira's obvious discomfort, I tried to lead the driver towards different topics, asking him about his role in the organisation. After several minutes' drive, he parked the car to run another errand, 'Won't be long!' he shouted as he left us with the motor running. The very moment he left, Kira spun around on her seat, questions pouring out of her: Who am I?

Why am I interested in surrogacy? Why in Russia? What have I done before? Do I like it here? Once she was satisfied with my answers, she began telling me about her experience, without a prompt on my side, but went quiet as soon as we could see the driver returning. She remained silent until we reached the destination.

Walking through the gates, the driver directed rather than asked Kira to show me around compound as he busied himself with her luggage. Inside, Kira ushered me into her very own (and too small for me) turquoise fluffy house shoes and led me upstairs to her room. She pointed out the soft carpet, the large windows, the shelf with knickknacks, the double bed with the colourful throw, the flat screen TV and most importantly, the fact of it being her own room. 'I had never had a room of my own before! At home I first shared with my brother, and then with my daughter. I felt like princess here!'

I was unable to interview her on that day, even though she was keen to do so, because the driver stayed present and monitored our interaction. Unfortunately, neither was I able to interview her before she left return to the Ukraine a few days later, nor to arrange to interview her over Skype. She had no computer or reliable Internet connection in her home village in southern Ukraine.

Oksana

Like Galina, I met Oksana (34) in the waiting room of a fertility clinic. She had agreed to meet me after being approached by her agency's manager, and together we had agreed that the first meeting and introduction would happen via her manager and take place at a monitoring appointment prior to her embryo transfer. On the day, I arrived ahead of time, and so had she. In fact, I had sat down next to her, not knowing who she was, while waiting for the manager to arrive. But before the manager arrived, Oksana had taken the initiative to tap me on the shoulder and asked whether I am Christina, 'the foreign woman who wanted to meet her' – my style of clothing had given her the idea it might be me, and she was curious to meet and share her surrogacy experience with me.

Oksana is one of the few surrogacy workers who contributed to my research and understanding of surrogacy work over several years: from our first meeting in the clinic that October 2012 during my first research visit, throughout my second research visit, to occasional messages over social media while writing up my PhD. During that time, she experienced several failed embryo transfers, an early miscarriage, one successful surrogacy pregnancy and the process of considering whether to try again, driven by financial needs.

Fieldnotes from accompanying her to her fourth embryo transfer (an exception granted by her agency upon the client parents' request) in January 2013 read:

Oksana is nervous. She is tired after a troubled night with little sleep caused by tormenting headaches which she attributes to the hormones she has been taking. I see her swollen red eyes and the worry lines on her forehead.

It is the morning of her fourth, and final, embryo transfer. Oksana is worried whether she will get pregnant, or whether the transfer will be unsuccessful, like the first and third time, or whether, and even worse, she might miscarry as she did with the second transfer. It happened early, in the sixth week, but she felt devastated. Another failure would ultimately mean being dismissed from the surrogacy programme and she would find herself in more financial difficulties and in a worse situation than before, when opting for surrogacy seemed a promising solution. It would also mean that for over a year, she would have juggled informal employment, making herself available for the appointments and going through the hormone treatment, all while hiding her surrogacy attempts from her social circle, for no gain, but only loss.

This fourth time, Oksana got pregnant and stayed pregnant. I wasn't in Russia when she delivered. But we met again, in September 2014, a year after she had given birth, and she insisted on me recording her story. It was a hot day and we sat outside, in a backyard under tall trees. After telling me about her long, difficult delivery, she lit a cigarette. 'During the pregnancy I didn't drink and didn't smoke! At all! I also didn't want to. But then problems started, and I started again'. The problems she referred to were related to her agency that withheld half of her payment at the end, not because she had committed any transgressions, but because her agency manager had mismanaged money and, without knowing anyone she could turn to, all Oksana could do was fret over whether she would ever be paid or whether she was being cheated. After sitting for a while in silence, looking at the first autumn colours in the trees, she said with a tired voice:

> It was difficult! Kristinika, it was very difficult to give up the child. I didn't think it would be so difficult, I didn't expect it. But it turned out to be so difficult – first the birth, they told me I'd be giving birth quickly, but it took longer, it took 5 hours. And then I was crying – everybody around me has a child, and I am lying in my room all alone, the TV wasn't working. It was – difficult, difficult. I usually don't tell this to anyone.
>
> (September 2014)

After those words, we sat together in silence for a while. Then, Oksana added 'I guess I am lucky I am too old to be considered a second time': having exceeded the age limit of 35 to become a surrogacy worker relieved her of making the decision.

Ilya

I met Ilya (33), a three-times surrogacy worker, who lived in a small town near Smolensk close to the Belarusian border, for the first time in November 2014. The setting was a clinic in St. Petersburg during one of her early pregnancy scans. Her client parents Nadezhda (32) and Arkady (33) had been introduced to me by their doctor after giving their informed consent, and asked Ilya on my behalf; Ilya agreed to be introduced to me, and following that, Ilya and Nadezhda offered to stay back after the embryo transfer to give me a first interview, whereas Arkady excused himself and left.

For Ilya, this was her third and last surrogacy pregnancy, and like in her previous surrogacy pregnancies, she commuted to St. Petersburg on a regular basis for appointments, and when she did, she stayed with the client parents. For Nadezhda, this was her first surrogacy attempt after surviving cancer. She was using her sister's eggs – a secret which was supposed to stay within the family. Over the course of my research period in St. Petersburg, both women offered me the opportunity to join their medical appointments when feasible, gave series of interviews and answered my questions over social media channels. I became a consistent part of their surrogacy experience. On one particular occasion in January 2015, I was invited to a monitoring ultrasound. Ilya had just arrived on a 17-hour-overnight train from Smolensk. The receptionist wasn't pleased with three women showing up for an appointment that was scheduled for one, but Ilya took charge and stated matter-of-factly that it just is how it is. 'My friends are coming in with me'. Likewise the doctor expressed her discontent, saying that the examination room was too small for such a 'caravan of support', but Ilya, without hesitation, walked us in and replied again that 'that's how it is'. While the doctor checked her details, Ilya began stripping down, first her tights, then her knickers and went over to the examination bench. When the doctor asked her whether it was her first child, my assumptions were confirmed: the doctor wasn't aware of the surrogacy arrangement and our respective roles. Ilya presented herself as the mother, and she played her role excellently. Sitting next to me, Nadezhda played her role as an excited friend as she watched the image of her baby on the screen, and I felt so relieved that I had followed my earlier gut feeling to not take out my fieldnotes diary. After the appointment, we went for lunch at a Chinese chain restaurant and Ilya insisted on paying with the free vouchers she had brought for the occasion.

A year after the child's birth, I received a surprise message from Nadezhda sending me a picture of her child and a big birthday cake.

Anina

In December 2012, I met Anina, a surrogacy worker in her early 20s, and Gulya, the client mother, in a fertility centre prior to an appointment. The meeting was arranged by a doctor with whom I had agreed the protocol to inform me when surrogacy workers were scheduled for appointment to be present and available in the waiting room. The doctor would inform the women about my research prior to or during their appointment, and if they agreed on meeting, he would introduce me. If women disagreed, they could leave anonymously. On this day in December 2012, the waiting room was unusually crowded as the doctor accompanied two women to the waiting room and indicated with a nod in my direction that it was me who he told them about. I guessed their respective identity as surrogacy worker and client mother by their clothing, age and behaviour. Once the doctor retreated, the client mother took charge and refused my suggestion to retreat to the quieter and more privacy-offering waiting area on the second floor. Instead, Gulya first ushered Anina to sit down on the couch and then gestured me to join them. I squeezed myself next to them. Our hips were pressing against each other, and to create a more intimate space, we hunched our backs and turned towards each other. The three of us sitting so unpleasantly close, and we could feel each other's breath in our faces, resulted in exactly what I intended to avoid: the curious attention of the other people in the waiting room. In an attempt to resolve this situation, I suggested in a low voice to postpone my questions. To my surprise, Anina shook her head, and then, with a nod demanded me to begin. My unease was growing with every second, but I felt that I couldn't just get up and leave, and so in an almost toneless whisper, I introduced myself and my research interest. In the very moment I said 'surrogate motherhood', Anina uttered a groan and flinched. Then she murmured, with a tremble in her voice: 'Everybody is looking at me already!' I felt guilty of putting her in this situation, and then, without a further word, slid to a newly empty seat away from both women, took out my phone and pretended to be busy. Anina moved away from Gulya and stared at the ground. The minutes leading up to her appointment passed excruciatingly slowly.

Looking back, it was obvious that Anina had not been comfortable with being exposed as a surrogacy worker to me when asked by the doctor. It is most likely the case that she did not feel comfortable to speak up about it in the presence of the client mother.

Uncomfortable transgressions like this happen in ethnographic research and research with gatekeepers. I have chosen to share this story to draw attention to them, so we can continue to prepare ourselves to learn from such experiences. In my case, I changed my recruitment approach (Weis, 2019).

Lyubov

I recruited Lyubov via one of my online recruitment calls on one of the surrogacy forums in March 2015. She was six months pregnant when we met and so it wasn't difficult to recognise her as she met at the train station of the 'electrichka', the suburban train, from where we walked to a nearby restaurant that she picked. She was in a cheerful mood and on the way told me that her two young children were at home, sleeping, and her husband was looking after them. When I asked her what motivated her to answer my ad, she replied that she liked talking to people and getting out, and that the latter didn't happen too often now that she was pregnant and tending to two toddlers. And meeting me was a bonus: not only did she have a reason to leave the house and her children with her husband for a research interview, but I was a foreigner, and she was curious to meet a foreigner.

Olesya

I was introduced to Olesya (29), a local to St. Petersburg, married and a mother of two, by her embryologist on the day of her embryo transfer appointment in September 2014. Retreating to a second, more private waiting room, I explained my research intentions to her, and Olesya expressed her interest and curiosity to participate. As her client mother and an agency staff member were also present at the clinic on that day, Olesya gave me her home address and phone number to contact her to meet and talk in private.

A week later, after enjoying a bowl of mushroom soup (prepared by her from mushrooms collected by her and her children), I recorded our first interview and from then on accompanied Olesya and her client mother Evgenya to their routine pregnancy checks. Between the appointments, Olesya and I stayed in touch over vkontakte, a Russian online social network. After two more medical appointments and many informal messages, Olesya asked me, 'So have you even been to a birth?', and upon my response that I haven't yet been to a surrogacy birth, invited me to attend hers. Then a few weeks later, she miscarried (see Appendix 3 for more details). After a couple of days, she wrote to inform me that she would try again in a few months and hoped I would still be in Russia to accompany her again.

On February 2015, Olesya and I met for her second embryo transfer. For her second attempt, her agency had matched her with new client parents who, to Olesya's dissatisfaction, had no intention to meet her in person or even be in contact via the agency. Coming to terms with the disappointment she asked me 'but you *are* joining me again to the other appointments, should I get pregnant, right? Your presence is permitted there! With you, it is more fun, and less scary'. Again, as with her first pregnancy, I accompanied Olesya to her appointment and stayed in regular contact. Several times she confirmed that she enjoyed being part of a research project and that she took pride in contributing to knowledge. It was a severe disappointment for both us when in April 2015, a few weeks before my research visited ended, a misunderstanding and miscommunication between the gynaecologist, the agency and Olesya and me severed my research access.

On April 2015, stuck in traffic, I was running late to an appointment and texted Olesya to let her know. Olesya, with the best intentions in mind, asked her gynaecologist to wait a few minutes. Her gynaecologist, however, called Olesya's agency to enquire who she was supposed to wait for and by the time I arrived, an agency worked had called Olesya and made a scene over the phone. 'She called me and lashed out at me!' Olesya then called back the number who called her, handed me the phone and while it was ringing instructed me 'Ask why she is against it, and even prohibits your visits if the director has given your her permission and I myself permit you to come along'. Ala, the secretary who answered the phone call, was in a rage as she heard my voice. She accused me of betraying Olesya by pretending to be a medical doctor. Olesya, who could hear the whole conversation, took back the phone and explained calmly that she had always been aware of me being a social scientist working on my doctoral degree – but after the call we sadly agreed for me to no longer come to any appointments so as to avoid risking any punishment for Olesya in form of payment cuts. Olesya immediately offered to keep me updated via text messages and still wanted to give a final interview before I left Russia in May 2015, but then had to withdraw her offer a few days later. She explained 'They are forbidding me to talk to anyone about anything regarding the pregnancy from now on, including my experience and my opinion'.

Appendix 3

Emotion Work

In this appendix, I share two distinct experiences of emotion work 'in the field'. I chose to share this personal and intimate account as genuine as possible in order to allow students in particular to gain an insight behind the scenes of published research and to encourage them to work with (their) emotions in research.

The first example is an account of participant observation during a surrogacy worker's control appointment that revealed that she had miscarried.

The second example are notes from my personal diary during fieldwork about feeling the emotional impact, cultivating working with my own emotions in research and learning to apply self-care, with all the setbacks and challenges it brought.

Liminality of the Researcher's Role

Fieldnotes, October 2014

Today I accompanied surrogacy worker Olesya and client mother Evgenya to their routine pregnancy check-up. It was the seventh week of Olesya's surrogacy pregnancy and today they wanted to measure the heartbeat, and Evgenya wanted to record it for her husband. During the previous appointment, the doctor was slightly dissatisfied with the embryonic development.

When I join these gynaecological check-ups, Olesya and Evgenya see in me the 'professional', the researcher. It seems to me that this role makes it easier for them to grant me access to these intimate moments, from the 20min gyn check up to their surrogacy experience at large. Joining for a third time, we have established a routine. In the examination room my presence is both acknowledged and subsequently overlooked as the attention turns to the examination. Mute, discreet and unobtrusive, I am in a corner, observing and listening, and recording my fieldnotes in my worn diary.

As the doctor started the examination, I was startled that she did not say a single word to either of us, unlike before. The soft clicking of the computer mouse and the peeping when taking measures of the ultrasound image on the screen felt ominous against the radio in the background. I could see the screen from where I stood (an angle I had chosen carefully to see the screen, but not be looking at or between Olesya's spread legs; this early on, the doctor took a transvaginal ultrasound.). The large black dot on the screen – the gestational sac – should not be solely black. It looked different to other images I had seen before. I began biting my lip. My heart was growing heavy as my throat tied up. I felt my blood pumping and reluctance to continue writing. Seconds in silence passed cruelly slowly. I had already understood what had happened, yet refused to acknowledge it: Olesya had miscarried, the embryo had stopped growing. Only the hormones that Olesya kept taking, the dosage of which the doctor had increased in the previous consultation, had prevented her body from having a natural spontaneous abortion.

The radio now played 'This land is your land, this land is my land' into the silence.

'No heartbeat, sorry', the doctor finally spoke. Her voice was factual. It carried no empathy. 'Where it was [last week], there it has remained' – she referred to the embryo growth. Notebook and pen felt awkward in my hand, too big, misplaced. I wished both would disappear. A split second later, I wished I would feel comfortable to continue writing to escape the scene, to take refuge in looking at the scene instead of being in it. Barely having finished that thought, I condemned myself for it, feeling a hot rush of embarrassment for being concerned about that amidst the news and their significance for Olseya and Evgenya. I was embarrassed for the intuitive wish to not be present. Nobody was saying a word and I was trying to think of something to say, something reasonable, or something comforting, but my brain refused to come up with anything sensible. I didn't want to anticipate such an event, I had not rehearsed what to say, in Russian. But I would not have known what to say in such a situation in German or English either.

'That is bad, right?' Evgenya's fearful question pierced the silence. She clinged to hope that her question would be denied. Then she burst into tears and rushed out of the room. The time kept crawling while the doctor completed the ultrasound report.

I looked at Olesya. She looked at me. Neither the doctor nor Evgenya had addressed her at all, and so she continued lying on her back with the ultrasound transducer inserted in her vagina. Throughout the examination she had not been spoken to or had said a word. Even though it was her who nourished the embryo, it was the black spot in the screen that everyone paid attention to.

Finally, the doctor had finished her examination. Only after Olesya had gotten up and was getting dressed, the doctor turned her attention to her and instructed her to stop taking the hormones and, if she was not going to have a natural abortion, arrange for a curettage. As Evgenya re-entered, eyes red from crying, cheeks flushed, the doctor explained that it was unlikely Olesya's fault that the pregnancy failed. Olesya began to cry. 'I just wanted to help someone, but instead' – but I could not understand her words in the sobbing.

After leaving the premises, we remained for a moment in front of the doors. I finally found words to express my empathy, and sadness over their loss. Olesya and Evgenya avoided looking at each other. Without any frozen embryos left, the sudden end of the pregnancy also marked the end of Evgenya's and Olesya's relationship. Without looking at her, Evgenya told Olesya that their agency would be in touch regarding finalising pay. Then the time had come to depart. In the past two visits, I took the metro with Evgenya as we have a similar journey home, but today I didn't feel like joining her or taking the metro. I cringed at the thought of descending underground and sitting crammed in a stuffy compartment with strangers and a crying woman, whose pain was breaking my heart. I also felt that Olesya might need my company more, so I indicated Evgenya that I needed to head in another direction. After Evgenya had left, Oleysa asked me where I was going and joined me. I knew that the direction I had chosen at random was not where Olesya lives. After a few steps, at first haltingly, then with growing confidence, she started recalling the examination, and her thoughts and feelings about surrogacy, and her concerns and reservations about trying again. And I listened, not with the ear of an anthropologist, but as a confidante.

On this day, during the visit at the doctor, witnessing the miscarriage and upon leaving, I faced two challenges: to reconcile the different roles of being a researcher and a confidante, and choosing whose confidante and support person to be. I realised that in order to be true to myself and to what I felt was the right thing to do, I had to step across the threshold from the boundaried role of the professional researcher that comes with professional detachment into accepting the responsibility of having entered into relationships with my participants, and in this case, Olesya in particular.

Venting Frustration and Practicing Self-care

Emotion Diary Fieldnotes, 14 October 2014

'It's exhausting, the "noes". "No!" here, "No." there... all those shades of "no": "Ne chotchet [she doesn't want to]" – "Nel'zya [you're not allowed]" – "Ne vozmozhno [it is not possible]" – or my [attention: irony!] favourite: laughing at me and hanging up on me on the phone. That is pretty obviously also a "no" – though I would rather have had a "no" than be laughed at and hung up upon.

"Knocking on doors" all over again is exhausting, investing energy and hope, keeping a positive attitude and a smile – even when all I get are sour looks and I am left to swallow up my disappointment yet again. I have to keep smiling and stay friendly and polite when my conversation partner is neither friendly, nor polite, nor even trying.

The uncertainty of success, or reward, is exhausting. Do those who say yes really mean it? And how long will their promise last? Every unanswered phone call triggers the thought they have had enough – but often they were just busy.

My feelings veer toward apprehension – and I turn it into pressure to perform better.

I have stopped counting the hours I have sat in a waiting room to not be informed that an appointment has been moved or cancelled, or that the doctor forgot about me and the surrogacy worker had left.

I cannot show my frustration – neither to the representatives of the agencies I approach nor to the receptionists of clinics if I want to get access and get through to a doctor with actual authority.

I feel I cannot show it – so I don't allow myself to show it! Not even to my friends'.

This emotional record of frustration and exhaustion opened my emotion diary three months into my fieldwork. My energies were drained; the immersion not only into surrogacy but also into the Russian language was challenging (and besides Russian, I was also speaking Dutch at the Netherlands Institute where I had a workspace, English when recording my fieldnotes, Romanian for communicating with the Moldovan surrogacy workers and German with family back home), and as winter approached, sunlight dwindled. Even though incidents of being denied access to research sites, or having access granted and then revoked, participants agreeing to an interview but then not answering my call or not showing up without notice were unrelated, they were cumulative, and I struggled to not perceive them as professional or even personal failures. The process of gatekeeping I had worked out with medical professionals in order to meet surrogacy workers – coming to appointments, making myself available by waiting in the waiting room and being introduced by the gatekeeper after their appointment if they agreed – resulted in countless visits and hours waiting in medical practices in vain as many women declined, or gatekeepers forgot about me in the hectic schedule. Often, I wouldn't know the reason for an unsuccessful visit.

In the first weeks of fieldwork during my second research visit in 2014/2015, when I was benefitting from revived social networks and was in the first rush of excitement of conducting fieldwork again, paying attention to my well-being did not seem important yet. When I started interviewing, transcribing, translating and writing ethnographic fieldnotes, I failed to allot time for these 'emotional reflections' aside from rants and comments in correspondence with friends. My days were busy and, returning home late, I wanted and needed 'time off'. Unintentionally, because I was negligent in cultivating a functioning and supportive habit of recording and reflecting on my emotions, I employed the opposite strategy from the one I intended; instead of engaging with my feelings towards 'my field' and research participants, especially the unpleasant or unwanted, I shoved them aside in order to rest.

Yet after almost three months of fieldwork, I experienced a key moment that helped dissolve the blockage that I had erected to protect myself and profoundly changed that attitude.

The trigger for me to face my frustrations came during a late evening walk with a friend and colleague after a long day filled with interviewing and writing up fieldnotes. Both of us had been working late and left our desks only to catch the last metro home. It wasn't the first time that we had left together, and we had cultivated the habit of conversing in German so that my friend could practice. That day, however, my friend said she was tired and her 'brain would not produce any German'. Though I offered to stick to her native Dutch, we trod along in silence, our necks tucked tightly between hunched shoulders in the cold, listening to the crunching of gravel under our shoes as we crossed the park. Then my friend picked up our conversation again – in English, 'Don't you feel just knackered sometimes as well?' With a huge sigh of relief, I replied 'Yes!'

I had been asked the well-intended question, 'Is your research progressing well?' a lot, and I usually confirmed that it was, even when it wasn't or when I would rather have complained about all the difficulties and frustrations. But, on the one hand, I felt I had brought the troubles and challenges onto myself by choosing to return to Russia and to surrogacy research and, therefore, restrained myself from complaining, which I perceived as showing weakness, and on the other hand, I didn't expect complaining to bring about a change. That evening my friend's readiness to share her vulnerability, prompted me to share mine and marked the turning point. From the park to my stop at the metro station, I vented my frustrations about all the things and people that ticked me off, my weariness at incessant rejections, my emotional exhaustion and my struggles with the winter darkness. And when I got home, I started writing about it. This is how I started my personal emotion diary. The quote above is the very first entry.

I began to record the numerous feelings triggered by my research: anger over the structural power imbalance to the disadvantage of the surrogacy workers; sadness and worries over miscarriages; anxiety over not doing enough research or not getting (good) enough data; joy over 'all-clear signals' that a pregnancy is no longer at risk, as well as successful births; and guilt for not knowing how to reciprocate more to my participants. Yet, while I was beginning to work with the emotions that the conversations and observations with participants triggered, I still had to learn a healthy way to engage with them. Although the initial step of recording my feelings was a way to vent frustration, it also meant longer 'work hours' to accommodate the additional note taking. In other words. working with the emotions triggered by my research wasn't the only lesson to learn. Like in any fieldwork, the dynamics of the field were unpredictable and made making my own plans – including 'time off' – a venture in vain. Appointments with surrogacy workers could not be planned more than a few days in advance, and were often at the risk of last minute cancellations, which I was sometimes informed of only when I arrived at the clinic or enquired after an hour of waiting, knowing that delays also tended to happen. With surrogacy workers, all kinds of eventualities came up that postponed or ruled out their attending an interview; the major ones included hospitalisation and miscarriages. Regularly, medical gatekeepers notified me of an appointment and meeting/recruitment opportunity with only an hour's notice, whereby agency staff – possibly as a way to consciously demonstrate their power and maintain a hierarchical setting – allowed themselves to cancel, come late, leave earlier or interrupt interviews by taking one phone call after another. In one particular incident, an agency manager answered three different phone calls and transacted an egg donation arrangement in the half hour she had allotted to me after weeks of negotiations for the interview appointment. To accommodate the unpredictability, I made myself available at all times, which put a lot of pressure and stress on me.

By the end of November, I had (emotionally) overworked myself. The emotions I had accumulated began to have a physical impact on me. It came in form of sleeplessness, physical exhaustion, loss of appetite, feeling leaden as if every move demanded an effort and suddenly being overcome by feelings of immense sadness and (for a week) unpredictable and unpreventable moments of crying. My body forced me to acknowledge what my mind had stubbornly ignored. My energies drained, I experienced what Everhart (1977, p. 13) called 'fieldwork fatigue', or the onset of a burnout.

The week that I experienced uncontrollable crying, I undertook a solo trip to Kavgolovo Lake, a few miles north of St. Petersburg (Fig. A3.1). Walking over the lake's frozen surface under a grey, misty sky, no sound was audible but the whisper of the wind sweeping soft layers of powered snow. Here, at − 10°, and with only the hunched figures of ice fishers on the horizon, my loneliness felt palpable. Confronting the reality that I had not told anybody where I had gone, I realised that it was nobody else's responsibility but mine to take care of myself and ensure my safe return. That thought energised me. By finally fully acknowledging not only the need of, but also entitlement to self-care, and my own responsibility to do that, I put this principle in action: caring research means not only caring for the research participants but also caring for oneself. Physical self-care and coping strategies meant accepting an increased need for sleep, good food and relaxation. I made time for regular visits to the *banya,* the Russian steam sauna, more yoga practice and for any extra moment I could spend in the sun (Fig. A3.2). In addition, I decided to take the risk of missing an opportunity for an interview by leaving the research sites for a day or two to gain the advantage of returning rested and with new drive and ideas. Emotional self-care involved positively censoring who I talked to about the challenges this fieldwork posed to me. Tired of justifying why I 'put myself through this' or why 'it concerned/affected me', I shared my emotional response only with those from who offered support and encouragement, and who I knew would not worry about me or doubt my abilities to emerge from this 'trial': local friends, friends far away and my supervisors. That helped me to get over the feelings of shame over 'failing' and the worry of not being professional, and to acknowledge my emotional response as an integral part of a research project that comprised hopes and desperation, risky pregnancies, miscarriages, inherent power inequalities and power abuse, challenges to my personal values through racist, sexist and homophobic narratives, compassion, confusion and empathy. In addition, I continued recording, observing and reflecting on my emotional responses to let them guide me in my research.

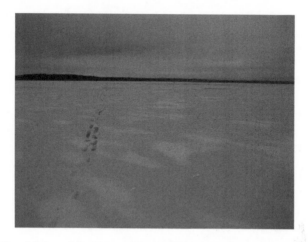

Fig. A3.1.   My Footprints on Frozen Lake Kavgolovo.
Source: Author, 06/12/2014.

Fig. A3.2.   Taking the Opportunity to Catch Some February Sun in a Park in St Petersburg. *Source:* Author, 15/02/2015.

Appendix 4

Surrogacy Workers' Accommodations

Fieldnotes on migrant surrogacy workers' agency-provided accommodation in St. Petersburg.

07 September 2012; waiting for surrogacy worker Marcella.

Today was the first meeting with Marcella, a migrant surrogacy worker from Moldova. I had arrived a bit too early at the meeting point, a bus stop near apartment blocks. Somewhere nearby she is sharing her agency-provided flat with two other pregnant women.

While waiting, I took the opportunity to have a closer look at my surroundings.

I am on a busy multiple lane street in a district somewhere south of St Petersburg's city centre. It took me about an hour to travel here. What immediately strikes me is how nothing here resembles the beautiful centre of St Petersburg with its light-coloured ornamented Baroque and neoclassical buildings, where the agencies and private fertility clinics are located. Here is what locals call a 'spalniy rayon' – a 'dormitory suburb' – featuring weathered, grey 7-15 story apartment blocks from the Soviet days, and amenities providing everyday necessities: schools, pharmacies, newspaper corner shops and super-market chains. This neighbourhood is not connected to the underground network, but only served by busses which make for a tedious rush hour commute. Some trees line the street, but the map shows that the next park is 2.5km from here. I am thinking of my research map on my wall at home, and the clear pattern it started revealing as I pinned my research sites and travels on it: the pins for agency offices and private fertility clinics cluster in the city centre, near metro stations and iconic architectural and cultural landmarks, whereas the pins for accommodation provided to migrant surrogacy workers are spread in the suburbs and alongside industrial areas (Fig. A4.1).

07 September 2012; after meeting Marcella.

Marcella did not invite me home to her accommodation as she had indicated when we arranged to meet. Instead, we walked around the blocks, for about an hour. Around the blocks, across backyards, along trodden pathways. As we walked, she told me how this resembles how she usually spends her days when she isn't called somewhere for an appointment related to the pregnancy. 'I take some walks. But I have never been to the inner city [on my own initiative], because the transport is too expensive to just go and see and go back. And it is also so far'.

Fig. A4.1.   Marcella's Neighbourhood. *Source:* Author, 07/09/2012.

13 September 2014; Visiting the agency accommodation at the outskirts of St. Petersburg.

To get to this accommodation for migrant surrogacy workers, which is located outside the city boundaries of St Petersburg, takes at least two means of transport – either by metro and an electritchka, the suburban train, or by metro and a marshrutka, a minibus. Both routes take over an hour, and neither the train or minibus departs more frequently than once every hour.

Taking the train, I observed the landscape changing from housing blocks and large grounds of garages to more trees and green areas until I have left urban St Petersburg. My station stop called at a small, unserviced platform outside the village. At first I was worried I had missed my stop – surely the accommodation for surrogacy workers could not be this far from the centre? But I got off correctly.

The accommodation for the surrogacy workers is at the edge of this village, on a narrow road edged with sprawling grass and young trees, about fifteen minutes to walk from the station (Fig. A4.2). The village houses, many wooden and dachas with large vegetable and flower gardens, are widely spaced between birches. The house for the surrogacy workers however stands out. Not only is it modern, large and newly built, it also is surrounded by a head-high wall, very visibly fitted with surveillance cameras and tinted windows on the first floor.

Fig. A4.2.   The Road Leading to the Agency Accommodation.
Source: Author, 13/09/2014.

As nobody was expecting me here today, I didn't want to draw attention to myself by standing on the road looking at this house. I had come here simply because I was curious and because the agency had given me the address. I therefore took a walk through the village and finally to the main square with the bus stop and a small, multipurpose shop, the only one I could spot in the village. The shop contained a bread counter, a meat and cheese counter, a counter for fruit and vegetables, and final one for toiletries, conserves and sweets. The same building also hosted a hairdresser, a furniture shop and a pharmacy. There was no public space, like a café, nor a bench to sit and rest (Fig. A4.3).

Preparing to leave, I asked a young man for the best way back to St Petersburg. In return he wanted to know my business for coming here, a foreigner in this village. 'By chance', I fibbed, 'I live in St Petersburg for work and explore the

Fig. A4.3.   The Village Square and Store. *Source:* Author, 13/09/2014.

surroundings on weekends'. He looked around and, nodding in the direction of the wooden houses, remarked 'ordinary people live here'. 'I've also seen new buildings' – I picked up, hinting at but not mentioning the accommodation for surrogacy workers. 'The rich ones are there' he responded as turned his gaze in the exact direction. Then he left me at the bus stop and walked off.

I know from the agency that the houses accommodate 15 women, all of whom are at different stages of pregnancy, and I wonder how comfortable they feel in leaving the premises to go for a walk and undertake a little shopping at the village store, or whether they prefer to stay put and leave the premises only when being picked up by the agency's driver for medical appointments in St Petersburg or to go shopping in a large mall in the suburbs. And I wonder, what they do all day long? How do they keep occupied? I also wonder, today is a sunny September day, but soon autumn will come, and then winter – and will there be any snow-clearing happening in a place like this?

References

Agadjanian, A. (2017). Tradition, morality and community: Elaborating orthodox identity in Putin's Russia. *Religion, State and Society, 45*(1), 39–60.

Ahmed, S. (2017). *Living a feminist life*. Durham, NC: Duke University Press.

Aigen, B. (1996). Motivations of surrogate mothers – Parenthood, altruism and self-actualisation (a three year study). Retrieved from https://doi.org/http://claradoc. gpa.free.fr/doc/87.pdf. Accessed on August 03, 2017.

van den Akker, O. (2003). Genetic and gestational surrogate mothers' experience of surrogacy. *Journal of Reproductive and Infant Psychology, 21*(2), 145–161.

Anderson, E. (1990). Is women's labor a commodity? *Philosophy & Public Affairs, 19*(1), 71–92.

Anderson, E. (2000). Why commercial surrogate motherhood unethically commodifies women and children: Reply to McLachlan and Swales. *Health Care Analysis: Journal of Health Philosophy and Policy, 8*(1), 19–26.

Andrews, L. (1988). Surrogate motherhood: The challenge for feminists. *The Journal of Law, Medicine & Ethics, 16*(1–2), 72–80.

Anleu, S. (1990). Reinforcing gender norms: Commercial and altruistic surrogacy. *Acta Sociologica, 33*(1), 63–74.

Ashwin, S., & Lytkina, T. (2004). Men in crisis in Russia: The role of domestic marginalization. *Gender & Society, 18*(2), 189–206.

Avilov, A. (2021). Russia considers banning surrogacy for unmarried people, foreigners – RBC. *The Moscow Times*. Retrieved from https://www.themosco wtimes.com/2021/01/20/russia-considers-banning-surrogacy-for-unmarried-people-foreigners-rbc-a72668. Accessed on March 09, 2021.

Belyakov, D. (2018). *No support. Russia's "gay propaganda" law imperils LGBT youth*. Report. Human Rights Watch. Retrieved from https://www.hrw.org/report/2018/ 12/11/no-support/russias-gay-propaganda-law-imperils-lgbt-youth. Accessed on March 09, 2021.

Berend, Z. (2012). The romance of surrogacy. *Sociological Forum, 27*, 913–936.

Berend, Z. (2014). The social context for surrogates' motivations and satisfaction. *Reproductive BioMedicine Online, 29*(4), 399–401.

Berend, Z. (2016a). 'We are all carrying someone else's child!': Relatedness and relationships in third-party reproduction. *American Anthropologist, 118*(1), 24–36.

Berend, Z. (2016b). *The online world of surrogacy*. New York, NY: Berghahn.

Berkhout, S. (2008). Bun in the oven. *Social Theory and Practice, 34*(1), 95–117.

Blam, I., & Kovalev, S. (2006). Spontaneous commercialisation, inequality and the contradictions of compulsory medical insurance in transitional Russia. *Journal of International Development, 18*(3), 407–423.

Blee, K. (1998). White-Knuckle research: Emotional dynamics in fieldwork with racist activists. *Qualitative Sociology, 21*, 381–399.

Block, F. (2012). Relational work in market economies: Introduction. *Politics & Society, 40*(2), 135–144.

Bocharova, M. (2020). Russian investigators single out gay fathers in latest crackdown on LGBTQ rights. *Coda*. Retrieved from https://www.codastory.com/disinform ation/russia-gay-fathers/. Accessed on March 23, 2021.

Bondar, J. (2017). Суд Обязал Суррогатную Мать Отдать Детей Заказчикам [The court ordered the surrogate mother to give the children to the customers]. Retrieved from https://medportal.ru/mednovosti/sud-obyazal-surrogatnuyu-mat-otdat-deteyzakazchikam/. Accessed on November 27, 2020.

Bourdieu, P. (1977). *Outline of a theory of practice*. Stanford, CA: Stanford University Press.

Bourdieu, P. (1986). The forms of capital. In J. Richardson (Ed.), *Handbook of theory and research for the sociology of education* (pp. 241–258). Oxford: Greenword Publishing Group.

Brednikova, O., Nartova, N., & Tkach, O. (2009). Assisted reproduction in Russia: legal regulations and public debates. In W. de Jong & O. Tkach (Eds.), *Making bodies, persons and families: Normalising reproductive technologies in Russia, Switzerland and Germany* (pp. 43–56). Münster: LIT Verlag.

Bridger, S., Pinnick, K., & Kay, R. (1996). *No more heroines?: Russia, women and the market*. New York, NY: Routledge.

Burfoot, A. (1990). The normalisation of a new reproductive technology. In M. McNeil, I. Varcoe, & S. Yearly (Eds.), *The new reproductive technologies. Explorations in sociology. British sociological association conference volume series* (pp. 58–73). London: Palgrave Macmillan.

Campbell, R., & Wasco, S. (2000). Feminist approaches to social science: Epistemological and methodological tenets. *American Journal of Community Psychology, 28*(6), 773–791.

Carroll, O. (2020). Gay men in Russia with surrogate children warned they face arrest. *The Independent*. Retrieved from https://www.independent.co.uk/news/world/europe/russia-gay-putin-arrest-lbgt-surrogate-b746395.html. Accessed on March 09, 2021.

Cassaniti, J., & Hickman, J. (2014). New directions in the anthropology of morality. *Anthropological Theory, 14*(3), 251–262.

Chauduri, M. (2013). New Indian visa rules exclude single people and gay couples from child surrogacy. *BMJ, 346*, f475.

Chen, S., Yang, J., Yang, W., Wang, C., & Bärnighausen, T. (2020). COVID-19 control in China during mass population movements at new year. *The Lancet, 395*(10226), 764–766.

Cockerham, W. (2007). Health lifestyles and the absence of the Russian middle class. *Sociology of Health & Illness, 29*(3), 457–473.

Colen, S. (1995). 'Like a mother to them': Stratified reproduction and West Indian childcare workers and employers in New York. In F. Ginsburg & R. Rapp (Eds.), *Conceiving the new world order: The global politics of reproduction* (pp. 78–102). Berkeley, CA: University of California Press.

Constable, N. (2009). The commodification of intimacy: Marriage, sex, and reproductive labor. *Annual Review of Anthropology, 38*(1), 49–64.

Cook, M. (2017). Russian surrogacy, controversial and unregulated. Retrieved from https://www.bioedge.org/bioethics/russian-surrogacy-controversial-and-unregulated/12528. Accessed on November 27, 2020.

Cooper, M., & Waldby, C. (2014). *Clinical labor: Tissue donors and research subjects in the global bioeconomy*. Durham, NC: Duke University Press.

Cromer, R. (2019). Making the ethnic embryo: Enacting race in US embryo adoption. *Medical Anthropology: Cross Cultural Studies in Health and Illness, 38*(7), 603–619.

Culley, L., Hudson, N., & Van Rooij, F. (2012). *Marginalized reproduction: Ethnicity, infertility and reproductive technologies*. London: Earthscan.

Cussins, C. (1998). Quit sniveling, cryo-baby, we'll work out which one is your mama!. In R. Davis-Floyd & J. Dumit (Eds.), *Cyborg babies: From techno-sex to techno-tots* (pp. 40–66). New York, NY: Routledge.

Dandan, N., & Shiyu, Z. (2020). The scramble to rescue China's stranded babies. *Sixth Tone*. Retrieved from https://www.sixthtone.com/news/1006460/the-scramble-to-rescue-chinas-stranded-babies. Accessed on February 19, 2021.

Davis, D.-A. (2019). *Reproductive injustice racism, pregnancy, and premature birth*. New York, NY: New York University Press.

Davis-Floyd, R. (1997). Conceiving the new world order: The global politics of reproduction. *Medical Anthropology Quarterly, 11*(3), 398–401.

Davis-Floyd, R. (2001). The technocratic, humanistic, and holistic paradigms of childbirth. *International Journal of Gynecology & Obstetrics, 75*(Suppl 1), S5–S23.

Davydova, D. (2019). *Between heteropatriarchy and homonationalism: Codes of gender, sexuality, and race/ethnicity in Putin's Russia*. Doctoral Dissertation, York University, Toronto, ON. Retrieved from https://yorkspace.library.yorku.ca/xmlui/bitstream/handle/10315/36777/Davydova_Darja_2019_PhD.pdf?sequence=2&is Allowed=y. Accessed on March 09, 2021.

Denton, S. (2020). Surrogate families separated by coronavirus travel restrictions. *Bionews*. March 30, 2020. Retrieved from https://www.bionews.org.uk/page_148783. Accessed on November 27, 2020.

Deomampo, D. (2013a). Gendered geographies of reproductive tourism. *Gender & Society, 27*(4), 514–537.

Deomampo, D. (2013b). Transnational surrogacy in India: Interrogating power and women's agency. *Frontiers, 34*(3), 167–188.

Deomampo, D. (2016). Race, nation, and the production of intimacy: Transnational ova donation in India. *Positions: East Asia Cultures Critique, 24*(1), 303–332.

Dow, K. (2017). "A Nine-month head-start": The maternal bond and surrogacy. *Ethnos, 82*(1), 86–104.

Dushina, A. D., Kersha, Y. D., Larkina, T. Y., Provorova, D. D. (2016). Легитимация коммерческого суррогатного материнства в России [Legitimation of commercial surrogacy in Russia]. *Экономическая социология. [Journal of Economic Sociology], 17*(1), 62–82.

Dworkin, A. (1983). *Right-wing women*. New York, NY: Perigee Books.

Dzhafarov, E. (2020). The invention of 'gay mutilators'. *Meduza*. October 5, 2020. Retrieved from https://meduza.io/en/feature/2020/10/05/the-invention-of-gay-mutilators. Accessed on October 5, 2020.

Einwohner, J. (1989). Who becomes a surrogate. In J. Offerman-Zuckerberg (Ed.), *Gender in transition. A new frontier* (pp. 123–132). New York, NY: Plenum Medical Book Company.

Ekman, K. E. (2013). *Being and being bought : Prostitution, surrogacy and the split self.* North Melbourne, VIC: Spinifex Press.

Emmel, N., Hughes, K., Greenhalgh, J., & Sales A. (2007, March). Accessing socially excluded people — trust and the gatekeeper in the researcher-participant relationship. *Sociological Research Online, 12*(2), 43–55.

EU-OCS. (2020). Russia to arrest individuals fathering children via surrogacy. Retrieved from https://eu-ocs.com/russia-to-arrest-individuals-fathering-childrenvia-surrogacy/. Accessed on March 09, 2021.

Everhart, R. (1977). Between stranger and friend: Some consequences of 'long term' fieldwork in schools. *American Educational Research Journal, 14*(1), 1–15.

Farrugia, A., Penrod, J., & Bult, J. M. (2010). Payment, compensation and replacement–the ethics and motivation of blood and plasma donation. *Vox Sanguinis, 99*(3), 202–211.

Fisher, A., & Hoskins, M. (2013). A good surrogate: The experiences of women who are gestational surrogates in Canada. *Canadian Journal of Counselling and Psychotherapy, 47*(4), 500–513.

Franklin, S. (2013). *Biological relatives: IVF, stem cells, and the future of kinship.* Durham, NC; London: Duke University Press.

Franks, D. (1981). Psychiatric evaluation of women in a surrogate mother program. *The American Journal of Psychiatry, 138*(10), 1378–1379.

Gerrits, T. (2016). 'It's not my eggs, it is not my husband's sperm, it is not my child': Surrogacy and 'not doing kinship' in Ghana. In C. Krolokke, L. Myong, S. W. Adrian, & T. Tjornhoj-Thomsen (Eds.), *Critical kinship studies* (pp. 65–81). London: Rowman & Littlefield.

Giddens, A. (1984). *The constitution of society: Outline of the theory of structuration.* Cambridge: Polity Press.

Ginsburg, F., & Rapp, R. (1995). *Conceiving the new world order: The global politics of reproduction.* Berkeley, CA: University of California Press.

Glenn, E. N. (1992). From servitude to service work: Historical continuities in the racial division of paid reproductive labor. *Signs: Journal of Women in Culture and Society, 18*(1), 1–43.

Gorshkova, I., & Klochkov, V. (2011). Economic analysis of development prospects for air transport in Russia's sparsely populated regions. *Studies on Russian Economic Development, 22*(6), 611–621.

Harrison, L. (2014). "I am the baby's real mother": Reproductive tourism, race, and the transnational construction of kinship. *Women's Studies International Forum, 47*, 145–156.

Harrison, L. (2016). *Brown bodies, white babies: The politics of cross-racial surrogacy.* New York, NY: New York University Press.

Haylett, J. L. (2015). *From contracted employee to fictive kin: U.S. commercial surrogacy as a case of relational work.* Doctoral Thesis. Retrieved from https://www.semanticscholar.org/paper/From-contracted-employee-to-fictive-kin%3A-U.S.-as-a-Haylett/7d8895530e526555cacb7fa11c08247e9acd55f1. Accessed on July 08, 2017.

HFEA. (2020). *Fertility treatment 2018: Trends and figures.* Human Fertilisation and Embryology Authority. Retrieved from https://www.hfea.gov.uk/about-us/publications/research-and-data/fertility-treatment-2018-trends-and-figures/. Accessed on September 25, 2020.

Hibino, Y. (2015). Implications of the legalization of non-commercial surrogacy for local kinship and motherhood in Vietnamese society. *Reproductive BioMedicine Online, 30*(2), 113–114.

Hochschild, A. (1979). Emotion work, feeling rules, and social structure. *American Journal of Sociology, 85*(3), 551–575.

Hochschild, A. (2003). *The managed heart: Commercialization of human feeling.* Berkeley, CA: University of California Press.

Hochschild, A. (2011). Emotional life on the market frontier. *Annual Review of Sociology, 37*(1), 21–33.

Hoffmann, E. (2007). Open-ended interviews, power, and emotional labor. *Journal of Contemporary Ethnography, 36*(3), 318–346.

Holland, J. (2007). Emotions and research. *International Journal of Social Research Methodology, 10*(3), 195–209.

Hoodfar, H. (1992). The veil in their minds and on our heads: The persistence of colonial images of Muslim women. *Resources for Feminist Research, 3*(3/4), 5–18.

Hudson, N. A. (2008). *Infertility in British South Asian communities: Negotiating the community and the clinic.* Doctoral Dissertation, De Montfort University. Retrieved from https://www.dora.dmu.ac.uk/xmlui/handle/2086/4817.

Humphrey, C. (2002). Subsistence farming and the peasantry as an idea in contemporary Russia. In P. Leonard & D. Kaneff (Eds.), *Post-socialist peasant? Rural and urban constructions of identity in Eastern Europe, East Asia and the former Soviet Union* (pp. 136–159). London: Palgrave Macmillan.

Imrie, S., & Jadva, V. (2014). The long-term experiences of surrogates: Relationships and contact with surrogacy families in genetic and gestational surrogacy arrangements. *Reproductive BioMedicine Online, 29*(4), 424–435.

Inhorn, M. C. (2011). Diasporic dreaming: Return reproductive tourism to the middle east. *Symposium: Cross-Border Reproductive Care – Ethical, Legal, and Socio-Cultural Perspectives, 23*(5), 582–591.

Inhorn, M. C. (2015). *Cosmopolitan conceptions: IVF sojourns in global dubai.* Durham, NC: Duke University Press.

Isakova, E., Korsak, V., & Gromyko, Y. (2001). Опыт реализация программы 'суррогатное материнство' [Experience of the realisation of the programme of 'surrogate motherhood']. Retrieved from http://www.fesmu.ru/elib/Article.aspx?id560747. Accessed on November 29, 2020.

Issoupova, O. (2012). From duty to pleasure?: Motherhood in Soviet and Post-Soviet Russia. In S. Ashwin (Ed.), *Gender, state and society in Soviet and Post-Soviet Russia* (pp. 30–54). London: Routledge.

Ivankiva, M. (2012). Russian surrogate moms attract foreigners. *The St Petersburg Times.* Retrieved from http://www.jurconsult.ru/smi/print/st_peter_times/12_09_2012.pdf. Accessed on January 22, 2017.

Ivolga, I. (2016). Adaption of the Russian food market to the contemporary geopolitical challenges: Bans vs liberalisation. In V. Erokhin (Ed.), *Global perspectives on trade integration and economies in transition* (pp. 185–211). Hershey, PA: Business Science Reference.

Jacobson, H. (2016). *Labor of love: Gestational surrogacy and the work of making babies.* New Brunswick, NJ: Rutgers University Press.

Jadva, V., Murray, C., Lycett, E., MacCallum, F., & Golombok, S. (2003). Surrogacy: The experiences of surrogate mothers. *Human Reproduction, 18*(10), 2196–2204.

Jaggar, A. (1989). Love and knowledge: Emotion in feminist epistemology. *Inquiry. An Interdisciplinary Journal of Philosophy, 32*(2), 151–176.

de Jong, W., & Tkach, O. (Eds.). (2009). *Making bodies, persons and families: Normalising reproductive technologies.* Münster: Lit Verlag.

Kanefield, L. (1999). The reparative motive in surrogate mothers. *Adoption Quarterly, 2*(4), 5–19.

Katchanovski, I. (2016). The separatist war in Donbas: A violent break-up of Ukraine? *European Politics and Society, 17*(4), 473–489.

Keaney, J., & Moll, T. (2020). Fertility care in the era of COVID-19. *ADI Policy Briefing Papers, 1*(6), 1–8. Retrieved from https://static1.squarespace.com/static/5b0fd5e6710699c630b269b1/t/5fae133b36358572f1186955/1605243747841/ADI+Policy+Briefing+Paper+-+Fertility+care+in+the+era+of+COVID-19.pdf. Accessed on March 19, 2021.

Khazova, O. A. (2013). Russia. In K. Trimmings & P. Beaumont (Eds.), *International surrogacy arrangements: Legal regulation at the international level* (pp. 311–324). Oxford; Portland, OR: Hart Publishing.

Khvorostyanov, N., & Yeshua-Katz, D. (2020). Bad, pathetic and greedy women: Expressions of surrogate motherhood stigma in a Russian online forum. *Sex Roles, 83*(7–8), 474–484.

Kiblitskaya, M. (2000). Russia's female breadwinners: The changing subjective experienceq. In S. Ashwin (Ed.), *Gender, state and society in Soviet and Post-Soviet Russia* (pp. 55–70). London: Routledge.

King, E., Dudina, V., & Dubrovskaya, S. (2020). 'You feel sick, you get sick, you still keep going': Central Asian female labour migrants' health in Russia. *Global Public Health, 15*(4), 544–557.

Kirillova, Y., & Bogdan, V. (2013). The role and significance of assisted reproductive technology in Russia's inheritance law. *Middle-East Journal of Scientific Research, 17*(12), 1641–1645.

Kirpichenko, M. (2017). Russian legislative practises and debates on the restriction of wide access to ARTs. In M. Lie & N. Lykke (Eds.), *Assisted reproduction across borders: Feminist perspectives on normalizations, disruptions and transmissions* (pp. 232–247). . New York, NY: Routledge.

Kirpichenko, M. (2020). Ideology of simulation: The material-semiotic production of the surrogate in the web worldings of Russian surrogacy. *European Journal of Women's Studies,* 1–17.

Kleinpeter, C., & Hohman, M. (2000). Surrogate motherhood: Personality traits and satisfaction with service providers. *Psychological Reports, 87*(3, 1), 957–970.

König, A. (2018). Parents on the move: German intended parents' experiences with transnational surrogacy. In S. Mitra, S. Schicktanz, & T. Patel (Eds.), *Cross-cultural comparisons on surrogacy and egg donation.* Cham: Palgrave Macmillan.

König, A., Jacobson, H., & Majumdar, A. (2020). 'Pandemic disruptions' in surrogacy arrangements in Germany, U.S.A., and India during COVID-19. *Medical Anthropology Quarterly.* Retrieved from http://medanthroquarterly.org/2020/08/11/pandemic-disruptions-in-surrogacy-arrangements-in-germany-u-s-a-and-india-during-covid-19/

Kozkina, A. (2018). Сложный ребенок. Как расставание двух влиятельных людей и суррогатное материнство обернулись уголовными делами и (возможно) жертвами [Difficult child. How the separation of two powerful people and surrogate motherhood turned into a criminal case with a (possible) victim]. Retrieved from https://zona.media/article/2018/03/05/mirimskaya. Accessed on November 29, 2020.

Krainova, N. (2013). Mizulina's surrogacy ban idea ridiculed. *The Moscow Times.* Retrieved from https://www.themoscowtimes.com/2013/11/11/mizulinas-surrogacy-ban-idea-ridiculed-a29455. Accessed on March 09, 2021.

Lafuente-Funes, S. (2020). Shall we stop talking about egg donation? Transference of reproductive capacity in the Spanish bioeconomy. *BioSocieties, 15,* 207–225.

Larivaara, M., Dubikaytis, T., Kuznetsova, O., & Hemminki, E. (2008). Between a rock and a hard place: The question of money at St. Petersburg women's clinics. *International Journal of Health Services, 38*(2), 357–377.

Leissner, O. (2012). From surrogacy to abortion and all that lies between them. *International Journal of Feminist Approaches to Bioethics, 5*(1), 133–159.

Lewis, S. (2019). *Full surrogacy now: Feminism against family.* London: Verso.

Liefert, W. (2004). Food security in Russia: Economic growth and rising insecurity. Food Security Assessment/GFA-15. Retrieved from https://www.cpc.unc.edu/projects/rlms-hse/publications/1449. Accessed on November 29, 2020.

Litvinova, M., Manuyilova, A., Veretennikova, K., & Makutina, M. (2021). Иностранцев посылают к иной матери. В Госдуме обсуждают нюансы суррогатного материнства [Foreigners are sent to another mother. The State Duma discusses the nuances of surrogacy]. *Коммерсантъ [Kommersant].* Retrieved from https://www.kommersant.ru/doc/4654340. Accessed on March 09, 2021.

Loktionova, M. (2020). Дело в клетке: суррогатному материнству прописали новые правила [A case in a cage: New rules have been prescribed for surrogacy]. *Газета [Gazeta].* Retrieved from https://www.gazeta.ru/social/2020/10/20/13326049.shtml. Accessed on March 08, 2021.

MacLeod, A. (1992). Hegemonic relations and gender resistance: The new veiling as accommodating protest in Cairo. *Signs, 17*(3), 533–557.

Majumdar, A. (2014). The rhetoric of choice: The feminist debates on reproductive choice in the commercial surrogacy arrangement in India. *Gender, Technology and Development, 18*(2), 275–301.

Majumdar, A. (2017). *Transnational commercial surrogacy and the (un)making of kin in India.* New Delhi: Oxford University Press.

Mamo, L., & Alston-Stepnitz, E. (2015). Queer intimacies and structural inequalities. *Journal of Family Issues, 36*(4), 519–540.

Marger, M. (2015). *Race and ethnic relations: American and global perspectives.* Stamford, CT: Cengage Learning.

Martin, T. (2001). *The affirmative action empire: Nations and nationalism in the Soviet Union, 1923–1939.* Cornell, NY: Cornell University Press.

McGregor, S. (2001). Neoliberalism and health care. *International Journal of Consumer Studies, 25*(2), 82–89.

McLachlan, H., & Swales, J. K. (2000). Babies, child bearers and commodification: Anderson, Brazier et Al., and the political economy of commercial surrogate motherhood. *Health Care Analysis: Journal of Health Philosophy and Policy, 8*(1), 1–18.

Mezentseva, E. (2005). Gender inequality in today Russia: Who bear the social costs of reforms? *Gender and Feminism Under Post-Communism Roundtable.* Retrieved from http://www.indiana.edu/~reeiweb/newsEvents/pre2006/mezentseva%20paper. pdf. Accessed on April 12, 2017.

Michaels, P. (2000). Medical propaganda and cultural revolution in Soviet Kazakhstan, 1928–41. *The Russian Review, 59*(2), 159–178.

Mitra, S. (2017). *Disruptive embodiments: An ethnography of risks and failures during commercial surrogacy in India.* Doctoral Dissertation, Social Science Faculty, University of Göttingen.

Mitra, S., & Schicktanz, S. (2016). Failed surrogate conceptions: social and ethical aspects of preconception disruptions during commercial surrogacy in India. *Philosophy, Ethics, and Humanities in Medicine, 11*(1), 1–16.

Moll, T. (2019). Making a match: Curating race in South African gamete donation. *Medical Anthropology: Cross Cultural Studies in Health and Illness, 38*(7), 588–602.

Nahman, M. (2008). Nodes of desire: Romanian egg sellers, dignity' and feminist alliances in transnational ova exchanges. *European Journal of Women's Studies, 15*(2), 65–82.

Nahman, M. (2013). *Extractions: An ethnography of reproductive tourism.* Hampshire: Palgrave Macmillan.

Näre, L. (2014). Agency as capabilities: Ukrainian women's narratives of social change and mobility. *Women's Studies International Forum, 47*(November), 223–231.

Nartova, O. (2009). Surrogate motherhood and sperm donorship in the Russian media: Normalising the body. In W. de Jong & O. Tkach (Eds.), *Making bodies, persons and families: Normalising reproductive technologies in Russia, Switzerland and Germany* (pp. 75–94). Münster: LIT Verlag.

van Niekerk, A., & van Zyl, L. (1995). Commercial surrogacy and the commodification of children: An ethical perspective. *Medicine & Law, 14*(3–4), 163–170.

Novoselova, E. (2006). Мама на девять месяцев. Суррогатное материнство поможет решить демографическую проблему [Mother for nine months. Surrogate motherhood helps to solve the demographic problem]. *Российская Газета [Rossiyskaya Gazeta].* Retrieved from https://rg.ru/2006/12/08/surrogatnaya-mat. html. Accessed on November 29, 2020.

Oliver, K. (1989). Marxism and surrogacy. *Hypatia, 4*(3), 95–115.

Ortner, S. (1997). *Making gender: The politics and erotics of culture.* Boston, MA: Beacon Press.

Ortner, S. (2006). *Anthropology and social theory: Culture, power, and the acting subject.* Durham, NC: Duke University Press.

Ortner, S. B. (2001). Specifiying agency. The Comaroffs and their critics. *Interventions, 3*(1), 76–84.

Oxford Dictionary. (2017). *Oxford Dictionary.* Retrieved from http://www.oed.com/ view/Entry/122086?isAdvanced=false&result=2&rskey=sffkSq&. Accessed on July 25, 2017.

Pachenkov, O. (2010). 'Caucasian' female labor migration in contemporary Russia: Changing patterns (case of St.-Petersburg). Retrieved from https://www.yumpu.com/ en/document/read/18240059/caucasian-female-labor-migration-in-contemporary-russia-. Accessed on November 29, 2020.

Pande, A. (2009). "It may be her eggs but it's my blood": Surrogates and everyday forms of kinship in India. *Qualitative Sociology, 32*(4), 379–397.

Pande, A. (2010). Commercial surrogacy in India: Manufacturing a perfect mother-worker. *Signs. Journal of Women in Culture and Society, 35*(4), 969–992.

Pande, A. (2014a). This birth and that: Surrogacy and stratified motherhood in India. *Philosophia, 4*(1), 50–64.

Pande, A. (2014b). *Wombs in labor: Transnational commercial surrogacy in India.* New York, NY: Columbia University Press.

Parker, P. (1983). Motivation of surrogate mothers: Initial findings. *American Journal of Psychiatry, 140*(1), 117–118.

Parker, P. (1984). Surrogate motherhood, psychiatric screening and informed consent, baby selling, and public policy. *Bulletin of the American Academy of Psychiatry & the Law, 12*(1), 21–39.

Pizitz, T., Joseph, M., & Rabin, A. (2012). Do women who choose to become surrogate mothers have different psychological profiles compared to a normative female sample? *Women and Birth, 26*(1), e15–e20.

Ragoné, H. (1994). *Surrogate motherhood: Conception in the heart.* Boulder, CO: Westview Press.

Ragoné, H. (1996). Chasing the blood tie: Surrogate mothers, adoptive mothers and fathers. *American Ethnologist, 23*(2), 352–365.

Ragoné, H. (1999). "The gift of life." Transformative motherhood: On giving and getting in a consumer culture. In R. Cook, S. D. Sclater, & F. Kaganas (Eds.), *Surrogate motherhood: International perspectives* (pp. 65–88). Oxford: Hart Publishing.

Ragoné, H. (2000). Of likeness and difference: How race is being transfigured by gestational surrogacy. In H. Ragone & F. W. Twine (Eds.), *Ideologies and technologies of motherhood: Race, class, sexuality, nationalism* (pp. 56–78). New York, NY: Routledge.

RAHR. (2015). Российская Ассоциация Репродукции Регистр ВРТ [Russian association of reproduction register]. Retrieved from http://www.http://www.rahr.ru/d_registr_otchet/registr_2015.pdf. Accessed on August 08, 2015.

RapsiNews. (2014). Russian lawmakers consider banning use of surrogate mothers by single men. Russian Legal Information Agency (RAPSI). Retrieved from http://www.rapsinews.com/legislation_news/20140204/270635433.html. Accessed on Novemmber 29, 2020.

RapsiNews. (2017). Bill banning surrogacy reaches Russian lower house of parliament. Russian Legal Information Agency (RAPSI). Retrieved from http://www.rapsinews.com/legislation_news/20170327/278106535.html. Accessed on March 09, 2021.

RapsiNews. (2020). Arrest of wanted defendant in surrogacy kids trade case in absentia upheld. Russian Legal Information Agency (RAPSI). Retrieved from http://www.rapsinews.com/judicial_news/20201209/306577379.html. Accessed on March 09, 2021.

Rathi, D. (2020). Critical analysis of the surrogacy regulation bill, 2016. *International Journal of Innovative Science and Research Technology, 5*(5), 751–756.

Reuters. (2020a). Russia Ramps up controls, shuts China border crossings over virus fears. Retrieved from https://www.reuters.com/article/us-china-health-russia-border/russian-regions-in-far-east-close-border-with-china-amid-coronavirus-fears-tass-idUSKBN1ZR0TU. Accessed on September 23, 2020.

Reuters. (2020b). 'There will be dad and mum': Putin rules out Russia legalizing gay marriage. Retrieved from https://www.reuters.com/article/us-russia-putin-constitution-idUSKBN2072DS. Accessed on March 24, 2021.

Rivkin-Fish, M. (2013). Conceptualizing feminist strategies for Russian reproductive politics: Abortion, surrogate motherhood, and family support after socialism. *Signs, 38*(3), 569–593.

Roberts, E., & Scheper-Hughes, N. (2011). Introduction: Medical migrations. *Body & Society, 17*(2–3), 1–30.

ROC. (n.d.). Основы социальной концепции Русской Православной Церкви: XII. Проблемы биоэтики [Fundamentals of the social concept of the Russian Orthodox Church: XII. Problems of bioethics]. Retrieved from https://mospat.ru/ru/documents/social-concepts/xii/. Accessed on August 26, 2020.

Roth, A. (2020). Up to 1,000 babies born to surrogate mothers stranded in Russia. *The Guardian.* Retrieved from https://www.theguardian.com/lifeandstyle/2020/jul/29/up-to-1000-babies-born-to-surrogate-mothers-stranded-in-russia. Accessed on September 01, 2020.

Rothman, B. K. (1988). Cheap labor: Sex, class, race – And "surrogacy". *Society, 25*(3), 21–23.

Rotkirch, A., Temkina, A., & Zdravomyslova, E. (2007). Who helps the degraded housewife?: Comments on Vladimir Putin's demographic speech. *European Journal of Women's Studies, 14*(4), 349–357.

Rudrappa, S. (2015). *Discounted life: The price of global surrogacy in India.* New York, NY: New York University Press.

Rudrappa, S. (2017). Reproducing dystopia: The politics of transnational surrogacy in India, 2002–2015. *Critical Sociology, 44*(7–8), 1087–1101.

Rudrappa, S. (2018). Why is India's ban on commercial surrogacy bad for women. *North Carolina Journal of International Law, 43*(4), 70–95.

Rusanova, N. (2013). Вспомогательные репродуктивные технологии в России: История, проблемы, демографические перспективы [Assisted reproductive technologies in Russia: History, problems, demographic prospects]. *Журнал исследований социальной политики. [The Journal of Social Policy Studies], 11*(1), 69–86.

Ryazantsev, S., Pismennaya, E., Karabulatova, I., & Akramov, S. (2014). Transformation of sexual and matrimonial behavior of Tajik labour migrants in Russia. *Asian Social Science, 10*(20), 174–183.

Sahlins, M. (1981). *Historical metaphors and mythical realities: Structure in the early history of the Sandwich Islands Kingdom.* Ann Arbor, MI: University of Chicago Press.

Saxinger, G. (2015). 'To you, to us, to oil and gas' – The symbolic and socio-economic attachment of the workforce to oil, gas and its spaces of extraction in the Yamal-Nenets and Khanty-Mansi autonomous districts in Russia. *Fennia, 193*(1), 83–98.

Saxinger, G., Oefner, E., Sakirova, E., Ivanona, M., Yakuvlev, M., & Gareev, E. (2014). «Я готов!», новое поколение мобильных кадров в российской нефтегазовой промышленности. Сибирские исторические исследования ["I am ready!": The next generation of mobile professionals in the Russian oil and gas industry]. *Сибирские исторические исследования. [Siberian Historical Research], 3,* 73–103.

Sevortian, A. (2009). Xenophobia in Post-Soviet Russia. *The Equal Rights Review, 3,* 19–27.

Shadrina, A. (2015). What is threatening 'traditional family values' in Russia today? *Open Democracy*. Retrieved from https://www.opendemocracy.net/en/odr/what-is-threatening-traditional-family-values-in-russia-today/. Accessed on March 09, 2021.

Shanley, M. (1993). 'Surrogate mothering' and women's freedom: A critique of contracts for human reproduction. *Signs*, *18*(3), 618–639.

Siegl, V. (2018a). Aligning the affective body: Commercial surrogacy in Moscow and the emotional labour of Nastraivatsya. *Tsantsa*, *23*, 63–81.

Siegl, V. (2018b). 'The ultimate argument': Evoking the affective powers of 'happiness' in commercial surrogacy. *Anthropological Journal of European Cultures*, *27*(2), 1–21.

Slezkine, Y. (2000). Imperialism as the highest stage of socialism. *The Russian Review*, *59*(2), 227–234.

Smietana, M. (2017). Affective de-commodifying, economic de-Kinning: Surrogates' and gay fathers' narratives in U.S. surrogacy. *Sociological Research Online*, *22*(2), 163–175.

Smietana, M., Rudrappa, S., & Weis, C. (2021). Moral frameworks of commercial surrogacy within the US, India and Russia. *Sexual and Reproductive Health Matters*, *29*(1), 1–17.

Sokolova, N., & Mulenko, A. (2013). Новеллы Российского законодательства о применении вспомогательных репродуктивных технологий [Innovations of the Russian legislation on ARTs]. *Медицинское Право. [Medical Law]*, *1*, 26–30.

Spar, D. (2006). *The baby business: How money, science, and politics drive the commerce of conception*. Boston, MA: Harvard Business School Press.

SPBdeti. (2020). Уполномоченный навестила малышей родденных суррогатнымы мамами [Commissioner visited babies born to surrogate mothers]. Retrieved from https://spbdeti.org/id8183. Accessed on November 10, 2020.

Speier, A. (2016). *Fertility holidays: IVF tourism and the reproduction of whiteness*. New York, NY: New York University Press.

Strathern, M. (1992). *Reproducing the future: Essays on anthropology, kinship and the new reproductive technologies*. Manchester: Manchester University Press.

Sunkara, S. K., Khalaf, Y., Maheshwari, A., Seed, P., & Coomarasamy, A. (2014). Association between response to ovarian stimulation and miscarriage following IVF: An analysis of 124 351 IVF pregnancies. *Human Reproduction*, *29*(6), 1218–1224.

Surrogacy.ru. (2021). Это моё кредо, мои принципы и убеждения, которые я отстаивал в России на протяжении последних 25 лет [This is my credo, my principles and beliefs, which I have defended in Russia over the past 25 years]. Interview with Konstantin Svitnev, January 01, 2021. Retrieved from https://surrogacy.ru/news/eto-moyo-kredo-moi-printsipy-i-ubezhdeniya-kotorye-ya-otstaival-v-rossii-na-protyazhenii-poslednih-25-let/. Accessed on March 15, 2021.

Svitnev К. (2007). Право на жизнь (ВРТ, суррогатное материнство и демография) [Right to life (ART, surrogate motherhood and demography)]. Националь-ная идентичность России и демографический кризис. Материалы Всероссийской научной конфе-ренции (20–21 октября 2006 г.) [Scientific Conference "National identity of Russia and demo-graphical crisis" (20–21 October 2006)]. Научный эксперт; 932–942. [Scientific expert, pp. 932–942].

Svitnev, K. (2011). Legal control of surrogacy – international perspectives. In J. Schenker (Ed.), *Ethical dilemmas in assisted reproductive technologies* (pp. 149–160). Berlin/Boston, MA: Walter de Gruyter GmbH & Co.

Svitnev, K. (2012a). New Russian legislation on assisted reproduction. *Open Access Scientific Reports*. Retrieved from https://www.omicsonline.org/scientific-reports/srep207.php. Accessed on March 09, 2021.

Svitnev, K. (2012b). "Socially infertile" single intended parents' motivation for gestational surrogacy: A preliminary report. *Human Reproduction*. Conference proceedings.

Svitnev, K. (2020). Konstantin Svitnev to the Ombudsmen, prosecutor general and chairman of the investigative committee of Russia: The first year of life cannot be returned. But at least now – help return the children to their parents! *Open Letter*. Retrieved from https://jurconsult.ru/en/news/konstantin-svitnev-to-the-ombudsmen-prosecutor-general-and-chairman-of-the-investigative-committee-of-russia-the-first-year-of-life-cannot-be-returned-but-at-least-now-help-return-the-children-to-their-parents/. Accessed on March 18, 2021.

Svitnev, K. (2021). Today we publish some abstracts from an extensive interview of RJC C.E.O. Konstantin N. Svitnev to Surrogacy.ru. Retrieved from https://jurconsult.ru/en/news/publikuem-vyderzhki-iz-programmnogo-intervyu-direktora-kompanii-rosyurkonsalting-konstantina-svitneva-portalu-surrogacy-ru/. Accessed on March 15, 2021.

SVPRESSA. (2013). Депутат Мизулина предложила запретить суррогатное материнство [Chairperson Mizulina proposes prohibiting surrogate motherhood]. *Свободная Пресса* [*Free Press*]. Retrieved from https://svpressa.ru/society/news/77217/. Accessed on March 08, 2021.

Takie Dela. (2021). В Госдуме разработали законопроект, запрещающий суррогатное материнство для иностранцев и неженатых россиян [The State Duma has developed a bill prohibiting surrogacy for foreigners and unmarried Russians]. *TakieDela.* Retrieved from https://takiedela.ru/news/2021/01/20/zhenispotom-rodish/. Accessed on March 09, 2021.

Teman, E. (2010). *Birthing a mother: The surrogate body and the pregnant self.* Berkeley, CA: University of California Press.

The Economist. (2021). Panic womb. Russia's liberal surrogacy rules are under threat. (No author). Retrieved from https://www.economist.com/europe/2021/03/18/russias-liberal-surrogacy-rules-are-under-threat. Accessed on March 24, 2021.

Tkach, O. (2009). Making family and unmaking kin in the Russian media: Reproductive technologies and relatedness. In W. de Jong & O. Tkach (Eds.), *Making bodies, persons and families: Normalising reproductive technologies in Russia, Switzerland and Germany* (pp. 135–157). Münster: LIT Verlag.

Tkach, O., & Brednikova, O. (2010). What means home for the Nomad?. *Laboratorium: Russian Review of Social Research, 3*, 72–95.

Toledano, S. J., & Zeiler, K. (2016). Hosting the others' child? Relational work and embodied responsibility in altruistic surrogate motherhood. *Feminist Theory, 18*(2), 159–175.

Twine, F. W. (2015). *Outsourcing the womb: Race, class and gestational surrogacy in a global market* (2nd ed.). New York, NY: Routledge.

Twine, F. W. (2017). The fertility continuum: Racism, bio-capitalism and post-colonialism in the transnational surrogacy industry. In M. Davies (Ed.), *Babies for sale? Transnational surrogacy, human rights and the politics of reproduction* (pp. 105–122). London: Zed Books.

Varisco, D. M. (2007). *Reading Orientalism: Said and the unsaid.* Seattle, WA: University of Washington Press.

Vasilyeva, N. (2020). Parents who used surrogates driven out of Russia amid crackdown on 'non-traditional' families. Retrieved from https://www.telegraph.co.uk/news/2020/10/11/gay-parents-driven-russia-government-targets-surrogacy-clinics/. Accessed on November 10, 2020.

Vasyagina, N., & Kalimullin, A. (2015). Retrospective analysis of social and cultural meanings of motherhood in Russia. *Review of European Studies, 7*(5), 61–65.

Vertommen, S., & Barbagallo, C. (2021). The in/visible wombs of the market: The dialectics of waged and unwaged reproductive labour in the global surrogacy industry. *Review of International Political Economy*, 1–41. doi:10.1080/09692 290.2020.1866642

Vertommen, S., Pavone, V., & Nahman, M. (2021). Global fertility chains: An integrative political economy approach to understanding the reproductive bioeconomy. *Science, Technology & Human Values.* doi:10.1177/0162243921996460

Vitebsky, P. (2005). *The reindeer people living with animals and spirits in Siberia.* New York, NY: Houghton Mifflin.

Vlasenko, P. (2020). Ukraine's surrogate mothers struggle under quarantine. *Open Democracy.* Retrieved from https://www.opendemocracy.net/en/odr/ukraines-surrogate-mothers-struggle-under-quarantine/. Accessed on June 10, 2020.

Watts, J. (2008). Emotion, empathy and exit: Reflections on doing ethnographic qualitative research on sensitive topics. *Medical Sociology Online, 3*(2), 3–14.

WCIOM. (2013). Суррогатные матери – героини или изгои? [Surrogate mothers - heroines or outcasts?]. Пресс-Выпуск №2479 [Press release Nr 2479]. Retrieved from https://wciom.ru/analytical-reviews/analiticheskii-obzor/surrogatnye-materigeroini-ili-izgoi. Accessed on November 30, 2020.

Weis, C. (2013). *'Born to birth'? Surrogacy workers in Saint Petersburg.* Master thesis, Utrecht University, Utrecht, The Netherlands. Retrieved from http://dspace.library.uu.nl/handle/1874/276628

Weis, C. (2017). *Reproductive migrations: Surrogacy workers and stratified reproduction in St Petersburg.* Doctoral Dissertation, De Montfort University. Retrieved from https://www.dora.dmu.ac.uk/handle/2086/15036

Weis, C. (2019). Situational ethics in a feminist ethnography on commercial surrogacy in Russia: Negotiating access and authority when recruiting participants through institutional gatekeepers. *Methodological Innovations, 12*(1), 1–10.

Weis, C. (2021). Changing fertility landscapes: Exploring the reproductive routes and choices of fertility patients from China for assisted reproduction in Russia. *Asian Bioethics Review, 13*, 7–22.

Weis, C., & Norton, W. (2021). 'My emotions on the backseat.' Heterosexually-partnered men's experiences of becoming fathers through surrogacy. *Journal of Diversity and Gender Studies, 7*(2), 35–49.

Weiss, G. (1992). Public attitudes about surrogate motherhood. *Michigan Sociological Review, 6*, 15–27.

Whittaker, A. (2016). From "Mung Ming" to "Baby Gammy": A local history of assisted reproduction in Thailand. *Reproductive Biomedicine & Society Online, 2,* 71–78.

Whittaker, A. (2018). *International surrogacy as disruptive industry in Southeast Asia.* New Brunswick, NJ: Rutgers University Press.

Whittaker, A., Inhorn, M., & Shenfield, F. (2019). Globalised quests for assisted conception: Reproductive travel for infertility and involuntary childlessness. *Global Public Health, 14*(12), 1669–1688.

Widdicombe, L. (2020). The stranded babies of the coronavirus disaster. *The New Yorker.* July 20. Retrieved from https://www.newyorker.com/news/news-desk/the-stranded-babies-of-the-coronavirus-disaster. Accessed on November 30, 2020.

Zakharov, N. (2015). *Race and racism in Russia. Mapping global racisms.* New York, NY: Palgrave Macmillan.

Zakirova, V. (2014). Gender inequality in Russia: The perspective of participatory gender budgeting. *Reproductive Health Matters, 22*(44), 202–212.

Zdravomyslova, E., & Tkach, O. (2016). Культурные модели классового неравенства в сфере наемного домашнего труда в России [Cultural patterns of class inequality in the realm of paid domestic work in Russia]. *Laboratorium: Журнал социальных исследований. [Journal of Social Research.*], *8*(3), 68–99.

Zelizer, V., Bandelj, N., & Wherry, F. (2012). Talking about relational work with Viviana Zelizer. *orgtheory.net.* Retrieved from https://orgtheory.wordpress.com/2012/09/06/talking-about-relational-work-with-viviana-zelizer/. Accessed on October 29, 2016.

Zelizer, V. A. (2012). How I became a relational economic sociologist and what does that mean? *Politics & Society, 40*(2), 145–174.

Zelizer, V. A. R. (2005). *The purchase of intimacy.* Princeton, NJ: Princeton University Press.

Zen, Y. (2018). Госдума: запрета на суррогатное материнство в России не будет [State Duma: There will be no ban on surrogacy in Russia]. *Yandex News.* Retrieved from https://zen.yandex.ru/media/nsovetnik/gosduma-zapreta-na-surrogatnoematerinstvo-v-rossii-ne-budet-5bec2a23cfec6100aea4cbba. Accessed on March 09, 2021.

Zimmerman, A. (2016). Thailand's ban on commercial surrogacy: Why Thailand should regulate, not attempt to eradicate. *Brooklyn Journal of International Law, 41*(2), 917–959.

Index